Strangers on the Earth

Strangers on the Earth

Philosophy and Rhetoric in Hebrews

James W. Thompson

CASCADE *Books* • Eugene, Oregon

STRANGERS ON THE EARTH
Philosophy and Rhetoric in Hebrews

Copyright © 2020 James W. Thompson. All rights reserved. Except for brief quotations in critical publications or reviews, no part of this book may be reproduced in any manner without prior written permission from the publisher. Write: Permissions, Wipf and Stock Publishers, 199 W. 8th Ave., Suite 3, Eugene, OR 97401.

Cascade Books
An Imprint of Wipf and Stock Publishers
199 W. 8th Ave., Suite 3
Eugene, OR 97401

www.wipfandstock.com

PAPERBACK ISBN: 978-1-5326-8401-2
HARDCOVER ISBN: 978-1-5326-8402-9
EBOOK ISBN: 978-1-5326-8403-6

Cataloguing-in-Publication data:

Names: Thompson, James W. (James Weldon), 1942–, author.

Title: Strangers on the earth : philosophy and rhetoric in Hebrews / by James W. Thompson.

Description: Eugene, OR: Cascade Books, 2020 | Includes bibliographical references.

Identifiers: ISBN 978-1-5326-8401-2 (paperback) | ISBN 978-1-5326-8402-9 (hardcover) | ISBN 978-1-5326-8403-6 (ebook)

Subjects: LCSH: Bible—Hebrews—Criticism, interpretation, etc. | Hellenistic culture and society | Hellenism

Classification: BS2775.52 T46 2020 (print) | BS2775.52 (ebook)

Manufactured in the U.S.A.   04/14/20

CONTENTS

Preface | vii

Introduction: The Strange New World of Hebrews | 1

1 The Hermeneutics of the Epistle to Hebrews | 11

2 The New Is Better: A Neglected Aspect of the Hermeneutics of Hebrews | 28

3 The Appropriate, the Necessary, and the Impossible: Faith and Reason in Hebrews | 39

4 Argument and Persuasion in the Epistle to the Hebrews | 54

5 What Does Middle Platonism Have to Do with Hebrews? | 73

6 *Ephapax:* The One and the Many in Hebrews | 92

7 "Strangers on the Earth": Philosophical Perspective on the Promise in Hebrews | 108

8 The Epistle to the Hebrews in the Works of Clement of Alexandra | 130

9 The Epistle to the Hebrews and the Pauline Legacy | 145

10 Insider Ethics for Outsiders: Ethics for Aliens in Hebrews | 155

11 The Ecclesiology of Hebrews | 169

Bibliography | 181

PREFACE

Unless otherwise noted, translations of Philo and Plutarch are from the Loeb Classical Library: *Philo with an English Translation*, translated and edited by F. H. Colson and G. H. Whitaker (12 vols.; Cambridge: Harvard University Press, 1962); *Plutarch's Moralia*, translated and edited by Frank Cole Babbitt (16 vols.; Cambridge: Harvard University Press, 1962).

Translation of the church fathers, unless otherwise noted, are from *The Anti-Nicene Fathers: The Writings of the Fathers Down to A.D. 325* (10 vols.; Edinburgh: T. & T. Clark, 1867–73).

All abbreviations are taken from the *SBL Handbook of Style*.

INTRODUCTION

THE STRANGE NEW WORLD OF HEBREWS

In my monograph *The Beginnings of Christian Philosophy* I observed that the reader of Hebrews enters a strange new world that distinguishes it from other NT writings.[1] I had first observed the unique character of this work during my graduate studies, when I turned to Hebrews after working with Pauline letters and the apocalyptic literature of the period. These observations led to the research in my dissertation, *That Which Abides: Some Metaphysical Assumptions in the Epistle to the Hebrews*, which I completed in 1974. My continued analysis led to the publication of the monograph in 1982, in which I expanded on the subject and traced the same themes. This collection of essays reflects my continued engagement with the strange new world of Hebrews after the completion of the earlier publication.

Previous scholars had observed the anomalous character of Hebrews. Franz Overbeck once declared that Hebrews is "like Melchizedek," a book without a family of origin,[2] and William Wrede described it as the riddle of the NT.[3] More recently, Knut Backhaus suggested that Hebrews is a "foreigner and a sojourner," a "guest worker" in the NT canon.[4] The anonymity, distinctive genre, structure, and setting make this book a mystery. Reflections on Melchizedek, the extended treatment of the sacrificial cult, and the threefold warning about the impossibility of repentance (6:4–6; 10:26–31; 12:15–17) add to the mystery of Hebrews. With its series of reflections on OT passages, it is the book most rooted in Jewish Scriptures, while its

---

1. Thompson, *Beginnings of Christian Philosophy*, 1–16.
2. Overbeck, *Zur Geschichte des Kanons*, 1.
3. Wrede, *Das literarische Rätsel des Hebräerbriefes*.
4. See Backhaus, "Der Hebräerbrief: Potential und Profil. Eine Hinführung," 1.

polished Greek makes it the most Hellenistic writing in the NT.[5] These unique features have occupied scholars for generations.

The distinctive feature that has occupied my research is a method of argumentation that is also without parallel in the NT. This homily includes a series of *synkrises* comparing Christ and the Christ event with OT people and institutions. While *synkrisis* is a common rhetorical device,[6] its dominance in the homily distinguishes it from other NT writings. The two levels of reality—the heavenly and the earthly—are the focus of the *synkrisis*. Angels (1:5—2:18), the priesthood (5:1–10; 7:1–28), the tabernacle (8:1–13), and the sacrifices belong to this creation (8:4; 9:11; 12:25; cf. 9:24); Christ is "better" because he has been exalted above the angels and the priesthood, and his sacrifice is better because he offered it in the heavenly sanctuary. According to the author's unique definition, faith is not directed toward Christ but to "things unseen" (11:1). The Sinai theophany belongs to the tangible world (12:18), while the community has approached the heavenly city that is apparently not tangible (12:22). The exalted Christ abides forever (1:10–11; 7:3, 24), along with the believer's ultimate possession (10:34; 12:27; 13:14), while angels and the Aaronic priests along with their sacrifices do not share in the exaltation and are impermanent. The sacrifice of Christ, offered in the heavenly sanctuary, was ἐφάπαξ (7:227; 9:12; 10:10; cf. ἅπαξ, 6:4; 9:26–28), while the many Levitical priests are continually replaced (7:23) and the sacrifices on earth are continually repeated (9:25–26).

The author does not speak with apostolic or prophetic authority, but makes rational arguments, punctuating his claims with terms that are familiar to one who is schooled in rhetoric but largely absent from other NT writings. Indeed, he describes the Christ event with terms that were common in Greco-Roman rhetoric. It was "fitting" (πρέπον) for God to redeem the people through Jesus Christ (2:10; 7:26). Where there is a covenant, it is necessary (ἀνάγκη) for a death to occur (9:16), and it was necessary (ἀνάγκη) that the heavenly sanctuary be cleansed (9:23). The ancient sacrifices were ineffective because it is impossible (ἀδύνατος) for the blood of bulls and goats to take away sins (10:4). The author stands within a Christian tradition that proclaims the saving significance of the death of Jesus and his exaltation to God's right hand but elaborates on this confession with assumptions and arguments that are unprecedented in the NT.

Because of the strangeness of this book, it has been resisted by some and neglected by others. With the exception of Tertullian, who welcomed its

---

5. Grässer, "Der Hebräerbrief 1938–63," 167.

6. See Martin and Whitlark, *Inventing Hebrews*, 23–51. Martin and Whitlark speak of the "syncritical backbone of Hebrews."

denial of a second repentance,[7] early believers in the West resisted it. Luther saw in it only "wood, straw, or hay mingled together" and placed it after 1 and 2 Peter and the Johannine letters.[8] Protestant scholars observed its distance from Paul's doctrine of justification and gave it little attention; it is barely noticed, for example, in Rudolf Bultmann's *Theology of the New Testament*.

Because of the letter's consistent appeal to the two levels of reality and to rational argument, the intellectual milieu in which the argument would be persuasive becomes a major issue. Traditional interpretation had read Hebrews as a commentary on OT passages without considering a wider milieu. Scholarship in the past century has been sharply divided over the intellectual and religious background of Hebrews. Looking at the same evidence, some scholars maintain the deeply Jewish nature of the book with roots in Jewish apocalyptic literature while others interpret Hebrews against the background of Hellenistic thought.

These alternatives were especially evident for decades in the Protestant faculty at the University of Tübingen. In *Das wandernde Gottesvolk*, Ernst Käsemann correctly observed the central focus on the pilgrimage of the people of God to the heavenly city, attributing this motif to a gnostic influence. Otto Michel wrote the commentary on Hebrews in the Meyer series, which went through numerous editions, demonstrating the apocalyptic and rabbinic background to Hebrews. Käsemann's view of the gnostic background of Hebrews has not received many followers, but Michel's view continues in current literature.

The major debate since the middle of the twentieth century has been over the alternative between Platonism, as represented primarily by Philo of Alexandria, and Jewish apocalyptic literature. Although Platonic influence on Hebrews had been suggested since the sixteenth century, Ceslas Spicq's monumental twentieth-century commentary argued for the influence of Philo on Hebrews, even suggesting that the author of Hebrews was a Philonist converted to Christianity.[9] Spicq provided an extensive catalogue of verbal parallels between Philo and Hebrews. The most extensive challenge to Spicq's claim was that of Ronald Williamson, who successfully demonstrated the major differences between Philo and Hebrews.[10] Williamson did not, however, acknowledge the factors that distinguish Hebrews from apocalyptic literature and minimized the similarities between Philo and Hebrews. In distinguishing Hebrews from Philo, he assumed that Platonism

---

7. See Backhaus, "Der Hebräerbrief: Potential und Profil. Eine Hinführung," 2.
8. Backhaus, "Der Hebräerbrief: Potential und Profil. Eine Hinführung," 2.
9. Spicq, *L'Épître aux Hébreux*, published in 1952.
10. Williamson, *Philo and the Epistle to the Hebrews*, 493.

and apocalyptic existed in two different worlds. Thus he did not acknowledge the multiple ways in which ancient writers synthesized elements from the OT and Hellenistic thought.[11]

In my dissertation and the research that followed, I acknowledged the fluidity of ancient intellectual traditions, recognizing that the alternative between apocalyptic and Platonic features was not satisfactory, for the two were blended in a variety of ways in antiquity. Nevertheless, I concluded that traditional Jewish apocalypses did not account for the distinctive metaphysical assumptions and rhetorical arguments in Hebrews. The focus on the two levels of reality and the stability of the heavenly world were commonplace in Middle Platonism, the philosophy that was incorporated into a variety of philosophical and religious systems in the Hellenistic age. Gnostic systems, the *Hermetica*, and numerous patristic writers incorporate elements of Middle Platonism, while Greek writers incorporated Middle Platonism into ancient myths.

The most prominent characteristic of Middle Platonism was the focus on the gap separating the transcendent, intelligible world, and the realm of sense perception. The transcendent world is stable and unchanging, while the realm of sense perception is subject to change and destruction. A wall separates these two worlds, but intermediate beings bridge the gap between the two realms. The deity is so separated from human language that it can be described only with negatives. The challenge for the individual is to see beyond the physical world and enter a relationship with the transcendent deity.

Representatives of Middle Platonism include Philo, who interpreted Scripture through the lenses of philosophy, Plutarch, who incorporated these philosophical assumptions into the Greek myths, Alcinus, and Antiochus of Ascalon. Thus the alternative is not between apocalyptic literature and the works of Philo, for Philo belongs to the wider stream of Middle Platonism. In order to understand the argument of Hebrews, the interpreter must look beyond Philo to others in the Hellenistic Age who incorporated Middle Platonism into their systems. While apocalyptic resources are present in Hebrews, philosophy has also shaped the arguments of Hebrews and others.

Since the publication of *The Beginnings of Christian Philosophy*, some interpreters have maintained the influence of Middle Platonism on Hebrews, while others have rejected any Platonic assumptions as a background to Hebrews. Concurrent with my earliest work on Hebrews and Middle Platonism, but unknown to me, Lala Kalyan Kumar Dey argued that the

---

11. See my extended critique in *Beginnings of Christian Philosophy*, 9–11.

emphasis on intermediaries between the intelligible and sense-perceptible world in Hebrews and Philo are rooted in the assumptions of Middle Platonism.[12] In numerous works, Knut Backhaus has argued convincingly that the originality of the author comes from his capacity for synthesis. While the OT and Jewish apocalyptic literature influence the argument, Middle Platonism also plays a role. The signs of Middle Platonism in Hebrews, according to Backhaus are 1) the emphasis on the ontological transcendence of the deity; 2) the gulf between the heavenly, invisible archetype and the earthly, visible copy; 3) the resulting need to bridge the chasm between the deity and humankind with an intermediary figure; 4) the goal of giving humankind a point of stability in the midst of insecurity; and 5) the appeal of religion to bridge the gap.[13]

Peter Busch argued also that, to discover the intellectual background of Hebrews, one must look beyond Philo to the larger world of Middle Platonism. Busch focused his comments on the initial description of the high priestly work of Christ in Heb 4:14—5:10. According to Busch, the work of Christ corresponds to that of the intermediary beings (*daimones*) in Middle Platonism. The intermediary beings live in ether, in the space between the place of the gods and the earth, and "pass through the heavens" (cf. Heb 4:14) The intermediary beings in Middle Platonism have a priestly function. In *def orac.* 417a, Plutarch describes the demigods (*daimones*) as λειτουργοί who oversee the offerings to the gods and the cultic activities (cf. Plato, *Sym.* 202).[14] Busch also notes that the qualification that the high priest be able to "deal gently" (μετριοπαθεῖν) with the wayward (Heb 5:2) has no OT background. However, he argues that, while the gods have no παθή, the demigods (δαίμονες) have human emotions and godlike power (πάθος θνητοῦ καὶ θεοῦ δύναμιν, *def. orac.* 416D). Apuleius made a comparable statement in *De deo Socr.* XII about δαίμονες who "perceive hate and love of certain men; the one they act favorably toward, the other they attack and strike down, they feel sympathy (*miserere*), have anger. They have all of the passions of the human soul." The passions of the δαίμονες are systematized in *De deo Socr.* XIII.[15]

---

12. Dey, *The Intermediary World and the Patterns of Perfection in Philo and Hebrews*, 44–45.

13. Backhaus, *Hebräerbrief*, 55.

14. Cf. Heb 1:7, according to which the angels are λειτουργοί. Cf. Plutarch, *Is. Os.* 361: "Plato calls this class of beings an interpretative and ministering class, midway between gods and men, in that they convey thither the prayers and petitions of men, and then they bring hither the oracles and the gifts of good things" (trans. Babbit in LCL).

15. Busch, "Der mitleidende Hohepriester," 25–27.

Ronald Cox examined the doctrine of creation and salvation in Middle Platonism and the NT, concluding that Middle Platonism, with its focus on the distance between the transcendent and material worlds was especially attractive to Hellenistic Judaism, which also adopted the concept of the intermediate being as the bridge between the two worlds. The intermediate being in Middle Platonism was active in the creation and sustaining of the physical world. Similarly, σοφία in the Wisdom of Solomon and the λόγος of Philo had a role in creating and sustaining the world. Cox demonstrates that this role is applied to Christ in Pauline passages (1 Cor 8:6; Col 1:15–17), the Johannine literature (John 1:1–5), and Hebrews. Indeed, the prologue of Hebrews identifies Christ with the terms and functions attributed to σοφία in the Wisdom of Solomon.[16]

Wilfried Eisele wrote a major monograph on the transformation of eschatological expectation in Hebrews by Middle Platonic thought.[17] After analyzing texts on the parousia in Hebrews and comparing them to similar NT texts, Eisele concludes that the focus of the parousia expectation in Hebrews was not in a detailed description of the parousia but in the distinction between the shakable and unshakable worlds. Believers live in the shakable world but participate already in the unshakable world. The task of the believer is to persevere, holding on to that which cannot be shaken, the world that abides forever.

Eisele gives an extended analysis of three Middle Platonic thinkers: Philo, Plutarch, and Alcinus. He demonstrates that all three writers maintain the distinction between the intelligible and perceptible worlds and that all three speak of mediating powers between the transcendent world and the world of the senses. Hebrews shares with them the distance between the visible and invisible worlds, the view that the believer is a stranger on the earth, the idea of a mediator between two worlds.

Luke Timothy Johnson has also maintained that the arguments in Hebrews reflect the influence of Middle Platonism. In his commentary, he argues that Hebrews shares the "worldview" of a specific stream within Greek philosophers associated with Plato. The term "worldview" is appropriate, for by the first century CE, Plato's classic metaphysical theories, expressed in *Resp.* 509–521B and *Tim.* 27–29, had been filtered through many schools and permutations and had been appropriated through many others. In broad terms, this is a view of reality that draws a sharp distinction between the phenomenal world, which is the realm of materiality, characterized by movement, change, and corruption—always passing away . . . and

---

16. Cox, *By the Same Word*, 193–222.
17. Eisele, *Ein unerschütterliches Reich*.

the noumenal world, characterized by changelessness and incorruptibility. The Platonic realm is "better."[18] According to Johnson, "It is not a great leap required to identify the heavens with the Platonic world of forms."[19] The Platonic world of Hebrews is real, but it "is a Platonism that is stretched and reshaped by an engagement with Scripture."[20]

Gregory Sterling acknowledges that the author of Hebrews does not exhibit a profound understanding of Plato. He nevertheless employs Platonic categories in Heb 8:1–5. Sterling notes that while some of the terms used in this passage (τύπος, σκία, ὑπόδειγμα) could be derived from diverse backgrounds, "the ensemble is Platonic."[21] Sterling maintains that the "thrust of the argumentation in Hebrews is the imposition of an eschatological perspective on Platonizing exegetical traditions.[22]

The argument for the influence of Platonism (including Middle Platonism) on Hebrews has met considerable resistance. The focal point of the argument is the analysis of Heb 8:1–5. Here the language of the earthly sanctuary as a shadow of the divine archetype is evocative of Plato's theory of ideas. Lincoln D. Hurst, however, examined the proposed backgrounds of Hebrews, comparing it to Philo, Qumran, and other NT writings. In a chapter on Philo, he examined the apparent Platonic terminology (σκία, 8:5; ὑπόδειγμα, 8:5; ἀντίτυπος, 9:24, ἀληθινός, 8:2; 9:24), demonstrating that, while Plato spoke of the σκία on earth (cf. Plato, *Resp.* 514–17), such terms as ὑπόδειγμα and ἀντίτυπος are foreign to Plato. Hurst concludes that the author of Hebrews developed OT themes within an apocalyptic context.[23]

Hurst concludes that my argument goes back to a "pre-Barrett" point of view, assuming that C. K. Barrett had resolved the issue of Platonism and apocalypticism. However, he ignores the advances since Martin Hengel's *Judaism and Hellenism* that demonstrate the synthesizing of traditions in antiquity. Platonism and apocalyptic were synthesized in a variety of ways. Moreover, Gregory Sterling has demonstrated that Platonists used such terms as τύπος and ὑπόδειγμα in a variety of ways.[24]

Other scholars have rejected the influence of (Middle) Platonism on Hebrews, offering a critique similar to that of Hurst. Edward Adams also challenged a Platonic and dualistic reading of Hebrews. Like Hurst, he

18. Luke Timothy Johnson, *Hebrews*, 18.
19. Luke Timothy Johnson, *Hebrews*, 19.
20. Luke Timothy Johnson, *Hebrews*, 21.
21. Sterling, "Ontology versus Eschatology," 194.
22. Sterling, "Ontology versus Eschatology," 208.
23. See Hurst, *The Epistle to the Hebrews*, 7–41.
24. Sterling, "Ontology versus Eschatology," 195.

maintains that the heavenly sanctuary of Hebrews is indebted to apocalyptic rather than Platonic thought. He argues that Hebrews does not share Plato's expectation that the cosmos will last forever (cf. Plato, *Tim.* 32C–33A). He also points to the absence of typical Platonic language in Hebrews,[25] which nowhere speaks of the intelligible and perceptible worlds. Adams concludes that the cosmology of Hebrews is derived from the OT.

Kenneth Schenck acknowledges that a weakness in the analysis of the background of Hebrews is the "tendency to pigeonhole the epistle into a single ideological background,"[26] citing Hurst as an example of this approach. He agrees that the author consistently argues from the two levels of reality, placing OT institutions within the created realm.[27] However, while he recognizes that no wall separated Jewish and Hellenistic thought, he concludes that the Platonic reading of Hebrews is to be rejected. Following Hurst's argument, he regards Heb 8:1–5 as the *locus classicus* of a Platonic reading of Hebrews but agrees with Hurst that the language is not Platonic, inasmuch as the relationship of the archetype to the copy is temporal rather than vertical.[28]

Arguments against the influence of Middle Platonism have focused primarily on the apparent Platonic language in the description of the tabernacle (8:5) and the contrast between the archetype (τύπος) and the copy (ὑπόδειγμα) and shadow (σκία). While those who reject a Platonic background correctly note that these terms do not portray orthodox Platonic language, they do not consider that Middle Platonists employ a range of terms for archetype and copy. Moreover, the claim for the influence of Middle Platonism does not rest on the obvious Platonic language in 8:1–5. The contrast between the two spheres of reality, including the denigration of the earthly high priesthood (ch. 7), tabernacle (9:1, 24), and sacrifice (9:1–11), suggests metaphysical assumptions that are unprecedented in apocalyptic literature. As I argue in this book, the contrast between the one and the many—between the final sacrifice of Christ and the repeated sacrifices of the Levitical cult—reflects the Platonic distinction between the one and the many. Moreover, the claim that the ancient Hebrews were "strangers on the earth" (Heb 11:13) who saw the invisible one (11:27) echoes Platonic language.

The question remains: What audience would have found the author's argument persuasive? While apocalyptic expectation is present in Hebrews (cf. 12:25–27), it does not account for the argument of Hebrews. Similarly, Philo's

---

25. Adams, "The Cosmology of Hebrews," 195.
26. Schenck, *Cosmology and Eschatology in Hebrews*, 3.
27. Schenck, *Cosmology and Eschatology in Hebrews*, 143.
28. Schenck, *Cosmology and Eschatology in Hebrews*, 120.

argumentation departs from Hebrews at numerous points but exhibits similarities with Hebrews in other instances. Indeed, this homily is distinguishable from both Philo and apocalyptic literature. The strange new world of Hebrews is the author's own creative synthesis of ancient traditions.

In the following essays I depict the features that distinguish the argument of Hebrews. In the first four articles, I analyze the hermeneutical and rhetorical features of Hebrews. In "The Hermeneutics of Hebrews" (ch. 1), I argue that, while Hebrews exhibits features in common with the hermeneutics of Second Temple Judaism and other NT writers, the author moves beyond the familiar promise and fulfillment or typological exegesis. In "The New is Better" (ch. 2), I observe a hermeneutical principle that has little precedent in Jewish hermeneutics but reflects the legal arguments of the period. In "The Appropriate, the Necessary, and the Impossible" (ch. 3), I demonstrate that the appeal to rationality reflected in these categories reflects the author's rhetorical training, even though the author appeals to a rationality based on his prior Christian convictions. Similarly, "Argument and Persuasion in the Epistle to the Hebrews" (ch. 4) demonstrates the author's indebtedness to Hellenistic Rhetoric.

In chapters 5–8, I argue that, while the author undoubtedly appropriates apocalyptic thought patterns, the distinctive argument is indebted to the assumptions of Middle Platonism. In "What does Hebrews Have to Do with Middle Platonism?" (ch. 5), I observe the features of Middle Platonism that cohere with the argument of Hebrews: the dualistic distinction between the heavenly and earthly realms, the transcendence of the deity, the role of a mediator, and the distinction between the eternal and the transitory. In "*Ephapax*, The One and the Many in Hebrews" (ch. 6), I demonstrate that Hebrews' theme of the once-for-all nature of the sacrifice of Christ is based on the Platonic distinction between the one and the many. "'Strangers on the Earth': Philosophical Perspective on the Promise in Hebrews" (ch. 7) is a demonstration that the theme of being a stranger in the world is a common theme in Middle Platonism. "The Epistle to the Hebrews in the Works of Clement of Alexandria" (ch. 8), I demonstrate that an Alexandrian tradition that connected biblical faith with Middle Platonism extends from Philo to Clement of Alexandria. Hebrews has affinities with this tradition and is a major source for Clement.

The final articles reflect on theological and ethical contributions of Hebrews. In "The Epistle to the Hebrews and the Pauline Legacy" (ch. 9), I demonstrate that the points of convergence between Paul and the author of Hebrews suggest that we have no compelling reason to consider the author of Hebrews a student of Paul or to place the homily within the reception of Pauline theology. In the "Ecclesiology of Hebrews" (ch. 10), I maintain that

Ernst Käsemann's description of the community as "the wandering people of God" is an appropriate term for the community in Hebrews. The author addresses the marginalization of the community, reminding the hearers that, while they are the objects of ridicule in the present, they are united, not only with ancient Israel but also with the Son as they share both his sufferings and his exaltation in the present, living in hope for the ultimate realization of the promise. In "Insider Ethics for Outsiders" (ch. 11), I argue for the relationship between Hebrews and earlier NT ethics and the coherence of the ethics with the author's earlier argument.

CHAPTER 1

THE HERMENEUTICS OF THE EPISTLE TO THE HEBREWS

As the author of a "word of exhortation" (Heb 13:22) to a discouraged community, the writer of Hebrews appeals to the OT more consistently than any other writer of the NT, becoming one of the first writers to establish the meaning of the OT for the church. Indeed, Hebrews consists largely of a series of reflections on a variety of texts that are applied to the situation of the recipients. As the literature on Hebrews indicates, one may examine the hermeneutics of Hebrews from more than one perspective. One may analyze the Greek textual basis of the citations,[1] the role of the citations in the structure of Hebrews,[2] the exegetical methods,[3] and the hermeneutics in the homily.[4] Most studies of the author's hermeneutics have focused on the intellectual environment. James Moffatt,[5] Ceslas Spicq,[6] and Stefan Svendsen,[7] for example, argue that the author of Hebrews employs the allegorical method of Philo of Alexandria. L. Goppelt, in *Typos*, argues that the author's exegetical work is most dependent on typology.[8] Herbert Bateman

---

1. Revised and expanded from *Restoration Quarterly* 38 (1996) 229-37. See Gheorghita, *The Role of the Septuagint in Hebrews in Heb 10:37*; Steyn, *Quest for the Assumed LXX Vorlage of the Explicit Quotations in Hebrews*.

2. Jordaan and Nel, "From Priest-King to King-Priest."

3. Cf. Schröger, *Der Verfasser des Hebräerbriefs als Schriftausleger*.

4. Otto, "Hermeneutics of Biblical Theology, History of Religion, and the Theological Substance of Two Testaments," 3-26.

5. Moffatt, *A Critical and Exegetical Commentary on the Epistle to the Hebrews*, xlvi, "The exegetical methods which the author took over from the Alexandrian school are not ours."

6. Spicq, *L'Épître aux Hébreux*, 1.330-50.

7. See also Svendsen, *Allegory Transformed*.

8. Goppelt maintains: "It is significant that Hebrews, the NT book that has the most quotations from the OT, makes the most intensive use of typology." *Typos*, 176.

concludes from his analysis of Heb 1 that the use of Scripture reflects rabbinic methods.[9] S. Kistemaker, in *The Psalms Citations in the Epistle to the Hebrews*, suggested that Hebrews employs the pesher style of interpretation that was characteristic of the Dead Sea Scrolls. According to Kistemaker, "Nearly every chapter of Hebrews reveals the peculiar features of midrash pesher."[10] Otto Michel also argued for the similarities in the exegetical method of Hebrews and the Dead Sea Scrolls.[11]

F. Schröger has written a detailed study of the exegesis of Hebrews, analyzing each citation of Hebrews in order to determine what methods of exegesis were employed. He concludes:

> In Hebrews one finds the interpretation of the OT passages according to rabbinic rules, according to the method of midrash pesher employed by the Qumran community, according to the perspective of promise-fulfillment with the view that the Old Testament includes an imperfect hint of the events which have taken place in Christ. In a few cases the allegorical method is also to be found.[12]

The major concern of those who have examined the use of the OT in Hebrews is reflected in Schröger's conclusion. The focus has been on the identification of the exegetical techniques employed by the author. More recently, Susan E. Docherty has given a comprehensive examination of the exegetical method of Hebrews against the background of hermeneutical practice in Second Temple Judaism. Giving attention to recent Septuagintal and midrashic studies, she identifies exegetical techniques that previous scholarship had not recognized.[13] While this emphasis on identifying the type of exegesis in Hebrews (e.g., allegorical, typological, pesher) is informative, it provides an incomplete analysis of the author's hermeneutic. Inasmuch as the author does not use the categories of typology, allegory, pesher, or promise and fulfillment, his interpretative work is not likely to fit neatly into these categories. Moreover, studies in the hermeneutics of Hebrews have rarely placed the author's interpretation of Scripture within the larger context of his theology and pastoral purpose.[14] This chapter is an examination of the author's distinctive hermeneutic within that context.

9. Bateman, *Early Jewish Hermeneutics and Hebrews 1:5–13*.
10. Kistemaker, *The Psalm Citations in Hebrews*, 174.
11. Michel, *Der Brief an die Hebräer*, 76.
12. Schröger, *Der Verfasser des Hebräerbriefs als Schriftausleger*. For a detailed study of the history of scholarship on the Epistle to the Hebrews, see Docherty, *The Use of the Old Testament in Hebrews*, 61–82.
13. Docherty, *The Use of the Old Testament in Hebrews*, 201–6.
14. Rascher, *Schriftauslegung*, 10. See also Son, *Zion Symbolism in Hebrews*, 8.

Hebrews and Early Christian Interpretation

The author both stands within the early Christian exegetical tradition and departs from it in his appeal to the OT. Following earlier interpreters, the author cites Ps 110:1, the passage most frequently cited in the NT, as a reference to the exaltation of Christ (1:3, 13; 8:1; 12:2; 10:12).[15] He also cites Ps 2:7 as a declaration that Jesus is the Son of God (1:5; 5:5) in accordance with early Christian interpretation (cf. Matt 3:17par; Acts 13:33). In linking Ps 110:1 with Ps 8:5-7 (Heb 2:5-9), the author follows early Christian tradition (cf. 1 Cor 15:27; Eph 1:22). While only Hebrews cites the prophecy of the new covenant (Jer 31:31-34) at length (8:8-12; 10:16-17), the author is dependent on early Christian tradition in describing the events inaugurated by Christ as the new covenant (cf. Matt 26:28par; 1 Cor 11:25; 2 Cor 3:1-6). Like Paul, he cites Hab 2:4 (Heb 10:37-38), but his interpretation is independent of Paul. He also shares with the earlier exegetical tradition the frequent use of the Psalms (cf. Ps 103:4LXX/Heb 1:7; Ps 44:7LXX/Heb 1:8; Ps 101:26-28LXX/Heb 1:10-11; Ps 21:23LXX/Heb 2:12; Ps 95:7-11/Heb 3:7-11; Ps 40:7-9/Heb 10:5-8). However, he departs from early tradition in citing psalms that had not been employed by the known predecessors (cf. Ps 95:7-11/Heb 3:7-11; Ps 110:4/Heb 7:3).[16] He also reflects independence from previous tradition in his appeals to the Pentateuch and Proverbs (cf. 3:1-6/Num 12:7; 4:2/Gen 2:2; 7:1-3/Gen 14:17-20; 9:1-10; Lev 16; 12:5-11/Prov 3:11).

Hebrews and the OT Narrative World

The author's interpretation is evident not only in the specific citations but also in the OT narrative world that he assumes. The opening words of this homily describe both the continuity and discontinuity of the community with ancient Israel. The God who has spoken "in many and various ways to the ancestors" has also spoken to the community ("to us") "in these last days" (1:2). As hearers of the word of God, the community stands in continuity with its ancestors. However, "these last days" mark the discontinuity

---

15. For the earlier usage of Ps 110:1, see Matt 22:44; 26:46 par.; Acts 2:34; Rom 8:34; 1 Cor 15:25. For the function of Ps 110:1 in Hebrews, see Compton, *Psalm 110 and the Logic of Hebrews*.

16. Gert Steyn observes that Hebrews is the only known literature in early Judaism and early Christianity to make use of Ps 94:7-11LXX. Human and Steyn (eds.), *Psalms and Hebrews*, 194-228.

between the readers and ancient Israel, for God's speech "in a Son" is qualitatively different from God's earlier revelation.[17]

The OT narrative world includes the beginning (1:2, 10; 9:26; 11:3), "these last days" (1:2; cf. 6:5) inaugurated by the Christ event, and the end (cf. 3:14; 9:27; 12:25-27). While the author does not mention the origin of evil, he assumes the existence of the devil (2:14) and humanity burdened by sin from the beginning (cf. 1:3). The God who has spoken to the community "in a Son" (1:2) first spoke to their ancestors through the prophets (1:1), including Moses (3:1-6; 8:1-5) and Jeremiah (8:7-13). The ancestors (1:1; 11:2) include the catalog of heroes from the past (6:12-15; 11:1-39) as well as those who were negative examples (3:7—4:11; 12:15-17). The Levitical cultus belongs to the old age that is now obsolete "and growing old and to the point of disappearing" (8:13). In this old age the way into the sanctuary is not yet open (9:8) but awaits the time of reformation (9:9).

Like the readers of the Pauline epistles the community now lives "in the last days" (1:2; 6:5). The new covenant has been inaugurated (8:8-13; 10:15-17) in the incarnation (10:5-8) and the sacrifice of Christ in the heavenly sanctuary (9:11-22). The way into the sanctuary is now open for believers (10:19-22). However, the hope of entering the promised land still lies in the future. As a result of the entry of Christ into the heavenly world, the community can now draw near to the throne of grace. In the present, the community has a high priest who has passed through the heavens (4:14) and sits at the right hand of God (8:1-2), giving hope that is an anchor of the soul (6:19). The author never says that the promises have been fulfilled, but he assures the readers that the exalted high priest is the guarantee of the promise (7:22). Thus while the promises have not been fulfilled, they have been guaranteed. The challenge to the readers is to endure to the end (3:14).

The community lives in continuity with the Israelites in the wilderness, for the promised land that ancient Israel did not enter remains open for the listeners (4:1-11). Indeed, the ancestors who lived in faith without seeing the promise will only "be made perfect" when the listeners complete their journey (11:40). This "cloud of witnesses" from the OT now surrounds the readers as they complete the race (12:1-3).

Freedom in the Citation of Texts

A hermeneutical circle determines the author's use of Scripture. He expresses the saving significance of the Christ event with the language of the written text. At the same time, the Christ event leads to a new understanding

---

17. Rascher, *Schriftauslegung und Christologie im Hebräerbrief*, 47-48.

of Scripture.[18] This hermeneutical circle extends to the author's freedom in the citation of texts. For example, he has inherited from early Christian tradition the theme of preexistence, incarnation, and exaltation (cf. 2 Cor 8:9; Phil 2:6–11). By pressing the meaning of βραχύ τι as "little while" (Heb 2:9; cf. Ps 8:5), the author affirms this tradition, giving a christological interpretation that includes the descent and ascent of Christ (cf. also Heb 1:3). Psalm 8 is not a reflection on the place of humankind in the creation but about the humanity and suffering of Christ. When he cites Ps 95:7–11, he inserts διό, altering the LXX (and MT) citation from "they had seen my work. For forty years I was angry with that generation" to "they saw my works for forty years. Therefore (διό), I was angry with that generation" (Heb 3:10). The author has probably altered the citation to speak to his church, which is in danger of failing to reach the promised land. Moreover, the conclusion that Israel did not enter God's rest prepares the way for the author's argument for the community's opportunity to enter the promised land.[19] In the qualifications for the high priesthood (5:1–5), the author indicates that the high priest must "be able to deal gently with the ignorant and wayward, since he himself is beset by weakness" (5:2) but offers no OT reference for this claim. In chapter 11, the catalog on the heroes of faith consistently indicates that each acted "by faith," although in the OT faith is attributed only to Abraham (Gen 15:6). As the opposite of the faith that looks to "things unseen" (11:1), the author recalls that Esau sought a "place of repentance but did not find it" (12:17), apparently following haggadic traditions rather than the OT. Thus the author frequently reshapes citations to reinforce his message. He cites Hag 2:6 (Heb 12:26), "I will shake the heavens and the earth and the sea and the dry land," but reduces the citation to "I will shake not only the earth but also the heavens." The citation reflects the author's consistent distinction between the heavens and the earth. Thus the author's theology has shaped his citation of Scripture.

The author both chooses and arranges passage that advance his theological purpose. In the catena of passages in 1:5–13, for example, while the author does not comment on the passages, he establishes a comparison between the angels and the exalted Christ, choosing psalms that express the contrast between the creation, which will be destroyed, and the Son, who abides (διαμένει), and attributing passages related to God to the exalted Son (1:1; cf. Ps 101:26–28). Similarly, he contrasts the order of Melchizedek,

---

18. Rascher, *Schriftauslegung*, 1.

19. According to Christian Frevel, Heb 3:7—4:11 is a "violent reinterpretation"—going against the sense of the Pentateuch and Psalms contexts—and the author of Hebrews' "inexcusable hermeneutical sin," since it excludes present Israel from the promise. Frevel, "σήημερον—Understanding Psalm 95 within, and without, Hebrews," 166.

which abides forever (μένει ἱερεὺς εἰς τὸ διηνεκές) (6:20; 7:3, 8, 17, 21, 28; cf. Ps 110:4), with the impermanence of the Aaronic priesthood (7:8, 17, 21, 28). The author cites passages selectively, omitting the parts that do not advance his argument.

The Theology of the Word

The theology of the word expressed in the opening words of Hebrews is a central feature of the entire homily and the presupposition for its hermeneutic. God's word "in a Son" forms an *inclusio* with the claim that "the word of God is living and active" (4:12), marking the first major division in the homily. The Sinai theophany, described near the end of the homily (12:18–29), was a word event; the people could not bear "the voice whose words made the hearers beg that not another word be spoken to them" (12:19). In coming to Mount Zion, however, the community now hears "the sprinkled blood that speaks better than the blood of Abel" (12:24). At Sinai, the Israelites heard a voice from the earth, but now the community hears the warning from heaven (12:25). While the voice at Sinai shook the earth, the divine word promises the shaking of heaven and earth (12:26), so that only that which cannot be shaken remains (12:27).

Just as God's word to the ancestors was inseparable from the divine deeds, God's word in a Son involves the entire Christ event, God's ultimate revelation. As the focus on the divine deeds indicates in 1:2b–4, God has spoken in the Christ event.[20] He interprets this event with the words of Scripture, indicating that the God who has spoken in the past now speaks through the Scripture. The manner in which the author introduces citations is significant in demonstrating how the OT now functions for the church. The citations are introduced as words of God (1:5–13; 12:5–6), of Christ (2:12–13; 10:5–8), and of the Holy Spirit (3:7; 10:15), not of a human author.[21] The citation of Psalm 8 in Heb 2:6–8 is introduced as God's "witness" about the humiliation and exaltation of Jesus. In the citations introduced in 2:12–13, the Son speaks to God in language derived from the OT. Similarly, in 10:5–7, words from Psalm 40:6–8 are quoted as the words of the incarnate Son.

The author of Hebrews does not speak of promise and fulfillment, and his citations are never introduced as the fulfillment of prophecy. The words of the OT are in fact God's words to the church in the last days (1:2).

---

20. Wider, *Theozentrik und Bekenntnis*, 32.

21. Hübner, in *Biblische Theologie des Neuen Testaments*, 19, speaks of the trinitarian revelation of God.

In the catena of citations in chapter 1, God speaks through OT texts to the Son (1:5, 8, 10, 13) and to the angels (1:7). All of the sayings of the catena are living, heavenly words of God to the Son, and almost all begin with σύ. God's words in the past are now spoken to the Son at the exaltation. Similarly, God addresses (λαλήσας) the exalted Christ, "you are my Son; today I have begotten you" (5:5; cf. Ps 2:7) and "you are a high priest after the order of Melchizedek" (5:5; cf. Ps 110:4) at the exaltation. When he comes into the world (10:5), Jesus describes his sacrifice in the words of Ps 40. The promise of a new covenant has become a reality in the sacrifice of Christ (8:7-13; 10:15-18).

One may note also that the author's introductory formulae in citing the OT provide a clue to his view of the word of God. Forms of λέγειν are preferred to the familiar "it is written" (1:5; 13; 4:3-4; 5:5-6; 7:20; 8:8; 5:10; 13:5).[22] The author has a decided preference for the present tense (cf. 1:6-8; 2: 12-13; 3:7). When he introduces the citation with "it says somewhere" (4:4), the human author and the exact reference is unimportant, for it is *God* who speaks.[23] As Graham Hughes has said, the author sees such a close conformity between the OT and the NT forms of the word of God that the former can now be appropriated to give expression to the latter.[24] The author reads the Bible as "God's word in a son."

Psalm 110:1 is the cornerstone of this series of midrashim. It is the frame for the catena of passages in 1:5-13 and the reflection on Ps 8 in 2:5-18. The exaltation is assumed in the promise of entering God's rest in 3:7—4:11. With subordinate passages, Ps 110:1 provides the portrayal of the work of Christ in 7:1—10:18.[25] The cultic section assumes activity in the heavenly world (8:1—10:18). Jeremiah 31:31-34 and Lev 16 describe the work of Christ. The homeland of Heb 11 assumes that Christ has already entered.[26]

The Hermeneutic Task

The author, who describes his work as a "word of exhortation" (13:22), is one in a series of leaders who have "spoken the word of God" (13:7) to this community, thus confirming the word that was originally spoken by the Lord (2:1-4). To speak a "word of exhortation" is to address the community

22. See Rascher, *Schriftauslegung*, 31.
23. Rascher, *Schriftauslegung*, 34.
24. Hughes, *Hermeneutics*, 62.
25. See Son, *Zion Symbolism in Hebrews*, 176-84.
26. See Attridge, "The Psalms in Hebrews," 198-99.

with the word of God, the λόγος of Scripture that speaks to the readers of the author's own time. Thus Hebrews consists of a series of interpretations of the Bible and the author's comments on the hermeneutical task.

Observers have often noticed the pervasiveness in Hebrews of terms for speaking, which suggest the author's role in speaking the word of God. Indeed, the first major unit of the book begins with the reference to the God who has spoken "in a Son" and concludes with a reference to the "word of God," which is living and active. At 5:11 the author introduces his readers to a "word" that is "difficult to explain." This term refers to the central section of the epistle. Near the end of the book the author refers to the one "who is speaking" (12:25). These references indicate the significance of the author's work in the task of hermeneutics. This "word of exhortation" is based on words that continue to speak through the author's own voice.

Hebrews 1:1–3

The opening lines of Hebrews, which have been described as the "overture" or exordium to the entire sermon,[27] introduce the problem that will occupy the author throughout this "word of exhortation": the relationship between God's word in the past and in the "last days." This programmatic statement implies both the continuity and discontinuity of the two periods.[28] Continuity is suggested by the identification of the recipients of the former revelation as "fathers" (1:1; cf. πρεσβύτεροι in 11:1) and by the fact that the same God initiates the action in 1:1 and 1:2. Furthermore, both in the present and in the past "God has spoken." The emphasis on God's speaking, a major emphasis of the entire epistle (cf. 2:1; 4:1–2; 12:25), provides the point of continuity between the present and the past. The church, like Israel, has received the "λόγος of hearing" (4:2). The prophets were, according to 1:1, the instruments of God's word. The institutions and words of the OT have their origin in the words of God. Consequently, the author consistently cites the OT as the word of God.

The antithetical parallelism of "in the past" and "in these last days" indicates the continuity and discontinuity in God's revelation. The old revelation was πολυμερῶς καὶ πολυτρόπως, "partial and piecemeal."[29] The introduction here anticipates the argument of the rest of the book, for the author consistently indicates the superiority of the work of Christ. Unlike the OT institutions, which are regularly described as incomplete and partial

---

27. Grässer, "Hebräer 1,1–4. Ein exegetischer Versuch," 187.
28. Hughes, *Hebrews and Hermeneutics*, 35.
29. Hughes, *Hebrews and Hermeneutics*, 6.

(cf. 7:1 1, 27; 10:1-4), God's word in the Son is final. Thus the word in the Son both corresponds to and surpasses the fragmentary and incomplete words of the past.

The exordium of 1:1–3 anticipates the arguments that are developed in the remainder of the epistle. It provides a hermeneutical key to the author's work, for the author consistently demonstrates the continuity and discontinuity of the revelation of God. The OT is obviously the word of God, for the author appeals to it regularly. It provides the author's points for comparison, and its people are the church's predecessors in hearing the word of God (cf. 4:2; ch. 11). At the same time, the author argues consistently that God's word in the Son surpasses his words of the past. In the remaining references to God's activity in speaking, the author indicates more precisely what is meant by "in a son."

Hebrews 4:12–13

The first major unit of Hebrews concludes, after a series of reflections on OT texts, with a hymnic meditation on the word of God. This meditation recalls the overture to the epistle. The opening line of the book and 4:12–13 thus begin and end with reflections on the word of God. Although 4:12–13 appears at first to be an isolated unit, the context of Hebrews suggests the author's meaning. Γάρ in 4: 12 indicates that these reflections grow out of the author's commentary on Ps 95, which has been the subject of 3:7—4:1 1. In the author's reading of the wilderness story, the disobedience of Israel was total, and "all" who left Egypt failed to enter the promised land (3:16-19).[30] Israel, a "model" (ὑπόδειγμα) of disobedience,[31] did not enter the promised rest. The Psalm citation "They shall never enter my rest" (Heb 3:11; Ps 95:11) is understood as evidence that the rest was never attained. The author employs the well-known rabbinic hermeneutic rules, *gezera shewa*, to show that the "rest" of Ps 95 and Gen 2:2 ("God rested" on the seventh day) was the transcendent world (cf. 3:1; 11:14, 16; 13:14).[32]

The words of the psalmist, understood within the framework offered by Gen 2:2, now become "sharper than any two-edged sword" for the church. A hermeneutical principle, which the author uses twice elsewhere (7:11; 8:7), allows him to conclude that the full benefits of salvation

---

30. Paul likewise recalls the wilderness period as a time of failure.

31. The OT offers both positive (6:12; cf. chap. 11) and negative (cf. 12:15–17) examples for the church.

32. The *gezera shawa* argument was one of the seven hermeneutical rules attributed to Rabbi Hillel. Cf. Strack, *Introduction to the Talmud and Midrash*, 94.

were never attained in the OT. Hence, the OT texts reflect an awareness of imperfection and a lack of fulfillment and imply "another day" (4:8). For the author of Hebrews, the "today" of the psalm is the time of the church (3:12–13, 15; 4:7, 8). The OT text addresses the church with both warning (3:12) and promise (4:1–11). The church has heard the same "word of hearing" (4:2) and stands under the same promise that was heard by Israel (4:1). The author does not claim that the promise has been fulfilled in the church. Instead, the psalm now functions as God's oath to the church ("I swore in my wrath . . ."), providing both warning and assurance that "there is a sabbath for the people of God" (4:9).

The fact that the words of the OT address the church "today" suggests that the "word of God" in 4:12 is to be identified with the words that God has spoken in his Son. God has previously spoken to Israel but has now addressed the church (4:2). There is, as 1:1–2 indicates, a continuity in the revelation of God's word. However, the word of God has been spoken with finality in his Son (1:1–2; 2:3). Consequently, the community that hears the word is summoned to pay attention (3:1), to hold on (3:6, 14), to fear (4:1), and to make every effort (4:11) to maintain its fidelity. Indeed, the Christians are to "encourage one another" (3:12–13) and thus to continue the author's own work of providing a "word of exhortation" (13:22). Because of Israel's example (4:11), the community knows that it cannot trifle with the word of God, which both penetrates the inner recesses of the heart and calls for a word in return ("to whom we give an account," 4:13).

Hebrews 5:11–14

In 5:11–14 the author makes a third major statement about the word of God in the life of the community. The statement that "there is much to say which is hard to explain" is the opening line of a paraenesis that interrupts the discussion of the high priesthood in 5:1–10. The subject of the high priesthood after the order of Melchizedek is resumed in 6:19. The concern of 5:11–14 is, as Hughes has pointed out, hermeneutics.[33] The accusation against the lethargic church in 5:11–12 focuses on its incompetence in the word of righteousness, its inability to teach and its intellectual sluggishness. The lethargy of the church, which is frequently attested in the epistle, is here related to its lethargy with respect to the word of God.

For such a community, the solid food and word of righteousness is hard to explain. This "difficult word" is not esoteric, for it should be the property of the whole community. Indeed, just as the whole community is

33. Hughes, *Hermeneutics*, 47–51.

"dull of hearing," the mastery of the "difficult" word is available to all who will exercise their faculties with the solid food (5:14).

The "word that is hard to explain" is the treatment of the heavenly high priesthood, which is developed from the use of Ps 110:4 and other texts in 7:1—10:18. The author is thus aware that Christ speaks a "beginning word" (6:1) and a "difficult" or "sublime" word.[34] A church that has endured into the second generation needs the stability that is derived from the "word that is hard to explain." The texts of the OT, especially Ps 110:4, are also the words of Christ to the community.

Hebrews 6:13—10:18

The hermeneutical procedure of the author of Hebrews is to be seen in the "word that is hard to explain," which is introduced in 6:13-20. The author begins this section by indicating that Abraham is the paradigm of fidelity in attaining the promise (6:12-15). After indicating the importance of oaths in providing assurance (6:16), the author indicates that Christians also have received an oath, which provides the encouragement to seize the hope that has been laid out (6:18). This oath is not, however, the same oath that Abraham received. The oath and the promise, the "two unchangeable things" that offer encouragement to the church, were made available with the exaltation of Christ (6:19-20), when Christ became the high priest after the order of Melchizedek. The oath spoken to the church is apparently connected with God's oath recorded in Ps 110:4: "The Lord has sworn, and will not change his mind, 'You are a priest forever'" (cf. 7:21). The author places such a significance on the oath that the church has received that the Christian message is described as "the word of the oath" (7:28). The consistent references to God's oath are to be understood within the larger context of the introductory statement of Hebrews. God's "word in a son" includes both the words spoken by Jesus (2:1-4) and the entire event of the death and exaltation. Indeed, God's deed in the exaltation is also his word of oath to the church, his final and definitive form of the promise.[35]

Unlike Paul, the author of Hebrews never says that "all of the promises of God find their 'yes' in him" (cf. 2 Cor 1:20), for in Hebrews God's promise still remains (cf. 4:1). Indeed, Jesus Christ continues to speak to the church

---

34. The term δυσερμήνευτος was used in antiquity for a sublime message. Origen uses the term λόγος δυσερμήνευτος, particularly against Celsus's criticism of Christian belief, to describe the sublimity of the Christian message. Cf. Thompson, *Beginnings of Christian Philosophy*, 31.

35. Hughes, *Hermeneutics*, 53.

through the words of the OT (cf. 12:25). Promises spoken to Israel once more offer hope to this discouraged church (cf. 12:26). God speaks in the event of Jesus Christ, confirming his oath, and the church continues to await the fulfillment of the promise (cf. 12:26), in continuity with ancient Israel.

The Interpreter of Scripture

The author offers a window into his hermeneutical method in the description of the high priestly work in the sanctuary in 9:1-14. He continues the comparison between the earthly and heavenly sanctuaries (cf. 8:1-5), now contrasting the earthly sanctuary (ἅγιον κοσμικόν, 9:1) with the "greater and more perfect tent" (9:11) in order to establish the correspondence between the entry of the high priest into the earthly sanctuary (9:6-10) and the entry of Christ into the heavenly sanctuary (9:11-14). The description of the earthly cultus draws selectively from the OT texts (Exod 25:31; 26:31, 33-34; Heb 9:5) to focus on the annual entry of the high priest on *yom kippur* (Lev 16:2, 14; Heb 9:7).[36] The focus on the first and second tent (9:7-8) is indicated in the author's interpretative comment in 9:8: "The Holy Spirit indicating (δηλοῦντος τοῦ πνεύματος τοῦ ἁγίου) that the way of the sanctuary has not yet been revealed (πεφανερῶσθαι) as long as the first tent is still standing, which (ἥτις)[37] is a symbol [παραβολή] of the present time" (9:9). The first tent has a parabolic sense, signifying that access to God was limited under the old covenant.

Having said earlier that the Holy Spirit speaks through Scripture (3:7) and has confirmed the word through signs and wonders (2:14), the author now maintains that the Holy Spirit discloses the significance of the OT cult. The reference to the Holy Spirit is not simply an allusion to the divine inspiration of the scriptural account but an indication of the contemporary relevance of its message.[38]

Forms of δηλόω are used in 9:8 and 12:27 for the task of interpretation. In both instances the present tense is used. The term signifies the hidden meaning of a revelation (cf. 1 Cor 3:11; 1 Pet 1:22; 2 Pet 1:14).[39] The

36. Rascher, *Schriftauslegung*, 152. The author says little about the actual rite on *yom kippur*. He does not mention the garments of the high priest, the animals sacrificed, or the goat that is sent into the wilderness.

37. Interpreters debate whether ἥτις refers to the whole situation described in 9:8 or to the first tent (πρώτη σκηνή). Here it refers to the first tent, the symbol of the present time. See Grässer, *Hebräer*, 2.134.

38. Attridge, *Hebrews*, 240.

39. Backhaus, *Hebräerbrief*, 309. BDAG 222. In the LXX it is used for the divine revelation. God declares his name (Exod 6:3), his plans (Exod 33:12), his secrets (Ps 50:6;

language indicates the continuing activity of the Holy Spirit in interpreting the hidden meaning of Scripture. The Holy Spirit, rather than the author himself, is the interpreter of Scripture. Otto Michel comments on 9:8:

> Here in the order of cult and priestly service lies the intent and the announcement of the Holy Spirit, who speaks to us in signs and parables in a way different from the Jewish understanding of the word. The Holy Spirit is thus the living word of God, who can speak also to us through the word of the law.[40]

This interpretation is a παραβολή of "the present time" (καιρὸς τὸν ἐνεστηκότα) in which gifts and sacrifices are offered that cleanse only the flesh until the time of reformation (μέχρι καιροῦ διορθώσεως, 9:9). Παραβολή, a term that is used outside the Gospels only in Hebrews (cf. 11:19), is frequently used among rhetoricians to describe an example or symbol that points beyond itself.[41] It symbolizes the lack of access to God and the inadequacy of the sacrifices in the old cultus. The first and second tents symbolize the provisional nature of the old cultus and point toward a better cult that takes place in the superior sanctuary.[42] Consistent with the author's announcement of "these last days" (1:2), he gives an eschatological and christological interpretation of Scripture, contrasting two καιροί: the "present time" with the "time of reformation." The latter is the time of the new covenant, which has already become a reality.[43] The new covenant both corresponds to and surpasses the old covenant. Gudrun Holtz speaks of the "double hermeneutic" of correspondence and superiority (German: Entsprechung und Überbietung).[44]

Throughout the "word that is hard to explain" (7:1—10:18), the author reads the OT from the perspective of the "last days" (cf. 1:1–2), which have dawned with the Christ event (cf. 1:2; 9:9; 10:1), the decisive moment in salvation history. Indeed, Ps 110:1, 4, the church's favorite exaltation text, provides the framework for the entire section (cf. 7 passim; 8:1, 2;

Dan 2:28). Philo uses the formula ὡς δηλοῖ τὸ λόγιον (*Fug.* 157'; *Migr Ab.* 85'cf. 92) to denote the revelation given in the OT. In Daniel 2:5–7 it is used for the interpretation of dreams. In *Barn.* It is used for the allegorical interpretation of the OT (9:8; 17:1). See Bultmann, "δηλόω."

40. Michel, *Der Brief an die Hebräer*, 306.

41. BDAG, 759. In rhetoric παραβολή is a "more or less developed comparison in which two things or processes from different fields are set side by side so that in virtue of the similarity the unknown may be elucidated by the known." Hauck, "Παραβολή." See Quintilian, *Inst. Or.* 5.11.23.

42. Backhaus, *Hebräerbrief*, 310; Rascher, *Schriftauslegung*, 155.

43. Stefan Svendsen, *Allegory Transformed*, 174.

44. Holtz, "Besser und doch gleich," 159.

10; 10:11–14), and Christ is presented as the exalted high priest in the heavenly sanctuary. Other passages, including the Yom Kippur ceremony of Lev 16 and Exod 25:40, are employed to fill the portrait of Christ the heavenly high priest. The decisive moment is Christ's entry (cf. 6:19, 20; 9:12, 24) into the heavenly world. The variety of OT texts is read in the light of God's revelation in Christ. The author knows apart from the OT that Christ "died for our sins" and that he is exalted to the presence of God. The OT is then interpreted to illuminate the portrait of Jesus Christ, the exalted one, and to provide the categories for describing him. Although the institutions of the OT are ineffectual, since they are associated with a "fleshly" (7:16) or "earthly" (9:1) sphere, they provide the framework or "parable" for understanding the exalted work of Christ. Thus the OT is the word of God when it is read in the light of the Christian confession, even though it describes inadequate institutions.

Indeed, the author announces the divine appointment of Jesus as Son and high priest at the exaltation "in these last days," using the words of Scripture (1:5–13; 5:5; 8:10). The "today" of Ps 95 is not only spoken to ancient Israel but also to the church (3:13), which now lives in the new covenant announced by Jeremiah (8:7–13; 10:15–18). This eschatological and christological interpretation of Scripture is reminiscent of that of other NT writers (cf. 1 Cor 9:19; 10:11) and has similarities to the pesher method of interpretation at Qumran.

While some scholars describe the interpretation as typological, the author moves beyond typological interpretation, which focuses on the correspondence between the old and the new. The comparison of the old and new cultus in Hebrews is a *synkrisis*, a common rhetorical device. The author not only compares the old and the new, but also compares two levels of reality: the earthly sanctuary (9:1) and the greater and more perfect tent (9:11–14; cf. 8:1–5).[45] The παραβολή (9:8) not only points to the inadequacy of the earthly cultus (9:9–10) but also provides the language for describing the Christ event (9:11–14). This *synkrisis* conforms to the ancient type in which comparison is made between two items that are of a similar type, but one is superior.[46]

---

45. Svendsen, *Allegory Transformed*, 59. "It is significant that Christ emerged as a high priest centuries after the inauguration of the Levitical priesthood. But it is also significant that when he finally did, he appeared in the form of a heavenly high priest. As emerges from 9:23–25 he delivered his sacrifice in heaven, and even though he lived on earth for a certain period of time 7:26 and 8:5 inform us that he now resides in the word of heaven and performs his priestly duties there. What we have, then, is a combined hermeneutical movement from past to present and from earth to heaven."

46. According to Theon, "Synkrises are not comparisons of things having a great difference between them. Comparisons should be of likes and where we are in doubt

The author thus engages in a hermeneutic of correspondence and superiority.[47] The superior reality for Hebrews belongs to the heavenly world, while OT institutions belong to the physical world. Thus while the author employs an eschatological hermeneutic that had been employed in early Christianity and Judaism, his interpretation also has points of contact with the hermeneutic of Philo, who also interpreted the tabernacle as a symbol (cf. *Ebr.* 132–34). For him it was a symbol of wisdom (*Her.* 112–13; *Congr.* 116) and virtue (*Ebr.* 133–34),[48] terms that Philo uses interchangeably (cf. *Congr.* 114; *Leg.* 3. 46–48). "Let us conceive, then, of the tabernacle and altar as 'ideas,' the first being a symbol of incorporeal virtue, the other a symbol of the sensible image" (*Ebr.* 134). According to Svendson,

> Although Philo's analyses are not always consistent, a general picture emerges according to which the Holy of Holies signifies the realm of transcendence (*QE* 2.68f) and the Holy Place and the outer compartments of the tent the world of immanence. Thus the outer sections signify the world beneath the moon (2.69), whereas the Holy Place is an image of the physical sky (2.83).[49]

The author of Hebrews does not engage in the extended allegorical hermeneutic that is characteristic of Philo, but he shares with him the interpretation based on the two levels of reality. This hermeneutic is a consistent feature in Hebrews. In the first *synkrisis*, the words of Scripture declare that the exalted Son is greater than the angels (1:4), inasmuch as he is exalted into the unchanging heavenly world above the angels (1:5–13), and thus only he abides forever. The author makes a parallel argument in comparing the priesthood according to Melchizedek to the Aaronic priesthood (5:1–10; 6:19—7:28). As a priest forever according to the order of Melchizedek, the exalted Christ is a heavenly and abiding being (7:3, 16, 24, 28), unlike the Levitical priests who die and are replaced by others (7:23–25). The new covenant is the heavenly cultus in which the exalted and superior high priest offers a better sacrifice in a better sanctuary (9:1—10:18). Near the conclusion of the homily, the author compares the Sinai theophany unfavorably to the heavenly Jerusalem to

---

which should be preferred because of no evident superiority of one to the other." Cited in Kennedy, trans. and ed., *Progymnasmata*, 53 See also Kneepkens, "Comparatio." See the discussion in chapter 4, "Argument and Persuasion in Hebrews."

47. Holtz, "Besser und doch gleich—zur doppelten Hermeneutik des Hebraerbriefes," 159.

48. "When God willed to send down the image of divine excellence from heaven to earth in pity for our race, that should not lose its share in the better portion (*Her.* 112–13; Colson, LCL), he constructs as a symbol of the truth the holy tabernacle and its contents to be a representative of wisdom" (Colson, LCL).

49. Svendsen, *Allegory Transformed*, 165.

which the community has come (12:18–29). In each comparison, the author compares OT institutions unfavorably with Christ and the new covenant, indicating that the former belong to the physical world, while the latter belong to the heavenly and unchanging world.[50]

This *synkrisis* hermeneutic is common among Middle Platonists, including Plutarch and Philo, and reflects the influence of Middle Platonism on the author. Plutarch Plutarch (*Is. Os.* 373E) speaks of "The better (κρείττων) and more divine nature" and adds (*Is. Os.* 373): "For that which really is and is perceptible and good is superior (κρεῖττον) to destruction and change."[51] Philo, who employs *synkrisis* in many instances, frequently employs this rhetorical device in describing the two levels of reality. In a comparison of Leah and Rachel, he says that Rachel is mortal, while Leah is immortal, adding, that all things that are precious to the senses are inferior in perfection to beauty of soul, they are many and it but one" (*Sobr* 12).[52]

The *synkrisis* is the *basis* for the frequent *qal wachomer* arguments, which appear in the exhortations in the homily. In 1:4–13, the author argues that the exalted Christ is "greater than the angels" (1:4) and concludes with a comparison between the punishments given in the respective eras. Appealing to a premise that the author apparently shares with his readers, he recalls that disobedience to the "word delivered by angels" carried a severe punishment. Then he draws the logical conclusion with the question, "How shall we escape if we neglect such a great salvation" (2:4). That is, the "great salvation" is the result of the exaltation of Christ above the angels (cf. 1:4–13) in "these last days" (1:2). Thus the word "delivered by angels" is inferior to the word "spoken by the Lord" (2:1–2). Disobedience to the greater salvation results in a greater punishment.

A similar use of the *qal wachomer* appears at the conclusion of the extended *synkrisis* in 7:1—10:31. The comparison of high priest, sanctuary, and sacrifice is followed by the *qal wachomer* interpretation in 10:26–31. Once more the author maintains that the greater punishment is given to those who have "spurned the Son of God and profaned the blood of the covenant" (10:29–30). That is, the two covenants correspond in punishing disobedience. However, inasmuch as the new covenant is greater than the old one, the punishment for disobedience is also greater. The *qal wachomer* argument indicates the logical consequence of the *synkrisis* in 7:1—10:18.

A third use of the *synkrisis* associated with the *qal wachomer* appears in the final *synkrisis* in Hebrews. In 12:18–24, the author has contrasted the

---

50. Theobald, "Vom Text zum 'lebendigen Wort,'" 788.
51. See ch. 6 for Plutarch and Philo.
52. See ch. 6.

divine voice that shook the earth at Mount Sinai with the blood of Christ, which speaks greater than the blood of Abel. The first voice came from the earth, while the divine voice now warns from heaven. Indeed, if the Israelites did not escape when first voice shook the earth, "how much more is this the case for those who are warned from heaven." The *qal wachomer* once more follows the *synkrisis*.

The Word of God as the Word of Encouragement

The ultimate purpose of the author's interpretation of Scripture is to offer a "word of encouragement," as he indicates at the end of the book. The significance of encouragement in the lengthy interpretation of the OT is also suggested by the fact that the introductory words to this "word that is hard to explain" point to the "encouragement" that is offered to Christian "refugees" as they seize the hope that is set before them. The end of the section also (10:19-39) is a challenge for Christians to hold fast to their hope and to offer encouragement to each other (10:23-25). Thus both the introduction and the conclusion of the section refer to the encouragement and hope that are offered by the Christian interpretation of the OT. A "word of exhortation" (13:22) is thus an exercise in hermeneutics, a demonstration of the fact that ancient words continue to offer encouragement to a weary church.

The author is not the only one who offers a word of encouragement, for his words suggest also that the whole community engages in the task of encouraging each other (3:12; 10:25). Just as encouragement is the task of all, hermeneutics is the task of all, according to 5:11-14, for the author summons all to be teachers, to become "skilled in the word of righteousness," to "train the faculties" with the "word that is hard to explain" and thus to be able to distinguish good from evil (5:14). The task of hermeneutics is not reserved for a special class within the church, for the author appears to be challenging his readers to become teachers of the word of God, in continuity with him and with the past teachers (13:7). This discouraged church can find its encouragement and hope only as the members jointly involve themselves in the hermeneutical task. Only an encouragement that is based on the word that continues to speak to the church will offer a genuine "word of exhortation."

CHAPTER 2

THE NEW IS BETTER

A NEGLECTED ASPECT OF THE HERMENEUTICS OF HEBREWS

One of the distinguishing features of the argument of Hebrews is amplification, the recycling of themes that the speaker has already developed (Aristotle, *Rhet.* 3.19.1–2).[1] A significant example of the author's use of this practice is the repeated appeal to unstated premises that he apparently expects to be an effective means of persuasion. Consistent with this normal argumentation, on four occasions the author appeals to one premise and draws a logical conclusion as part of a hermeneutical procedure within the exposition of one or more texts. Thus he argues:

> "If Joshua had given them rest, he would not have spoken of another day." (4:8)

> "If there were perfection under the Levitical priesthood, . . . what need was there for another priesthood to arise according to the order of Melchizedek and not according to the order of Aaron?" (7:11)

> "For if that first [covenant] were blameless, he would not have sought a place for the second." (8:7)

> "In saying 'new' he made the first obsolete; but what is becoming obsolete and growing old is near to disappearing." (8:13)

> "He takes away the first in order to establish the second." (10:9)

In each instance, the author cites a specific passage to demonstrate the finality of the new and the inadequacy of the old, assuming that the new

---

1. Originally published in *Catholic Biblical Quarterly* 73 (2011) 547–61. Olbricht, "Hebrews as Amplification," 375–89.

passage cancels an older one when a conflict between the two is evident. In three of the four instances, he employs a contrary-to-fact conditional sentence to contrast the later passage with the earlier one. Similarly, in three of the passages, a psalm supersedes the Torah, while in the fourth passage Jer 31:31–34 supersedes Exod 24:8.[2] The author finds within the Psalms and Jeremiah the announcement of God's new deed in Christ, arguing that the new passage nullifies earlier passages. Thus he employs a specific hermeneutical procedure to argue that the announcement of the new is both a critique and a nullification of the old.

Contrary to traditional interpretations, this procedure does not belong to a polemic against Judaism but is a reaffirmation of commitments that the community has already made. As part of his persuasive strategy to convince the readers that it is worthwhile to hold firmly to the confession (4:14; 10:23), the author frequently employs *synkrisis* to demonstrate the greatness of the new revelation in Christ, comparing it to the old revelation "in the past" (1:1). This hermeneutical procedure, which appears at pivotal moments in the argument, has no parallel among other NT writings. Although NT writers consistently portray the Christ event as the culmination or fulfillment of Israel's story, they do not employ this particular hermeneutical method. Nor does this hermeneutical procedure have a direct analogue with the pesher exegesis of Qumran or the rules for hermeneutics established in the rabbinic literature.

F. Schröger has offered numerous examples of the author's appeal to rabbinic hermeneutical practices,[3] demonstrating that he uses the first two hermeneutical methods established by Rabbi Hillel, *qal wachomer* and *gezera shewa*.[4] Indeed, he uses the *qal wachomer* on at least three occasions. Schröger has also noted the four passages listed above as distinct hermeneutical category under the heading, "A new act of God cancels the old one,"[5] indicating that it also belonged to rabbinic hermeneutical rules but does not offer clear examples of parallels in rabbinic exegesis. One proposed parallel is the statement of Rabbi Dimi that "[one] will nullifies [another] will"

---

2. The author is often indefinite in identifying the earlier passage. One may assume that Heb 4:8 recalls the passages in Deuteronomy and Joshua that claim that Israel had rest (Deut 12:10; 25:19, Josh 1:13, 15; 21:44; 22:4; 23:1). In 7:11, he sets the reference to the priesthood of Melchizedek over against the earlier priesthood, but does not identify the passage. The contrast in 8:7, 13 between the new and old covenants may be a reference to Exod 24, cited in Heb 9:15–22. The citation in 10:9 refers to the old sacrificial system, but not to a specific passage.

3. Schröger, *Der Verfasser des Hebräerbriefes als Schriftausleger*, 258.

4. *Qal wachomer* is used in 2:2–3; 10:26–31; 12:25–28; *gezera shewa* is used in 4:4–8.

5. Schröger, *Der Verfasser des Hebräerbriefes als Schriftausleger*, 258 ("eine neue Tat Gottes hebt die alte auf").

(*BB* 135b; 152b).⁶ This comment, indicating that a dying man may cancel a bequest to one person by making a second will to another person, was one of many comments made in a discussion of the validity of wills, not an established rule of biblical interpretation. Despite the attempts to discover a rabbinic provenance for this argument, the claim that the new nullifies the old has no precise parallel. The author does not speak of the fulfillment of prophecies in Christ but consistently appeals to later passages to argue that the announcement of the new is an implied critique of the old. Nevertheless, this hermeneutic is a cornerstone of the author's argument and is consistent with his claim that God has spoken the ultimate revelation in Christ.

The argument is especially remarkable against the background of the assumption that the old is better, a commonplace in ancient discourse. In the *Timaeus*, Plato cites a Pythagorean text, according to which τὸ πρεσβύτερον κάρρον (=κρεῖττον).⁷ In both philosophical discourse and daily life, ancient people shared the opinion that the old is better and that the new is dangerous. Socrates is condemned because he introduced καιν δαιμόνια (Xenophon, *Mem.* 11.1; cf. Plato, *Apol* 24 b 8–c 1). Thus, according to the common understanding, "Things which happened or did not happen in a remote past, and especially at the beginning itself, are decisive for the whole and forever."⁸ Indeed, one of the major challenges faced by the apologists was to respond to the ancient charge that Christianity was new.⁹

The NT provides examples of the appeal to the primordial as a norm for the community, arguing that the new was, in fact, a return to the beginning. In the Synoptic tradition, Jesus argues in a way that is opposite the argument in Hebrews. Placing the creation story alongside the divorce law of Deut 24:1–4, he argues that the primordial has precedence over the Torah (Mark 10:2–9). Similarly, he answers questions about the Sabbath by giving precedence to the creation story over the Sabbath law (cf. Mark 2:23–28). Paul also argues that of "the new creation" (2 Cor 5:17), maintaining that this event is the restoration of the primordial.

Inasmuch as effective persuasion involves moving from shared assumptions toward a specific outcome, one may assume that the author is appealing to premises that are plausible to the readers. Since the argument that the new nullifies the old has no apparent parallel in the NT, rabbinic literature, or the Dead Sea Scrolls, one must ask what premises the author

---

6. Strack and Billerbeck, *Kommentar zum Neuen Testament aus Talmud und Midrasch*, 3.549.

7. Pilhofer, *Presbyterion Kreitton*, 18.

8. Van Groningen, *In the Grip of the Past*, 16.

9. Pilhofer, *Presbyterion Kreitton*, 221.

shares with the audience that would make the argument effective. Thus the purpose of this paper is to locate the world of assumptions in which this argument could be persuasive.

Old and New in Philo of Alexandria

Because of the numerous parallels between the arguments of Hebrews and the works of Philo of Alexandria, the latter is an obvious place to begin in a search for parallels. Philo discusses the relationship between the old and new on numerous occasions. In political discussions he argues for the maintenance of old traditions and against the introduction of new practices.[10] He goes to great lengths to prove that the teachings of Moses preceded the discoveries of the Greeks (cf. *Her.* 214; *Leg.* 1.105; *QG* 4.152; *Prob.* 57).[11] Nevertheless, on other issues Philo insists on the greater value of the new over the old, claiming that the virtuous person moves beyond the ancient traditions toward the new teaching from God. For example, in *Her.* 278, Philo discusses Gen 15:15, taking note of the fact that after the words "thou shalt depart" come the words "to thy fathers." Philo asks what fathers are referred to in the text. He concludes that the passage could not refer to the fathers in the land of the Chaldeans, who were the only kinsfolk Abraham had. Philo reads further in the Genesis text, "The Lord said unto Abraham, 'depart from thy land and from thy kinsfolk and from the house of thy father unto the land which I shall shew thee, and I will make thee into a great nation'" (Gen 12:1, 2). He concludes,

> Was it reasonable that he should again have affinity with the very persons from whom he had been alienated by the forethought of God? Or that he who was to be the captain of another race and nation should be associated with that of a former age? God would not bestow on him a fresh and in a sense a novel race and nation, if he were not cutting him right adrift from the old. . . . So we are told to bear out the old from the face of the new (Lev 26:10). Rightly, for how shall they on whom the rain of new blessings has fallen in all its abundance, sudden and unlooked for, still find profit in old-world lore and the ruts of ancient customs?

That is, Philo argues that the new replaces the old.

---

10. *Flacc.* 18, 24, 41, 73.
11. Pilhofer, *Presbyterion Kreitton*, 181–83.

Philo makes a similar argument in *Sacrifices* 76f, discussing the command to bring the firstfruits to God (Lev 2:14). Philo argues,

> Wherefore, "If you bring an offering of firstfruits," make such divisions as Holy Writ prescribes (Lev 2.14). First the new, then the roasted, then the sliced, and last the ground. The new is for the following reason. To those who cling to the old-world days with their fabled past and have not realized the instantaneous and timeless power of God, it is a lesson bidding them accept ideas that are new and fresh and in the vigour of youth. It bids them feed no more on effete fables, which the long course of the ages has handed down for the deception of mortal kind, and thus be filled with false opinions, but rather receive in lull and generous measure new, fresh, blessed thoughts from the ever ageless god. So shall they be schooled to understand that with Him nothing is ancient, nothing at all past, but all is in its birth and existence timeless.

Philo draws wide-ranging conclusions from Lev 2:14. He sees here the new ideas that one should receive rather than be imprisoned in old ones. He adds comments on Lev 19:32, "Thou shalt rise up away from the head of the hoary and thou shalt honour the head of the elder." Nevertheless, he advocated that one should both love ancient truths and welcome new ones.

> No doubt it is profitable, if not for the acquisition of perfect virtue, at any rate for the life of civic virtue, to feed the mind on ancient and time honored thoughts, to trace the venerable tradition of noble deeds, which historians and all the family of poets have handed down to the memory of their own and future generations. But when, unforeseen and unhoped for, the sudden beam of the self-inspired wisdom has shone upon us, when that wisdom has opened the closed eye of the soul and made us spectators rather than hearers of knowledge, and substituted in our minds sight, the swiftest of senses, for the slower sense of hearing, then it is idle any longer to exercise the ear with words. And so we read "ye shall eat the old and older yet, but also bear out the old from the face of the new" (Lev 26.10). The meaning is this. We must not indeed reject any learning that has grown grey through time, nay, we should make it our aim to read the writings of the sages and listen to proverbs and old-world stories from the lips of those who know antiquity, and ever seek for knowledge about the men and deeds of old. For truly it is sweet to leave nothing unknown. Yet when God causes the young shoots of self-inspired wisdom to spring up within the soul,

the knowledge that comes from teaching must straightway be abolished and swept off. Ay, even of itself it will subside and ebb away. (*Sacr.* 78–79)

These texts indicate that Philo held a complex view of the relationship between the old and new. Although scholars have offered these passages as possible parallels to the argument in Hebrews,[12] Philo's argument does not intersect with the argument of Hebrews in significant ways. It does not have obvious parallels to the comparison of two texts and the use of the later text to nullify the earlier one. Thus we look elsewhere for the background to the argument of Hebrews that the new nullifies the old.

Old and New in Legal Discourse

The argument of Paul in Galatians 3 offers an intriguing parallel to the hermeneutical procedure of Hebrews, although Paul takes the argument in the opposite direction. Faced with opponents who insist that gentile converts be circumcised, Paul confronts the apparent conflict between two passages—the promise to Abraham (Gen 15:1-6) and the command for Abraham's circumcision (Gen 17:1-8). Behind this portrayal is the conflict between two parties, each of whom calls on a different passage. The opponents of Paul appeal to the law of Moses, while Paul appeals to the promise to Abraham (Gen 13:15).[13] Paul resolves the issue by claiming that the later passage cannot nullify the earlier one. In 3:15 he says, "No one invalidates (ἀθετεῖ) a covenant that has been put into effect." He adds, "a law that is given 430 years after the covenant has been ratified cannot nullify the promise" (Gal 3:17). Thus Paul raises the question, which law has greater antiquity? The case is clear that the older law has greater weight because it cannot be cancelled by the latter.[14]

Like the argument of Hebrews, Galatians 3 appeals to assumptions that are not readily apparent. Paul assumes that the audience will accept the premise that the older law has priority over the later one. J. S. Vos has shown that Paul's hermeneutical dilemma is reminiscent of discussions in rhetorical handbooks about proper arguments when two laws contradict each other.[15] This issue has a firm place in the stasis theory of the rhetorical handbooks developed by Hermagoras of Temnos. The context of the

12. Cf. Grässer, *An die Hebräer*, 2.103. Grässer cites also Justin, *Dial.* 11:2.

13. Vos, "Die hermeneutische Antinomie be Paulus (Galater 3.11-12; Römer 10.5-10)," 265. See also Vos, *Die Kunst der Argumentation bei Paulus*, 127-29.

14. Vos, "Die hermeneutische Antinomie be Paulus," 265.

15. Vos, "Die hermeneutische Antinomie be Paulus," 260.

argument over conflicting laws is the courtroom in which two parties stand over against each other and appeal to different laws or different paragraphs of the same law. This discussion involves not only laws in the strict sense but other legal documents, including testaments and contracts (Cicero, *Topica* 26.96; Quintilian, *Inst Orat* 7.5.6).[16] In the case of a collision of laws the handbooks offer lists of questions, from which one can determine which had the greater weight. Standard questions included: Which of the two laws is more stringent? Does the law concern gods or men? The state or private individuals? Which law is older? (Quint *Inst Orat.* 7.7.8; Cicero *De Inv.* 2.145). The handbooks are in conflict over the resolution of questions involving conflicting laws. According to Aristotle (*Rhet.* 1.15.25), one must ask a number of questions when laws or contracts are in conflict with each other. One must ask whether the law in question is contrary to any written law or to other previous or subsequent contracts. "For either the latter are valid and the former are not, or the former are right and the latter fraudulent; we may put it in whichever way it seems fit."[17] According to Cicero's *De Inventione* (2.145), the later contract takes precedence.

> The conclusion from this is that if two laws (or whatever number there may be if more than two) cannot be kept because they are at variance, the one is thought to have the greatest claim to be upheld which has reference to the greatest matters. In the second place, he should consider which law was passed last, for the latest law is always the most important; then which law enjoins some action and which permits, for that which is commanded is necessary, that which is permitted is optional.[18]

According to the *Rhetoric ad Herennium* (2.15), when two laws conflict, one must ask a variety of questions. For example, one must determine whether their disagreement is such that one commands and the other prohibits, or whether they have been superseded or restricted, or whether one commands and the other allows. One must also consider which law was passed last. The author adds, "It is a meagre defence for a person to show that he has observed the obligation of a law which has been superseded or restricted, without heeding the obligation of the later law."[19] Thus it was a common topos in rhetorical theory that the most recent law was considered binding.[20]

16. Vos, "Die hermeneutische Antinomie be Paulus," 260.
17. Trans. Freese, LCL.
18. Trans. Hubbell, LCL.
19. Trans. Caplan, LCL.
20. See Anderson, *Rhetorical Theory and Paul*, 143.

Vos argues that Paul's argument in Gal 3:15-18 follows a course of action that was recommended in the rhetorical handbooks in the case of conflicting laws. A legitimate argument was to appeal to the original law. This procedure has parallels in Jewish hermeneutical practice, according to which interpreters claimed that the commands of the Torah correspond with features of the creation story.[21]

The Legal Context of Hebrews

This legal discussion provides the background for determining the place of the author's hermeneutic within the legal discussions. In the first appearance of this argument for the later passage, the author says, "If Joshua had given them rest, he would not have spoken of another day" (4:8). The one who has spoken is God, who has spoken with an oath (3:11; 4:3), a theme that the author develops at great length in the homily (cf. 6:13-20; 7:20-22). The author assumes a conflict between Ps 95 and Deuteronomy/Joshua, according to which the Israelites experienced rest in the promised land (Deut 12:10; 25:19, Josh 1:13, 15; 21:44; 22:4; 23:1). Despite the claims of Deuteronomy and Joshua, the word of God in the psalm nullifies the earlier passages. The "other day" (Heb 4:8) points to "these last days" in which God has spoken (cf. 1:1-2). Thus an eschatological dimension is important to the author's argument. Insofar as he assumes an eschatological reading of Ps 95, his interpretation has points of contact with pesher exegesis. However, the new dimension is the claim that God's word is an oath that has invalidated previous statements. The author apparently assumes that the readers will acknowledge the legal topos that the new will nullifies earlier decrees.

The author's claim that God's oath in the psalm (4:8) nullifies earlier statements anticipates the subsequent appeals to this argument in the central section of the homily (4:14—10:31), where it appears three more times to support the claims for the ultimacy of God's word. In this instance, the juristic frame of reference is evident in 7:11, which the author interprets with a range of legal terminology. In this instance, he is exploring the significance of Ps 110:4, in which God also swore an oath (cf. 7:20-22). According to 7:11, the oath, "You are a priest forever according to the order of Melchizedek," implies a contrast to previous divine utterances, although the author does not identify a particular OT text. His focus in this instance is that Ps 110:4 points to another τάξις of priesthood. Once more he uses the contrary-to-fact statement to indicate that the Levitical priesthood belonged to a τάξις that did not bring perfection, a claim that

---

21. See Berger, *Die Gesetzesauslegung Jesu*, 539-57.

he makes directly in 7:19, creating the inclusio in 7:11, 19. Without arguing the case, the author assumes that the psalm declares a μετάθεσις in the priesthood, and then makes the logical step characteristic of the homily, according to which ἐξ ἀνάγκης[22] this change is also a μετάθεσις in the law. Contrary to the common expectation that the Aaronic high priesthood was perpetual,[23] and Philo's claim that laws are unshakable and immortal (*Vit. Mos.* 2.14), the author claims a μετάθεσις in the law. Μετάθεσις has a range of meanings; it is used by the author for the "taking up" of Enoch (11:5) and the change in the creation (12:27). In Heb 7:12, however, it is used in the technical juridical sense of a change in the law (cf. Plato, *Minos* 7 [3l6c]; 2 Macc 11:24; Josephus, *Ant.* 12.387; *C. Ap.* 286; *Arist.* 8.162).[24] The μετάθεσις in God's law is contrasted to the ἀμετάθετον τῆς βουλῆς αὐτοῦ (6:17). In this instance, the author draws the conclusion that the announcement of the new oath indicates the imperfection (7:11, 19), weakness, and uselessness (7:18) of the law and its replacement by a law that is not only new but qualitatively different. The contrast between God's new oath and the previous order of priesthood is analogous to Dio Chrysostom's contrast between law (νόμος) and custom (ἔθος). The former has been repealed (ἀνῃρημένος) because it was bad (πονερός), while the latter lasts permanently (*Or.* 76.2).[25] In the case of Hebrews, the earlier law is weak because it belongs to the sphere of the flesh, while the latter is associated with immortality and transcendent reality.

Again employing technical legal terminology, the author speaks of the annulment (ἀθέτησις) of the commandment.[26] In describing the annulment of the law, the author speaks in opposite terms to Paul's statement in Galatians 3:15 that no one can nullify a law that has been put into effect. Annulment is the opposite of βεβαίωσις, the confirmation of an oath (cf. 6:16). The latter word is also a legal *terminus technicus*.[27] Having established earlier that the Christ event is God's oath given for βεβαίωσις (6:16), the author now maintains that the confirmation of the oath received by Christians is also the annulment of the previous law. The legal terminology suggests that the argument is rooted in Hellenistic discussions about laws and

22. On the argument from necessity, see 7:27; 8:3; 9:16, 27. Argument from necessity, appropriateness, and possibility are commonplace in Greco-Roman rhetoric and philosophy. See Thompson, "The Appropriate, the Necessary, and the Impossible." See also Löhr, "Reflections on Rhetorical Terminology in Hebrews," 199–210.

23. See Jub. 13:25ff.; 32:1f.; T. Lev. 8:3; 18:8.

24. Weiss, *Der Brief an die Hebräer*, 396.

25. On ἀναιρειν as a legal term in Hebrews, note comments on 10:9 below.

26. For ἀθετέω, ἀθέτησις as technical legal terms, cf. BDAG, 24.

27. BDAG, 173. See also Spicq, *Theological Lexicon of the New Testament*, 1.280.

contracts, according to which the later version of a testament indicates the inferiority of the earlier.

In 8:7, the author moves from the topic νόμος and ἐντολή to the announcement of the new covenant (διαθήκη), using a term that was often synonymous with νόμος in the LXX.[28] Although the promise of the new covenant in Jer 31:31–34 is a favorite passage in the Dead Sea Scrolls and in the NT, the author makes a hermeneutical move found nowhere else. He introduces the citation from Jer 31:31–34 with his own commentary, again using the familiar contrary-to-fact form: "If the first were blameless, he would not have sought a second place." Just as the announcement of a new priesthood was an implied comment on the inadequacy of the old priesthood (7:11), the announcement of the new covenant implies the inadequacy of the old one. "If the first covenant were blameless" implies the flaws in the first covenant similar to the point in 7:11. He offers the second hermeneutical comment after the citation, concluding "In saying new, he made the first obsolete." He does not say "old" but chooses to speak of *first* and *second* and concludes with two present participles παλαιούμενον and γηράσκον to describe the obsolescence of the first (8:13), indicating that, just as the priesthood was impermanent, the accompanying covenant was also.

The author has equated the oath (ὅρκος, 6:13, 16–17), the law (νόμος, 7:12, 19), the promise (6:16–17), and the covenant (διαθήκη, 8:6, 8; 9:15–22). His understanding of διαθήκη is rooted in his understanding of Hellenistic law, as 9:15–22 indicates.[29] In appealing to the assumption that a διαθήκη is only in force after the testator dies, the author is not assuming the biblical concept of covenant but the Hellenistic understanding of wills and testaments.[30] Thus he once more employs the legal frame of reference to indicate the change from a flawed to a flawless διαθήκη. This argument would make sense within ancient legal discussions.

The author concludes the central section of Hebrews, discussing the nature of the διαθήκη, once more appealing to a later passage to nullify an earlier passage. In this instance, he appeals to Ps 40, a passage that contrasts sacrifices and burnt offerings with doing the will of God. The author introduces Jesus as the speaker of the psalm who has come, not to offer the burnt offerings but to do God's will. Once more, the author employs his own hermeneutic in the commentary on the passage, concluding "He takes away the first in order to establish the second," once more preferring the terms "first" and "second." Here he speaks, not of the change (μετάθεσις) or the

---

28. Backhaus, *Neue Bund*, 147.
29. Spicq, *Theological Lexicon of the New Testament*, 281.
30. BDAG, 228.

annulment (ἀθέτησις) of the covenant but concludes that God "takes away" (ἀναιρεῖν) the first and establishes (ἵνα τὸ δεύτερον στήσῃ). The word pair ἀναιρεῖν-ἵστημι is common in Hellenistic legal terminology for the abolition of one law and the establishment of another. Ἀναιρεῖν was commonly used for the dissolving of a law or wills,[31] and ἵστημι is used for the establishment of a law or covenant.[32] Although he refers to the psalm, this passage has the larger frame of reference of the Levitical system of sacrifices over against the ultimacy of the sacrifice of Christ. Once more, he appeals to technical legal language to establish his point.

Conclusion

Ancient rhetoricians recognized the potential of the law court for making a rhetorical argument.[33] Throughout the homily, the author has described the Christ event with legal categories. In 2:1–4, the author introduced the legal categories with the claim that God's ultimate word was "validated" (ἐβεβαιώθη) and "attested" (συνεπιμαρτυροῦντες). The author repeatedly claims that God's word is an oath, which provides legal confirmation (βεβαίωσις) to the community (6:16). This claim is consistent with the repeated insistence that a change of laws has taken place. The argument cannot be reduced to the legal frame of reference, inasmuch as it is intertwined with the eschatological claim that God has spoken in these last days, reflecting points of contact with pesher exegesis. However, he moves beyond pesher exegesis, making claims that no one else makes. He does not speak of the fulfillment of prophecy but of the divine voice that declares the validation of the new covenant. The logical conclusion drawn by the author, based on the legal argument that subsequent wills invalidate earlier ones, is the claim that God's message in the last days is a testament invalidating earlier testaments. Thus the author appeals to legal premises that he assumes his audience will accept.

---

31. Aeschines, *Contra Ctesiph.* 3.39; Isaeus 1.14; LSJ 106. See also Luke Timothy Johnson, *Hebrews: A Commentary*, 252. For the "dissolving" of laws, see Aristotle, *Athenian Constitution* 29.4; Dio Chrysostom, *Or.* 76.2; Josephus, *JW* 2.4. For the dissolving of a will, see Demosthenes, *Or* 28.5.

32. LSJ 841.

33. Quintilian, *Inst. Orat.* 5.11.32, 34; See Backhaus *Der neue Bund und das Werden der Kirche*, 195.

CHAPTER 3

THE APPROPRIATE, THE NECESSARY, AND THE IMPOSSIBLE

FAITH AND REASON IN HEBREWS

The legacy of patristic theology is the use of Greek philosophy to interpret and defend the Christian credo on rational grounds for the benefit of both the cultured despisers and the faithful.[1] Adolf Harnack said of Irenaeus that he did not merely confine himself to describing the fact of redemption, "but he also attempted to explain the peculiar nature of this redemption from the essence of God and the incapacity of man, thus solving the question of *cur deus homo* in the highest sense."[2] C. J. De Vogel makes a similar comment about Clement of Alexandria, who employed the metaphysics of Plato and the logic of Aristotle to demonstrate the truth of Christian claims. De Vogel says that Clement more than anyone else "quite consciously laid the foundation on which in the Middle Ages Thomas Aquinas constructed his theology built on the substructure of natural reason."[3] A Christian philosophy, therefore, began in the second century and dominated Western thought until the Reformation.[4]

Although Clement played a pivotal role in the appropriation of Greek rationalism, he actually built on the foundation of his predecessors in Alexandria, Aristobulus and Philo.[5] They, along with others in the Alex-

---

1. Originally published in Abraham J. Malherbe, Frederick W. Norris, and James W. Thompson, eds., *The Early Church in Its Context: Essays in Honor of Everett Ferguson*, 302–17. Supplements to Novum Testamentum 90. Leiden: Brill, 1998.
Meijering, "Wie platonisierten Christen?" 1 7.

2. Harnack, *History of Dogma*, 2.289.

3. De Vogel, "Platonism and Christianity," 22.

4. De Vogel, "Platonism and Christianity," 1.

5. On Clement's indebtedness to Philo, see Runia, *Philo in Early Christian Literature*, 137–43.

andrian school, employed philosophy to ensure that the interpretation of Scripture was in accord with reason. Clement inherited the traditions of his Alexandrian Jewish predecessors. My purpose in this article is to examine the extent to which this tradition, which extends from the background to the foreground of the NT, is present in a meaningful way also within the NT. Because the Epistle to the Hebrews has numerous linguistic contacts with Philo and later becomes an important book in Alexandrian Christianity,[6] it provides a potential link in the Alexandrian tradition that employed philosophy to explain and defend the faith. Consequently, the focus of this article is on the place of the Epistle to the Hebrews within this Alexandrian tradition that Clement inherited. With this study I wish to honor my esteemed colleague and former teacher Everett Ferguson, who, through his publications and his university courses, has been a major contributor to our knowledge of the NT, its background and its foreground.

Rational Argument in Hebrews

Previous studies of the relationship of Philo and Hebrews have analyzed the affinities between the two authors in vocabulary, exegetical traditions, and exegetical method. In this study, I shall examine an aspect of the argumentation of Hebrews that has been noted but not examined in detail: the author's appeal throughout the book to axiomatic principles that appear to be self-evident to the readers. In addition to his appeal to Scripture, he consistently appeals to principles that are "beyond dispute" (cf. 7:7). These principles involve specifically the categories of the *fitting*, the *necessary*, and the *impossible*. With these categories, the author has introduced into the argument an appeal to reason that has no parallel in the Old and New Testaments.

Like his successors in the patristic period, the author supports the Christian confession on rational grounds. In one of the initial soteriological statements, the author says of God that "it was fitting for him" (ἔπρεπεν τῷ αὐτῷ) to make the pioneer of our salvation perfect through suffering" (2:10). In 2:17 he says that the Savior "ought" (ὤφειλεν) to be like his brothers. In 7:26 he argues that "it was fitting for us" (ἡμῖν καὶ ἔπρεπεν) that we should have the high priest whose qualities are described.

The author never explains why it was fitting for God to provide this salvation through suffering.[7] Instead, he consistently appeals to "the same

---

6. See Greer, *The Captain of Our Salvation*.

7. Dunnill, *Covenant and Sacrifice*, 117: "It is one of the most striking features of sacrificial customs that they persistently defy explanation, yet this author repeatedly refers to ritual matters without explanation or with only a dogmatic reason which itself

curious logic"[8] when he affirms the necessity of the sacrifice of Christ and the introduction of a new priesthood. A change in the priesthood "of necessity" involves a change in the law. According to the law, the daily sacrifices were necessary (7:27), and the cleansing of the copies of the things in the heavens at the ritual of the Day of Atonement was also necessary (ἀνάγκη, 9:23). The author argues also that death is necessary for the ratification of the covenant (9:16).

Although, according to the author, the Levitical sacrifices were necessary to "cleanse the copies of the heavenly things," a better sacrifice was necessary in order to cleanse "the heavenly things" (9:23). Without the once-for-all sacrifice, the Savior "would have had to suffer repeatedly" (ἐπεὶ ἔδει αὐτὸν πολλάκις παθεῖν, 9:26). The author argues his point by appealing to the category of the impossible to demonstrate the necessity of the sacrifice of Christ. The Christ event, which included both the death and exaltation of Christ, is the oath of God, for whom "it is impossible to lie" (ἀδύνατον ψεύσασθαι, 6:18). Only his sacrifice was effective because Levitical sacrifices were "not able (οὐδέποτε δύναται) to perfect those who drew near," inasmuch as "it is impossible for the blood of bulls and goats to take away sin" (10:4). The believer responds in faith because "without faith it is impossible to please God" (11:6). For the believer who has once been enlightened and then falls away, "it is impossible to restore this person to repentance" (6:4-6).

The author explains neither why salvation is "impossible" without the sacrifice of Christ and the faith of the believer (1 1:6) nor why this sacrifice was both "necessary" and "fitting for God." The argument rests, not on Scripture, but on self-evident principles that the author assumes that his readers share. Both divine deed and human response, therefore, are determined by necessity.

Although the language of appropriateness and necessity has faint echoes elsewhere in Scripture, only the author of Hebrews employs it to argue that the Christian confession conforms to necessity. Forms of πρέπειν are employed in the LXX of the Psalms to describe the "holiness that befits God's house" (93:5) and in ethical contexts where the term is used with Stoic overtones to describe appropriate human conduct (1 Cor 11:13; 1 Tim 2:10; Titus 2:1).[9] Neither ἀνάγκη nor ἀδύνατον is used outside Hebrews in a soteriological context. The pervasiveness of this argument,

---

needs to be explained."

8. Dunnill, *Covenant and Sacrifice*, 118.

9. On the significance τὸ Πρέπον in ethical contexts, see M. Pohlenz, "τὸ Πρέπον. Ein Beitrag zur Geschichte des griechischen Geistes," 1.100–115.

which W. Übelacker calls "metapropositional,"[10] suggests that the author is appealing to common assumptions that are based on the structure of reality.[11] Unlike the apostle Paul, who acknowledges that the cross is wisdom to the initiated but foolishness to the world (1 Cor 2:6), the author appeals to rational argument to persuade his readers and to provide the basis for his exhortations.

The argument represents such a remarkable departure from the common soteriological reflection in Scripture that one must ask who would have been persuaded by it. The linguistic associations with Philo are so great that numerous scholars have suggested that Philo and the larger philosophical tradition provide the context in which the argument would be persuasive. C. Spicq commented on the use of πρέπειν, for example, "The theological argument of appropriateness, ἔπρεπεν θεῷ, unknown in the Bible, is employed by ancient writers, especially Philo."[12] This view is also held in the commentaries of Windisch,[13] Hans-Friedrich Weiß,[14] E. Grässer, and others.

When one compares Hebrews with Philo and the wider philosophic tradition on precisely what was fitting for God, one must ask how the argument of Hebrews would have been persuasive, for the claim of Hebrews that the sacrifice of Christ was "fitting for God" is a remarkable tour de force in the ancient context, where the association of God with human suffering would have been abhorrent. E. Fascher has correctly said that what Hebrews claims of God "is the very thing which calls into question the deity of God."[15]

The extraordinary claim of Hebrews presses the question of this article further: Does the author of Hebrews reflect developments within a tradition that extends from Philo to Clement? Ronald Williamson concluded, on the basis of a comparison of ἔπρεπεν θεῷ in Hebrews and Philo, that the similarities between the two authors were merely verbal. "But what the Writer of Hebrews says 'it behoved' God to do is something that to Philo was utterly abhorrent and repugnant. Philo could never have said it was fitting for God to do what the writer of Hebrews says He has fittingly done

---

10. Übelacker, *Der Hebräerbrief als Appell*, 166.

11. Grässer, *An die Hebräer*, 1.90.

12. Spicq, *L'Épître aux Hébreux*, 1.53 ("L'argument théologique de convenance ἔπρεπεν θεῷ, inconnu de la Bible, est employé par les écrivains profanes et particulièrement par Philon").

13. Windisch, *Der Hebräerbrief*, 21.

14. Weiß, *Der Brief an die Hebräer*, 204.

15. Fascher, "Theologische Beobachtungen zu δεῖ," 27, Cf. Attridge, *The Epistle to the Hebrews*, 82: "The use of the term in this context is a rather bold move, since in Greek and Greco-Jewish theology it would not have been thought 'proper' to associate God with the world of suffering."

by means of the sufferings of Christ."[16] As persuasive as Williamson's case may sound, it is weakened by his use of a very small sampling of verbal parallels in Philo where forms of πρέπειν are used, thus ignoring a wide range of passages in Philo where synonyms are used to express a major concept. Ancient writers used a variety of synonyms to express what is "fitting for God," including προσήκω, θέμις, ἁρμόττον, and ἄνοικεν.[17] One can assess the evidence only through an examination of the wider range of expressions in the relevant literature and through an understanding of the larger purposes of the respective authors.

Appropriateness and Necessity in the Philosophical Literature

Arguments from necessity, appropriateness, and (im)possibility were commonplace in Greco-Roman rhetoric and philosophy.[18] Indeed, as W. Jaeger recognized,[19] this argument extended from the rationalism of Xenophanes in the sixth century BCE to the church fathers. The argument is actually directed against the Christians by the heirs of the Platonic tradition. For Celsus, the Christian claim of the incarnation contradicts the most basic assumptions about the deity. Celsus argues:

> God is good, beautiful, happy, he lives in the most ideal circumstance. If he comes down to humankind, then a change (μεταβολή) would be necessary, that is a change from good to bad, from the beautiful to the shameful, from happiness to misery, from the best to the worst. But who would choose such a change? The nature of the mortal is to be changed, but the nature of the immortal is to remain always the same. Thus God would not assume such a change.[20]

---

16. Williamson, *Philo and the Epistle to the Hebrews*, 92.

17. Dreyer, *Untersuchungen zum Begriff des Gottgeziemenden in der Antike*, 152.

18. Martin, *Antike Rhetorik*, 68. Appeals to the possible (or impossible), necessary (ἀναγκαῖον), that which is not in our power, and appropriate were commonplace in Greek oratory. See also Pohlenz, "Τὸ Πρέπον," 106–9. See Mitchell, "The Use of Πρέπειν and Rhetorical Propriety in Hebrews 2:10," 681–701, for the rhetorical concept of propriety in speech. Contrary to Mitchell's view, the issue in Hebrews is an argument based on propriety, necessity, and (im)possibility, not on God as persuasive speaker.

19. Jaeger, *The Theology of the Early Greek Philosophers*, 50.

20. Origen, *Contra Celsum* 4.14, cited in Maas, *Unveränderlichkeit Gottes*, 133. Dreyer, *Gottgeziemenden*, 21.

In directing his argument against the Christian understanding of the incarnation, Celsus employed the rational critique that began with Xenophanes and continued throughout late antiquity, eventually being adopted also by the Christian apologists. The foundation of the argument was that the gods were not like humankind. Xenophanes said of the deity, "He always remains in the same place, never moving, and it is not appropriate for him to move from place to place." This criterion became the center of Xenophanes's critique. Hence, he criticized Homer for attaching "to the gods everything that is blameworthy when practiced by humans: stealing, adultery, and betrayal." All of these deeds are ἔργα ἀθέμιστα (frg. 12), deeds that violate human law. What is not θέμις for humankind is not permitted for the gods.[21]

Subsequent philosophical critique developed Xenophanes's criticism of the anthropomorphic depiction of the gods. Most of the discussion was cast in the negative as the philosophers described what was both inappropriate and impossible for the gods. The result of the critique was that Plato and his heirs argued the banishing of such inappropriate stories while the Stoics chose to save them through allegory. Celsus's metaphysical argument was based on Plato's words in *Resp.* 380. This understanding of God as perfect and immutable became the criterion for appropriateness in Plato's critique of the gods of Homer and Hesiod. For Plato, the more perfect something is, the less it is subject to change. Thus the deity is unchangeable and, hence, without πάθος. Consequently, Plato argued that, since change is impossible for the gods who want no change (*Rep.* 381 c; 383a), all accounts that portray the gods contrary to this nature are inappropriate. Gods do not lament and cry (*Resp.* 388b). Stories of revenge and cruelty are to be buried in silence (*Resp.* 378a). Nor are stories of the wars of the gods to be permitted (*Resp.* 378c). Similarly inappropriate are stories of Hera's fettering by her son and the hurling of Hephaestus by his father when he was trying to save his mother from a beating (378d). Nor can gods lie; the god Apollo cannot lie, for it is not appropriate (οὐ γὰρ θέμις αὐτῷ).

Plutarch's role as priest of Apollo makes him of special interest in the developments of the rationalist critique. With Plato, Plutarch affirms that God is good and cannot be the source of evil. He attributes to Apollo the characteristics of deity. In his essay *De Iside et Osiride*, he also attributes to Osiris the characteristics of deity. Osiris is free from corruption and death (382E) and is superior to destruction and change (373B), above change (373A). These characteristics determine what is not appropriate or possible for God. Because the deity is immutable and without passion, he cannot beget since "begetting contradicts the unchangeableness of the divine no

---

21. Dreyer, *Gottgeziemenden*, 21.

less than being born, for procreation is a change and a passion" (πάθος). Moreover, ἡδονή and ὀργή are inappropriate for the gods, as is bodily union between gods and humans.[22]

Although Plutarch held to the separation of gods from humankind, he struggled with the question of whether Plato could be the son of Apollo. When Tyndares the Lacedaemonian said, "it is fitting (ἄξιον μεν ἐστιν) to celebrate Plato with the line, 'He seemed the scion not of mortal man but of a god,'" Plutarch went to great lengths to preserve the account of Plato's origins. Such a birth, Plutarch concedes, is a change and a πάθος (*Quaest. conviv.* 8.1.3.717F), appropriate only for mortals. Plutarch, however, preserves the story by explaining that Plato was conceived, not by a physical relationship like a man's but by some other kind of contact or touch, by other potencies that are suitable for a god.[23] Here one notes the extent to which Plutarch's religious commitment comes into conflict with his philosophical position. When faced with accounts of the gods that conflict with his Platonic philosophy, he declares that the gods do their deeds in another way, thus preserving his religious convictions from the effects of the rationalist critique.

Philo of Alexandria

Philo is the heir of a Jewish philosophical tradition that had already attempted to reconcile revelation and reason and to describe what is appropriate for God. His predecessor Aristobulus had already adopted the Stoic tradition of allegory in order to overcome the problems created by anthropomorphic portrayals of God. Aristobulus encouraged his readers to "hold fast the fitting (ἁρμάζουσαν) conception of God, and not to fall off into a fabulous anthropomorphic constitution."[24] What was most unfitting, according to Aristobulus, was the idea of the divine descent into human affairs. Philo shares with his predecessor the concern for appropriate concepts of God; thus he employs the concepts of the fitting (τὸ πρέπον, πρέπειν), the impossible (τὸ ἀδύνατον), and the necessary (ἀναγκαῖον) to speak of God and the human response to God. As the tractate *Quod Deus immutabilis sit* indicates, Philo has appropriated the Platonic conception of the transcendent and immutable God, and he has found this basic conviction expressed in the Torah's claim that "God is not like man" (Num 23:19). Philo uses this criterion to determine what is fitting, necessary, and impossible for God. As

---

22. Maas, *Unveränderlichkeit*, 68; Dreyer, *Gottgeziemenden*, 581.
23. Dreyer, *Gottgeziemenden*, 57.
24. Eusebius, *Praeparatio evangelica* 8.10.2 (trans, Edwin H. Gifford, 407).

the transcendent one, God needs nothing from humankind (*De conf. ling.* 175; *Quod det. pot.* 55). "To be everywhere and nowhere is his property alone, . . . and it is against all principle (θέμις) to say that the Maker is contained in anything that he has made" (*De conf ling.* 136). The Existent One can contain but cannot be contained (οὐ περιέχεσθαι θέμις, *De mig. Abr.* 182). Philo follows the Platonic tradition in his claim that God is without passion (παντὸς πάθους ἀμέτοχος [*De Abr.* 202]).[25] God's distance from humankind is to be seen also in the fact that he can neither be deceived (οὐχ . . . διαψευσθῆναι) nor repent (*De vit. Mos.* 1.283) of his deeds.

This view of God is the basis for Philo's frequent comments about what is appropriate for God. God must (ἀναγκαῖον) be ever active and never passive (*Quod det. pot.* 61);[26] He acts but is never acted upon. Just as in human existence there is a subject and a servant, "so in the universe there must be one, who alone can rightly (πρεπῶδες) claim that all things are his possessions" (*De cher.* 83). Because God is absolute goodness, it is fitting (ἁρμόττον) that he give only good gifts (*De Abr.* 143) by his own agency, for "it may not be" (θέμις δὲ οὐδέν) that his gifts are imperfect (*Sacr.* 57; cf. *De Abr.* 268). In the same way, it is also fitting (πρέπει) for God to plant virtues in the soul (*Leg. all.* 148).

Philo's major task is to interpret the Bible in such a way as to avoid inappropriate portrayals of God. Philo consistently interprets stories in order to ensure God's distance from the world, for God's nature forbade (οὐ θέμις) that he touch limitless chaotic matter (*De spec. leg*, 1.329). Consequently, Philo frequently refers to the mediating powers that God commissioned to execute his will on earth. In *De conf ling.* 171 he describes how the one God employs numberless Potencies to execute his will. After Philo says in 174 that "it must not be" (οὐ θέμις) that his angelic powers desert the ranks, he adds in 175, "The king may fitly (ἐμπρεπές) hold converse with his powers and employ them to serve in matters which should not be consummated by God alone." Although God is not in need of anything, "yet seeing what was fitting (πρέπον) to himself and the world which was coming into being, He allowed his subject powers to have the fashioning of some things." Philo then applies this principle to the creation of humankind: "Thus it was meet and right (προσηκόντως) that when man was formed, God should assign a share in the work to His lieutenants, as He does with the words 'let us make

---

25. Cited in Maas, *Unveränderlichkeit*, 115. Cf. *Quod Deus immut.* 52: The existent cannot be seized by passion.

26. See also *De opif. mund.* 4–8 for the two primal principles. In describing the two primal principles, Philo's claim is very similar to that of Cicero, *Academica posteriora*, which summarizes the teachings of Antiochus of Ascalon. Thus Philo may be following Antiochus of Ascalon here. See Horsley, "The Law of Nature in Philo and Cicero," 45.

men'" (179). Philo makes a similar argument about the giving of the ten commandments, which well befitted (ἱεροπρεπῶς) his holiness. Philo adds, however, that "it was in accord with His nature (ἦν γὰρ ἁρμόττον αὐτοῦ) that the pronouncements in which the special laws were summed up should be given in His person, but the particular laws by the mouth of the most perfect of the prophets whom He selected" (*De decal.* 175).

Philo is especially concerned to demonstrate that all forms of punishment are inappropriate for God. Because God is the cause of good things only, "it best becomes Him (ἐμπρεπέστατον) that the work of His own hands should be akin to His nature, . . . but that the chastisement of the wicked should be through His underlings" (*De conf ling.* 180). Inasmuch as nothing that leads to destruction should have its origin in him whose nature is to save, "it was meet (ἔδει) while mankind was judged to deserve correction that the fountains of God's ever-flowing gifts of grace should be kept free . . . from evil" (*De conf ling.* 182).

In several of his tractates, Philo repeats the claim that God can be the source of neither punishment nor evil. According to *De fug.* 66, "it is unbecoming (ἀπρεπές) for God to punish, seeing that he is the original lawgiver." Consequently, "God deemed it necessary (ἀναγκαῖον) to assign the creation of evil things to other makers, reserving that of good things to Himself alone." In the same way, Philo insists in *De Abr.* 143 that, because it was fitting (ἁρμόττον) for the Existent to give good gifts by his own agency, he left the opposite of good gifts to his ministers. According to *De decal.* 178, "it befits (ἐμπρέπει) the servants and lieutenants of God that, like generals in wartime, they should bring vengeance to bear upon deserters who leave the ranks of justice, for it befits (ἐμπρεπές) the great King that the general safety of the universe be ascribed to Him." When Philo examines the account of the creation of humankind, which has an inclination for both virtue and vice, he likewise argues that "it is most proper (οἰκειότατον) to God the universal Father to make the excellent things by Himself alone, because of their kinship to him," and then concludes that "His subordinates are held responsible for thoughts and deeds of a contrary sort; for it could not be that the Father should be the cause (ἔδει γὰρ ἀναίτιον εἶναι) of an evil thing to His offspring (*De opif. mund.* 75).

In other instances Philo's concern for appropriateness serves to reduce the anthropomorphic significance of OT stories. For example, when Philo relates that God swore with an oath, he concedes that, for thousands, the oath "seems unworthy (ἀνοίκειον) of Him" (*Sacr.* 91). He concludes that, since God needs no one to guarantee his statements, the oath is merely a crutch for our weakness (92–96). Like the other human characteristics that "could never belong (ἀνοίκεια) to the Cause" (96), the oath is created for our weakness to ensure us of the reliability of God.

Although Philo repeatedly insists that God needs nothing, he nevertheless argues that God desires a relationship with humankind. He indicates that "it accords with God's ways (τὸ θεῖον ἄνω καλεῖσθαι θέμις) that those who have received His down-breathing should be called up to Him" (*De plant*. 23). Thus Philo frequently speaks of the human response to the God who needs nothing as humans offer a gift that is worthy of the Giver. In the creation story, "God says, 'Take ye for Me,' thus giving to Himself what is His due (τὰ πρέπονθ᾽ ἑαυτῷ)," and teaching us to guard the gifts in a way "worthy of the Giver" (ἀξίως τοῦ δόντος, *Quis rer. div. her.* 123). The human response, therefore, is to give God the gifts that are his (*De ebr.* 117). Philo comments, for example, in the narrative of Abraham's sacrifice of Isaac, that Isaac is, in fact, "the only trueborn offspring of the soul" (*Quod Deus immut.* 4). This sacrifice is "a fitting thank-offering" (ἀναγκαῖον καὶ ἁρμόττον χαριστήριον).

Philo's treatment of the sacrifice of Isaac corresponds to his interpretation of Jewish cultic practices. Here one observes that Philo's philosophical commitments do not preclude his loyalty to Judaism, for he consistently describes the necessity of Jewish cultic practices. Philo argues, for example, that both circumcision and the offering of sacrifices "were symbols of two necessary (ἀναγκαοτάτοιν) features of human well-being": the excision of pleasures and the removal of deceit (*De spec. leg.* 1.8). This loyalty to Judaism is especially evident in Philo's treatment of the sacrificial cultus. In keeping with his philosophical commitments, he argues (*De plant*, 126), "it is not possible genuinely to express our gratitude to God by means of buildings and oblations and sacrifices . . . for even the whole world were not a temple adequate to yield the honor due Him." He insists that "God found no worthier temple on the earth than the reasoning faculty" (*De virt*. 188).[27] That the soul is the essential house of God is Philo's consistent claim, in keeping with his philosophical commitments. Thus the Jerusalem temple is not appropriate for God.

Philo never abandons the Jewish practices that would be, under the rationalist critique, inappropriate for God. The temple and the sacrifices symbolize realities that are necessitated by the nature of reality and of God. Here Philo frequently employs forms of ἀνάγκη to describe this necessity, which is attributed to the law of nature. In *De Abr*. 249 he speaks of "nature's inevitable law." In *Leg. all*. 1.8 he says, "The universe must consist of two

---

27. On Philo's treatment of Jewish sacrifices, see Ferguson, "Spiritual Sacrifice in Early Christianity and Its Environment," 1159.

parts"; in 1.12 he says that the world must have had an origin. In 2.16 he says that "created things must of necessity go through change." Thus the reason of nature pervades the universe, determining its laws.[28] The injunctions of the Torah reflect nature's law.

Just as the laws of local cities are the "ordinances of nature" (θεσμοὶ τῆς φύσεως), so also the ordinances of the cult are necessary. In the construction of the temple, Philo says that "it was necessary in the framing of a temple of man's making—he should take substances like those with which that Ruler made the All" (*De vit. Mos.* 2.88). He adds, "Six names had to be engraved on each of the stones, since each of the hemispheres also divides the zodiac into two and appropriates six of the signs" (*De vit. Mos.* 2.123). The laws of Israel, including the Sabbath law (*De cher.* 87) and the sacrificial cultus, are based on a cosmic order.

Just as circumcision was necessary, so also are sacrifices, even if God does not need them, for sacrifices point to a higher form of sacrifice that is appropriate for God. Philo says, "For he who has been consecrated to the Father of the world must needs have that Father's son to plead his cause (ἀναγκαῖον γὰρ ἦν τὸ ἱερωμένον τῷ τοῦ κόσμου πατρὶ παρακλήτῳ χρῆσθαι), that sins may be remembered no more" (*De vit. Mos.* 2.134). The offering of the calf signifies that sin requires prayers and sacrifices to propitiate the deity (*De vit. Mos.* 2.147). Therefore, Philo commonly speaks of the offerings (*De vit. Mos.* 2.159; cf. *Quod Deus immut.* 4) which, like the Sabbath (*De cher.* 87) and other regulations, are necessary (*De decal.* 165, 170; *De spec. leg.* 1.34, 39, 113) or fitting. When Philo describes the flame that came forth as Moses and Aaron came from the tabernacle, he concludes that God had expelled from the shrine the fire of common use and "rained instead an ethereal flame from heaven," knowing that "it was fitting (ἥρμοττε) that fire of a more incorruptible nature" than the ordinary should accompany the sacrifices (*De vit. Mos.* 2.158).

As a loyal Jew, Philo did not abandon the boundary markers that identified his people, even if the rationalist critique suggested that he do so.[29] This fact is especially to be seen in his defense of the cultus, which conforms to the cosmic order that requires the sacrifice for sin. Moreover, as W. Maas has shown, one discovers in Philo a "biblical breakthrough" in which he moves from the God of the philosophers to the biblical view of the God who

---

28. Horsley, "Law of Nature," 37, cites *De Jos.* 29–31, "For this world is the Great City, and it has a single constitution and law, which is the reason of nature (λογος φυσεως). Cf. Cicero, *Rep.* 3.33: "True Law is right reason in agreement with nature; it is of universal application, unchanging and everlasting."

29. Dreyer, *Gottgeziemenden*, 136.

acts in history to keep his promises.[30] Nevertheless, Philo's philosophical convictions lead him to describe other means of approaching God in an appropriate manner. God's possessions are "sublime and worthy of the deity" (μεγαλοπρεπῶς καὶ θεοπρεπῶς), and all human sacrifices merely give to God his due (πρέποντα, *Quis rer. div. her.* 123). Sacrifices actually represent the giving of the self (*Quod Deus immut.* 4). One who has learned this lesson will offer to God faith, the greatest sacrifice of all (*De cher.* 8445). God's people will also respond to their Maker with continuous thanksgiving to show that "it dedicates its whole being" (*Quis rer. div. her.* 200) and with the joy that is worthy of God (*De Abr.* 202, 206). Philo, like Plutarch, maintained his commitment to his ancestral faith and attempted to harmonize it with Platonic philosophy. However, in describing Jewish laws that conformed to a cosmic order and the personal God whose nature is to maintain a relationship with his creatures and to summon them in faith, Philo was not an orthodox Platonist. His understanding of necessity and appropriateness was shaped not only by the tradition of the philosophers but by his commitment to Judaism as well. Amir contrasted Philo with the Stoics, whose rationalist assumptions Philo adopts, and concluded that the distinguishing factor in Philo's interpretation is that the revelation in Scripture has priority. "For the Stoics rationalism and philosophy are predominant, to which mysticism and theology are subordinated. For Philo mysticism and theology are undoubtedly predominant, to which philosophy and science are subordinated."[31] Thus Williamson and others are correct in saying that Philo and Hebrews have very different understandings of what was necessary and appropriate for God, for both are loyal to their religious commitments. Nevertheless, one finds in both writers an attempt to demonstrate the coherence between their religious claims and practices and the nature of reality. Philo represents "new wine in the old bottles of classical rationalism,"[32] and the author of Hebrews represents a similar approach, even if he is not as thoroughgoing in his approach as Philo.

---

30. Maas, *Unveränderlichkeit*, 18–21. In *De vit. Mos.* 1 .283, Philo paraphrases the narrative of the book of Numbers: "God cannot be deceived as a man, nor as the son of man does He repent or fail to abide by what He has once said. He will utter nothing at all which shall not certainly be performed, for His word is His deed." Maas comments, "Here, in the paraphrase of the biblical text, stands the 'immutability' of God in the horizon of salvation history. It is the immutability of God's faithfulness to his promises.... The 'abiding' of God, understood otherwise in Philo as immutability in the sense given by Greek philosophy, becomes the 'abiding' of God's covenant faithfulness in salvation history" (119).

31. Amir, *Die hellenistische Gestalt des Judentums*, 198.

32. Amir, *Die hellenistische Gestalt des Judentums*, 199.

Clement of Alexandria

The concern for an appropriate view of God is continued in the work of Clement of Alexandria. Although Clement never cites Philonic traditions when he discusses the concept of appropriateness, the category plays a significant role in his work. In keeping with the Stoic tradition, Clement employs forms of πρέπειν to describe appropriate human conduct.[33] In the apologetic context of the *Stromateis*, Clement develops the theme of what is appropriate both for God and for the human response to God.

Clement's interest in this subject is most thoroughly demonstrated in *Stromateis* 7, where he contrasts the gnostic's true understanding of God with the erroneous views of those who persecute Christians (7.1). He writes "to prove that the Gnostic alone is holy and pious, and worships the true God in a manner worthy of Him" (θεοπρεπῶς τὸν τῷ ὄντι θεὸν θρησκεύντα).[34] Worship fit for God (τῷ θεοπρέπει) is followed by loving and being loved by God (7.1.2). The highest object of worship is the Son.

The gnostic exhibits godliness (θεοπρέπεια), which is the habit that preserves what is becoming to God (τὸ πρέπον τῷ θεῷ). Thus the godly person alone (ὁ θεοπρεπής μόνος) knows what is becoming to God (τὸ πρέπον τῷ θεῷ).[35] The first step of faith, according to Clement, is to know God and God's Son, who "is nearest to Him who alone is the Almighty One." Clement describes the Son in words that echo the Greek rationalist tradition. Whereas Xenophanes criticized depictions of the gods who move from place to place, Clement says of the Son (7.2.5):

> For from His own point of view the Son of God is never displaced; not being divided, not severed, not passing from place to place; being always everywhere, and being contained nowhere; complete mind, the complete mind, the complete eternal light; all eyes, seeing all things, hearing all things, knowing all things, by His power scrutinizing the powers. To him is placed in subjection all the hosts of angels and gods.

Here Clement employs the common attributes of God that one finds in Philo to describe the Son. Indeed, although the passage betrays little evidence of the direct use of Hebrews here, some of the same themes appear. The reference to the subjection of angels and gods echoes Heb 1:1–4. Clement's claim in *Strom.* 7.2 that philosophy was delivered to the Greeks through inferior angels echoes the claim in Hebrews that the law was

---

33. See *Paed.* 2.1.10, 13; 2.4.40; 2.5.46; 2.12.127; 3,3.19; 3.4.30; 3.11.79 (GCS).
34. *Strom.* 7.1.2.
35. *Strom.* 7.1.3.

delivered by angels. The point of contact with Hebrews is especially to be seen in Clement's comments about the incarnation and subsequent status of the Savior. He describes the Son as one "who for our sakes assumed flesh capable of suffering." He loved human flesh, "despising not its susceptibility to human suffering; but investing himself with it, came for the salvation of men" (*Strom.* 7.2.6).[36] His care for all "is befitting for Him who has become Lord (καθήκει τῷ κυρίῳ γενομένῳ) of all." The true gnostic recognizes his exalted status, which is expressed in the language of Greek rationalism. The Savior can neither envy nor be hindered by another; he is without beginning and impassible.

Only the gnostic knows how to come to God in a way that is appropriate to him. In *Strom.* 7.4 Clement describes in great detail the improper concepts of the deity held by the Greeks, making full use of the criticism initiated by Xenophanes. The erroneous Greek views are then contrasted with the faith of the gnostic, who alone recognizes what response to God is appropriate to his dignity. In *Strom.* 7.4 Clement makes full use of the critique that began with Xenophanes in describing in great detail the improper concepts of the deity held by the Greeks. The Greek myths are then contrasted with the faith of the gnostic, who alone recognizes what response to God is appropriate for the one who needs nothing. The gnostics "rightly do not sacrifice to God." The church is the temple that "is better for the greatness and dignity of God." The sacrifice offered by the church is the word breathing an incense to God.

An important feature in Clement's contrast between the faith of the true gnostic and the erroneous ideas about God among the Greeks is the fact that Clement employs Greek rationalism in his critique of the gods of Greece without acknowledging that the same critique could and would be leveled against his own understanding of the incarnation. Clement could at the same time affirm that the incarnation was appropriate for the Savior and dismiss the numerous accounts among the Greeks of the gods who took on human qualities. As with Philo before him, his primary loyalty is to his confession of faith. Both writers used Greek rationalism when it was convenient to support convictions that were already held. As a Middle Platonist, Clement affirmed the traditional understanding of the impassibility of God and employed the rationalist critique initiated by

---

36. Clement's attempt to maintain a loyalty to both his Christian confession and his philosophical commitments is especially evident in his comments about the flesh of Jesus. Although he affirms the Christian claim that Jesus took on flesh, he says elsewhere that this flesh was not susceptible to pleasure or pain (*Strom.* 6.9.7 1). In *Strom.* 3.7.59.3 he quotes with approval a letter of Valentinus, where Valentinus says that the food Jesus ate did not pass out of his body. I am indebted to Dr. Ronald Heine for this insight.

Xenophanes to ridicule stories about the gods. As a Christian, he affirmed a belief in the incarnation of the Son.

Conclusion

H. Dörrie argued that Christianity and Platonism were two mutually exclusive and rival confessions and that the Christian use of Platonism involved no more than the use of metaphors, comparisons, and literary questions.[37] C. J. De Vogel has suggested, however, that Christianity and Platonism found common ground in their insistence on the transcendence of God and that the Christian response to Platonism extended from total rejection to far-reaching acceptance. Between the two were varying degrees of acceptance,[38] which one can observe in the developing Alexandrian tradition of Clement and his predecessors. Neither Clement nor Philo adopted Platonism uncritically; both were willing to accept "irrational" elements in their own traditions, which they would not permit among the Greeks. This complicated relationship between Christianity and Platonism provides the basis for our evaluation of the Epistle to the Hebrews in this developing appropriation of the language of Greek rationalism that is commonly identified with Alexandria. Besides citing Hebrews frequently, Clement demonstrates in his use of rational language that he is continuing a tradition that he shares with both Philo and Hebrews. These writers are by no means uniform in the extent to which they have appropriated Greek rationalism. Nevertheless, they share a tradition in which their faith commitment stands in tension with and commonly takes precedence over their philosophy. In this way Philo, Hebrews, and Clement of Alexandria share a common tradition.

---

37. H. Dörrie, "Was ist 'spätantike Platonismus'?" 300.
38. De Vogel, "Platonismus and Christianity," 19.

CHAPTER 4

ARGUMENT AND PERSUASION IN THE EPISTLE TO THE HEBREWS

In his magisterial study of ancient literature, Eduard Norden distinguished sharply between the simplicity of earliest Christian writings and the artistry of classical Greek literature. Agreeing with Paul's own self-assessment as ἰδιώτης τῷ λόγῳ (2 Cor 11:6), Norden commented, "Paul is a writer whom I understand with difficulty." Norden gave two reasons for the difficulty: 1) Paul's manner of argument is strange; and 2) his style is not Hellenic. He added, "This assessment is confirmed by the fact that at least I can read through the so-called letter to the Hebrews from beginning to end without difficulty. Interpreters since antiquity have recognized in this book a totally different style reflecting the influence of Hellenism."[1] Norden cited the well-known words of Origen:

> That the character of the diction of the epistle entitled To the Hebrews has not the apostle's rudeness in speech, who confessed himself rude in speech (ἰδιώτης τῷ λόγῳ, 2 Cor 11:6), that is, in style, but that the epistle is better Greek in the framing of its diction, will be admitted by everyone who is able to discern differences of style. (Eusebius, *Hist. eccl.* 6.25.11ff. LCL).[2]

Since the nineteenth century, scholars have catalogued the numerous examples of the rhetorical sophistication of the author of Hebrews, giving special attention to the Hellenistic style of the homily. Von Soden called attention to the numerous examples of stylistic refinement.

> The author is a versatile and well-educated spirit. He has at his disposal a rich vocabulary (140 *hapax legomena*) that includes

---

1. Originally published in *Perspectives in Religious Studies* 39 (2012) 361–77. Norden, *Die antike Kunstprosa vom vi. Jahrhundert*, 2.499.

2. Norden, *Die antike Kunstprosa vom vi. Jahrhundert*, 2.499.

numerous words that appear nowhere else in the Bible, but are common in daily Greek usage (e.g., νέφος, νόθοι, γάμος for marriage, ἔλαθον τινες, κλίνειν, προσφέρεσθαι τινι along with select compound words, verbs with -ιζειν, substantives with -σις, composites such as αἱματεκχυσία, μισθαποδοσία). The linguistic diction is skillful, florid, . . . rich in fine syntactic phrases, beautiful periods; [the author] loves plays on words (5:8; 9:15f, 10:38f; 11:37; 13:14), striking images (6:7; 12:1-3), and sharply delineated antitheses.[3]

As Norden observes, "the sevenfold use of μεν . . . δέ in chapter 7 also suggests the author's use refined use of Greek, for it appears in one chapter in Hebrews as often as in several Pauline letters together."[4]

In more recent years, the skillful arrangement of Hebrews has been the subject of numerous articles and books. Indeed, more books have been written on the structure of Hebrews in the last two generations than of any other NT book.[5] Thus an earlier generation focused on style, but more recently scholars have analyzed the arrangement. While scholars have reached no consensus on the arrangement of Hebrews, all have recognized that this homily is a carefully crafted work. The author moves from one topic to another, but he maintains a central focus that is most evident in the alternation between scriptural exposition and exhortation throughout the homily. Frequent *inclusios* provide boundaries for the sections,[6] while catchwords at the end of the units announce the next topic.[7]

Although interpreters in the modern era have given considerable attention to style and arrangement, two of the divisions of ancient rhetoric, little work has been devoted to invention, a third division of ancient rhetoric. Like the style and arrangement of the homily, much of the argument is without parallel in the NT and both unconvincing and incomprehensible to the modern reader. Inasmuch as effective arguments proceed from assumptions shared by the author and the reader, one may assume that the author expected the argument to be persuasive. My task in this article is to examine the argument to determine the author's means of persuasion. What widely recognized means of persuasion does he use that would be recognized in

3. Soden, *Hebräerbrief, Briefe des Petrus, Jakobus, Judas*, 6.

4. Norden, *Kunstprosa*, 2.500n.

5. See Vanhoye, *La Structure Littéraire de L'Épitre aux Hébreux*; Übelacker, *Der Hebräerbrief als Appell*; Guthrie, *The Structure of Hebrews*; Westfall, *A Discourse Analysis of the Letter to the Hebrews*.

6. Cf. the references to God's word in 1:1; 4:12; ἔχοντες . . . προσερχώμεθα in 4:14-16; 10:19-23.

7. Cf. ἀγγέλων in 1:4, 5; πιστός in 2:17; 3:2; πίστις in 10:39; 11:1.

the larger culture? Does the argument become comprehensible within the context of ancient rhetorical theory?

Argument and Persuasion in Antiquity

As one dimension of *inventio*, argumentation (Latin *argumentatio;* Greek πίστις) involves offering reasons that will move the listener from the points of agreement to the speaker's point of view.[8] To argue is to supply reasons in support of a thesis, to modify the listener's convictions, or to increase the acceptance of what is already accepted.[9] According to Aristotle, every speech consists of at least the thesis statement (πρόθεσις) and the argument (*Rhet.* 3.13.4).[10] The strength of the argument is not measured only by logic but by its effectiveness with the hearer.[11] Thus the argument begins with the common ground shared by the speaker and the hearer and provides reasons for the change that the speaker intends.

L. Thuren maintains that argumentation is aimed at changing or modifying the readers' thoughts while the goal of persuasion is action. "To that end a command is hardly enough, nor are good arguments, but the recipients must also be persuaded so that the audience will change its behavior."[12] Thuren adds, "In order to persuade, the author needs to give reasons for the change, to give such reasons and to justify them so that the recipients' opinions are affected is called argumentation. It becomes persuasion if the goal is also to create in the recipients a volition to act in some way."[13]

In the common structure developed by Aristotle, Cicero, and Quintilian, the *exordium* and *narratio* precede the *argumentatio* (or *probatio*; Greek πίστις),[14] which is then followed by the *peroratio*. Thus, while the *argumentatio* forms the intellectual core of every speech,[15] the other parts contribute to the persuasive task. Quintilian says, "What difference is there between a proof (*probatio*) and a statement of facts (*narratio*) save that the latter is a proof put forward in continuous form, while the proof is a

---

8. Eggs, "Argumentation," 1.914.
9. Alexandre, *Rhetorical Argumentation in Philo of Alexandria*, 28.
10. See Veit, "Argumentatio," 1.905.
11. Alexandre, *Rhetorical Argumentation in Philo of Alexandria*, 25
12. Thuren, "On Studying Ethical Argumentation and Persuasion," 468.
13. Thuren, "On Studying Ethical Argumentation and Persuasion," 468.
14. Cf. Lausberg, *Handbook of Literary Rhetoric*, §349.
15. Lausberg, *Handbook of Literary Rhetoric*, § 349. Veit, "Argumentatio," 905.

verification of the facts as put forward in the statement (*narratio*)?"[16] Thus the argument can be found throughout the speech.

The basic *argumentatio* (πίστις) may consist of one proof but normally consists of multiple *argumenta* (πίστεις) in support of the thesis.[17] Rhetorical theorists beginning with Aristotle catalogued the types of arguments under the two major categories of the "inartificial" (ἄτεχνοι) and artificial (ἔντεχνοι) proofs. The former appealed to the evidence from witnesses, testimony, oaths, and past judgments, and thus required no rhetorical art, while the latter appealed to rhetorical artistry. These included the argument from the speaker's character (ἦθος), the emotions of the audience (πάθος), and the logical consistency of the explanation (λόγος).[18] These proofs were further divided into subcategories.

Arrangement, Argument and Persuasion in Hebrews 1–4

The exhortations in Hebrews (2:1–4; 5:11—6:12; 10:19–39; 12:14–17; 13:1–6) offer a clear indication of the persuasive task of the author. His challenge is to persuade readers of the second generation to "hold fast the confession" (4:14; 10:23; cf. 6:18) and endure (10:36) in the midst of suffering (cf. 12:4–11) and marginalization (10:32–34). He hopes to dissuade the readers from falling away (3:12; cf. 2:1; 6:4; 10:26–31). The expositions that alternate with the exhortations provide the arguments for the response that the author desires from the readers. As the arrangement of Hebrews demonstrates, the homily is a sequence of *argumenta* in support of the basic *argumentatio* of the homily. The expositions are encomiastic praise of Christ and his saving work, while the exhortations contain deliberative features that focus on the community's response in the future.

The author states the thesis in the *exordium* of 1:1–4 and elaborates on it throughout the homily in a series of expositions, which provide the basis for the claim that the author makes on the readers.[19] *Inclusios* in 1:1—4:13 and 4:14—10:31 signal the tripartite division of the work. In 1:1—4:13, the

---

16. *Inst. Or.* 4.2.79 LCL.

17. Aristotle, *Rhet.* 1.2.2; Quintilian, *Inst. Or.* 5.1.1. See Lausberg, *Handbook of Literary Rhetoric*, § 349.

18. Lausberg, *Handbook of Literary Rhetoric*, § 349.

19. See L. Thuren, *Argument and Theology in 1 Peter*, 88–183 for a similar structure in the argument of 1 Peter. Thuren modifies the analysis of Stephen Toulmin (*The Uses of Argument*, 87–134)]. Toulmin describes the basic components of an argument as facts (D, data) and warrants (W) in support of the claim (C).

inclusio is provided by the references to God's word (1:1–2; 4:12–13), while the exhortations "Therefore having a great high priest (4:14) . . . let us draw near" and "Therefore having . . . a great priest . . . let us draw near" (10:19–22) provide the boundaries for the central section of the homily (4:14—10:31).[20] Parallels between the first section and the final section (10:32—13:25) result in a concentric arrangement of the homily. Negative and positive examples of faithfulness in 3:1—4:13 and 10:32—12:11 provide a frame to the central section on the cultic work of Christ. The contrast between the transitory creation and the abiding realities (1:10–12) anticipates the similar contrast near the end of the homily (12:25–29). Thus the final section consists largely of a climactic restatement of earlier themes.

Because the major *argumenta* are introduced in 1:5—4:13, this section serves as the *narratio* of the homily. After a *propositio* in 4:14–16, the author develops the theme of the cultic work of Christ, which was introduced in 2:17—3:1. This central section thus serves as the *probatio*. The final section (10:32—13:25) restates earlier themes, and thus serves as the *peroratio*. Because the author's distinct mode of argumentation appears in the *exordium* and *narratio* before being repeated in the *probatio* and *peroratio*, this paper will focus on the *argumenta* that comprise the argument in the first division of the book (1:1—4:13).

The Exordium (1:1–4)

The opening lines of Hebrews offer the key to the author's argumentative strategy. The carefully crafted period is intended to state what is not under dispute and introduce the themes: God the one who speaks (cf. 1:5–13; 4:12–13; 12:25–29), the one and the many (cf. 7:23–28; 9:23—10:18), the high priestly work of Christ (7:1—10:18), the exaltation (cf. 8:1; 10:12), and the Son's appointment to a new status (cf. 2:17–18; 5:5–10).[21] As the repeated exhortation to "hold firmly" (κατέχειν, 3:6, 14; 10:23; κρατεῖν, 4:14; 6:18) indicates, the author's challenge is not to change the opinions of the readers but to persuade them to remain committed to the confession (4:14; 10:23; cf. 3:1). Indeed, 1:1–4 may contain a form of the confession

---

20. Cf. Nauck, "Zum Aufbau des Hebräerbriefes," 205.

21. See Übelacker, *Der Hebräerbrief als Appell*, 224–28; 66–138. See Aristotle, *Rhet.* 3.14.6. "But in speeches and epic poems the *exordia* provide a sample of the subject, in order that the hearers may know beforehand what it is about, and that the mind may not be kept in suspense, for that which is undefined leads astray; then he who puts the beginning, so to say, into the hearer's hand enables him, if he holds fast to it, to follow the story." Cited in Olbricht, "Anticipating and Presenting the Case for Christ as High Priest in Hebrews," 357.

that the readers made at their baptism. Thus the author begins the homily with the common ground that he shares with the readers, proceeding from the agreed-upon to the renewed commitment and behavioral change (cf. 5:11–14) that he desires from the readers (cf. 2:1–4). In the arguments that follow, the author continues to proceed from the basic argument to the claim that he makes on the readers.

The overpowering periodic sentence is an argument from *ethos* and *pathos*. The powerful rhetoric, with its alliteration and assonance should instill confidence in the speaker's intellectual ability.[22] The poetic rhetoric is intended also to affect the emotions and the will of the reader.[23] The first person plural reference, a dominant feature of the book ("God has spoken to *us* in a son" (cf. 2:9–10; 4:15; 5:11; 12:4, 18, 22), maintains a bond with the readers throughout the homily. The use of the vocative (cf. 3:1, 12; 10:19) and the hortatory subjunctive (4:1, 11, 14; 6:18; 10:19–23; 13:13) also maintains a relationship with the readers.[24]

The exordium also contains the argument from *logos*, introducing the major argumentative strategy of the homily: the argument from disassociation and *synkrisis*. The contrasts provide disassociation.[25] The climax of the periodic sentence is the Son's new status as "greater than angels" (γενόμενος κρείττων τῶν ἀγγέλλων) with a name that is greater than theirs. This use of *synkrisis* will dominate the entire homily, for the *argumenta* consist of a series of comparisons that provide the basis for the claim that the author makes on the reader. Indeed, the author employs κρεῖττον thirteen times. He uses forms of μείζων four times and adjectives or substantives with the -οτερος ending fifteen times.[26] He also uses clauses with μεν ... δε (7:2, 5–6, 8, 20–21, 23–24; 9:1, 11; 10:11–12). Christ is superior to the angels (1:4), Moses (3:1–6), the Levitical high priest (7:4–28), Levitical sacrifices (9:1–14), and he serves in a better sanctuary (8:16; cf. 9:1–14). Consequently, the community has received a better covenant and better promises (8:6), has come to a better mountain (12:18–22), and hears a word that speaks better than the blood of Abel (12:25). Each of the three major sections of Hebrews employs *synkrisis* as the basis for the exhortation.

---

22. Übelacker, "Hebrews and the Implied Author's Rhetorical Ethos," 334.

23. Gorman, "The Power of Pathos: Emotional Appeal in Hebrews."

24. Conley, "Philo of Alexandria," 698. Philo also works with personal pronouns to create communion with his audience by using the first person plural (cf. *Leg. All.* 2.68–69; *Sacr.* 99; *Cher.* 113–14).

25. The one (in a son) and the many (many and various); "In the past–in these last days"; fathers–us; prophets–the Son.

26. Smillie, "Contrast or Continuity in Hebrews 1.1–2," 551.

Contrary to earlier interpretations of Hebrews, the *synkrisis* (Latin *comparatio*) does not signal a polemic but is one of the most widely used modes of argumentation in Greek rhetorical theory. *Synkrisis* is a rhetorical device that takes persons, objects, or abstract concepts that are comparable in order to demonstrate either their equality or the superiority of one over the other.[27] It was included in the progymnasmata, the exercises in composition practiced in grammar schools.[28] Indeed, Theon shares with Hebrews the use of κρεῖττον (114.16, 19; 115.2) to establish a comparison. In ancient literature the comparison of Greek and Roman heroes in the parallel biographies of Plutarch are the most famous examples. As Plutarch's *Parallel Lives* indicates, *synkrisis* can be the organizing principle of a speech.[29]

Synkrisis was employed in all types of literature,[30] but was most common in epideictic speeches,[31] especially encomia. The paradigm of all later ones is the speech of Isocrates about Euagoras (Isoc *Or.* 16).[32] Isocrates begins the encomium with a description of φύσις and εὐγένεια of Euagoras and describes his ἀρεταί, first as a child, and then as a man. Euagoras displayed both courage in battle and the cardinal virtues, and his good deeds ended with his apotheosis. The greatness of the achievements of Euagoras becomes clear from the comparison with others.[33] According to Isocrates, none (of the poets) have told of anyone who returned after such fearful dangers. While most of the rulers come to power through chance, cunning, or deceit, Euagoras combined virtue with power. When one compares him to historical personalities such as Cyrus, then the comparison is to the disadvantage of the latter. Isocrates says that no man and neither a half-God nor immortal attained his power with more honorable, dominating, and more divine right. Isocrates declared Euagoras superior to the demigods because he exhibited greater fortune.[34]

---

27. According to Theon, *synkrisis* is "language setting the better or the worse side by side." He adds, "Synkrises are not comparisons of things having a great difference between them.... Comparisons should be of likes and where we are in doubt which should be preferred because of no evident superiority of one to the other." Cited in Kennedy, trans. and ed., *Progymnasmata*, 53. See also Kneepkens, "Comparatio," 2.293.

28. Kennedy, *A History of Classical Rhetoric*, 78n.

29. M. Martin, "Philo's Use of Syncrisis," 281. See also Erbse, "Die Bedeutung der Synkrisis in den Parallelbiographen Plutarchs," 398–424.

30. See Focke, "Synkrisis," 328–49. *Synkrisis* could be used in fables, tragedies, popular philosophy, and history writing.

31. Lausberg, *Handbook of Literary Rhetoric*, § 404.

32. J. Martin, *Antike Rhetorik*, 188.

33. J. Martin, *Antike Rhetorik*, 189.

34. See Olbricht, "Hebrews as Amplification," 379.

Synkrisis was a useful means of amplification,[35] the rhetorical device of adding intensity to the proofs by elaborating on them. According to Aristotle,

> If he does not furnish you with enough material in himself, you must compare him with others, as Isocrates used to do, because of his inexperience of forensic speaking. And you must compare him with illustrious personages, for it affords ground for amplification and is noble, if he can be proved better than men of wroth. Amplification is with good reason ranked as one of the forms of praise, since it consists in superiority, and superiority is one of the things that are noble. That is why, if you cannot compare him with illustrious personages, you must compare him with ordinary persons, since superiority is thought to indicate virtue. Speaking generally, of the topics common to all rhetorical arguments, amplification is most suitable for epideictic speakers, whose subject is actions which are not disputed, so that all that remains to be done is to attribute beauty and importance to them. (*Rhet.* 1.9.38–40)

Amplification was also a device for repeating points that had already been made (Aristotle, *Rhet.* 3.19.1–2). The repetition has the cumulative effect of enabling the listener to grasp the message and accept it.[36] With the consistent use of *synkrisis* throughout the homily, the author amplifies the comparison made in 1:1–4.

Ancient writers employed a wide variety of topics for comparison. In the comparison of individuals, the most common points of comparison included the native city, family, birth, education, character, virtues, personality, circumstances, and deeds.[37] For Plutarch, *synkrisis* served the purpose of moral instruction, for he described virtues worthy of emulation. Consequently, he focuses on the virtues and vices of his subjects.[38]

In Hebrews, the basis for comparison is the argument from the two levels of reality that predominates in the homily. The exalted Son is greater

---

35. Aune, ed. *The Westminster Dictionary of New Testament and Early Christian Literature and Rhetoric*, 110.

36. Cf. Alexandre, *Rhetorical Argumentation*, 192.

37. Plutarch makes the point that he chose Cicero and Demosthenes not only because they were the greatest orators, but also because their careers showed common features (exile, death of a daughter) and their personalities common characteristics (political vigor and disinclination for war). See D. A. Russell, *Plutarch* 114. See also the discussion in M. Martin and J. Whitlark, "The Encomiastic Topics of Synkrisis as the Key to the Structure and Argument of Hebrews," 41–11.

38. H. Martin, "Plutarch," 724–25 (Cf. Plutarch, *Alex.* 1; *Nic.* 1; *Cim.* 2:2–5).

than the angels insofar as he is exalted and abides forever, while angels belong to this world (1:5–13). Similarly, the exalted high priest is greater than Levitical high priests because only he belongs to the heavenly realm and abides forever (7:3). The heavenly cultus (9:1—10:18) and heavenly assembly (12:18–29) are superior to their earthly counterparts. Thus the argument of Hebrews consists of a *synkrisis* based on the two levels of reality.

This means of comparison also appears in the works of Philo and Plutarch. Plutarch (*Is.Os.* 373E) speaks of "the better (κρεῖττον) and more divine nature" and adds (*Is. Os.* 373): "For that which really is and is perceptible and good is superior (κρεῖττον) to destruction and change." Philo, who employs *synkrisis* in many instances, frequently employs this rhetorical device in describing the two levels of reality. In describing the creation, he claims that the universe consists of two parts, the active cause and the passive subject. He concludes that the active cause is the mind of the universe, "transcending (κρείττων) virtue, transcending (κρείττων) knowledge, transcending (κρείττων) the good itself and the beautiful itself" (*Opif.* 8 LCL). He describes the archetype of earthly things as "the more excellent model" (κρείττονα ἰδέα, *Opif.* 22), later adding, "The more eminent (κρείττων) the maker is, so much better the work" (*Opif.* 140). In a comparison of Leah and Rachel, he says that Rachel is mortal, while Leah is immortal, adding, that all things that are precious to the senses are inferior in perfection to beauty of soul, they are many and it but one" (*Sobr.* 12).[39]

The author's progression from one *synkrisis* to another indicates its decisive importance for the structure of the book. Thus he follows ancient rhetorical practice as he introduces the *synkrisis* in the exordium and employs it as a structuring device. Rhetors commonly introduced the *synkrisis* in the exordium and expanded it throughout the oration.[40] Plutarch organizes the *Parallel Lives* around the comparison of equals.[41] Similarly, Philo frequently

---

39. The *synkrisis* based on two levels of reality is a consistent part of Philo's argumentation. Cf. *Leg. All.* 1.72, "The reasoning faculty is better (κρεῖττον), the lustful and the high-spirited inferior"; *Leg. All.* 2.50, "For when that which is superior (κρεῖττον), namely Mind, becomes one with that which is inferior, namely Sense-perception, it resolves itself into the order of flesh which is inferior, into sense-perception"; *Leg. All.* 3.203, "For God has nothing higher (κρεῖττον) than he"; *Leg. All.* 3.223, "It is always right that the superior (κρεῖττον) should rule and the inferior be ruled; and the Mind is superior (κρεῖττον) to sense-perception"; *Mig. Abr.* 193, "But the mind of all things has brought the universe into existence; and that which has made is superior to the thing made, so that it could not be included in its inferior"; *Mut. Nom.* 122, "The imperishable is higher and greater than the mortal κρεῖττον δὲ θνητοῦ), the acting cause than that on which it acts."

40. Erbse, "Die Bedeutung der Synkrisis," 406.

41. Larmour, "Making Parallels," 4156–57.

employs *synkrisis* as the organizing principle of his works, comparing superior subjects to praiseworthy but lesser ones.[42]

Developing the Argument: The Narratio (1:5—4:13)

The Supporting Argument from Scripture (1:5-14)

As Quintilian indicated, the *narratio* is a vital part of the argument insofar as it introduces the argument that will be confirmed in the *probatio*. In Heb 1:5—4:13 the author amplifies the thesis set forth in 1:1-4 with additional *synkrises* (cf. 3:1-6) and provides the supporting arguments for the claim that he will make on the readers (2:1-4; 3:7—4:11), anticipating the themes that he will restate in the *propositio* (4:14-16) and develop in the *probatio* (5:1—10:31). Γάρ in 1:5 indicates that the argument from Scripture is intended as support for the thesis announced in 1:1-4. Indeed, the repetition of themes in 1:5-13 indicates that the author is giving scriptural support to the basic thesis in 1:1-4.[43] The argument from Scripture is introduced with a rhetorical question (1:5-6) that elicits a response from the readers. Indeed, the rhetorical question establishes an inclusio between 1:5-6 and 1:14 and continues into 2:1-4. One may compare the rhetorical questions in 3:16-18. The rhetorical question creates a sense of expectation in the audience and invites their participation in the exposition.[44]

The argument from Scripture is pervasive in Hebrews. At one level, the argument from Scripture distinguishes the rhetoric of Hebrews and other Christian writers from the accepted rhetorical practices of antiquity, for the teachers of rhetoric did not conceive of texts with a privileged status

---

42. See M. Martin, "Philo's Use of Syncrisis," 291. See the examples of Philonic *synkrises* on pages xxx.

43. See Meier, "Structure and Theology in Heb 1:1-14," 176. The catena of Scripture quotations contains the same general plot of the preexistence, incarnation, and exaltation of Christ that appears in 1:1-4. The movement of thought begins with the exaltation of the Son (1:2b; 1:5-6) and then moves back to the Son's role in creation (1:2b; 1:10) before concluding with the exaltation of the Son and the quotation of Ps 110:1.

44. See Conley, "Philo of Alexandria," 698-701. In *Det Pot Ins*. 58-61, Philo poses questions in such a way as to create a sense of expectation in his audience and then fulfill that expectation, a strategy very like a playwright's in its handling of the audience. In a rather severely abridged form: What profit is there in the answer? . . . On the contrary, it must be said that such things cannot . . . . For what, one might say, would one say such things? . . . So the [soul] about to give answers . . . [?] . . . What that is praiseworthy could come of answering? Behold, he says, I have virtue. *Somn*. 2.145-46: Who that enters the arena of life remains untouched? Who has never been tripped up? . . . Who has never been ambushed by fortune?

as revelation.[45] The appeal to Scripture bears some resemblance to the ancient appeal to laws, witnesses, contracts, torture, and oaths (Aristotle, *Rhet.* 1.15.1–3). However, within a subculture that recognized the divine origin of Scripture, the appeal to it was the ultimate proof.[46]

The appeal to Scripture appears regularly in the argument to support the *synkrisis* and reinforces the author's emphasis on the God who speaks. Scripture is the voice of God (1:5–13; 7:21; 8:8; 10:37–38; 12:5; 13:5–6),[47] the Son (2:12–13; 10:5–8), and the Holy Spirit (3:7; 10:15). Through it the community now hears the divine voice that addresses the exalted Son (cf. 5:5–6) and the community (cf. 3:6, 12–13; 4:7; 12:5–6). Because the community lives within the narrative world of Scripture, the *exempla* provide compelling support for the author's case (see below).

A special feature of appeal to Scripture in Hebrews is the juridical language that the author employs to support the argument. God's revelation is a witness, testifying (cf. συνεπιμαρτυροῦντος, 2:4; διεμαρτύρατο, 2:6; μαρτυρούμενος, 7:8, μαρτυρεῖται, 7:17; μαρτυρεῖ, 10:15) to the saving events. Similarly, the author gives special emphasis to Scripture as God's oath, indicating that the divine oath provides certainty (βεβαίωσις, 6:16). God "swore" (ὤμοσεν) that the Israelites would not enter the promised land (3:11, 18), confirmed his promise to Abraham, "swearing by himself" (ὤμοσεν καθ' αὑτοῦ, 6:13), and "swore" (ὤμοσεν) to the exalted Christ, "You are a priest forever after the order of Melchizedek" (7:21). Indeed, in the Christ event God demonstrated the irrevocability of his promise when he "swore with an oath" (ἐμεσίτευσεν ὅρκῳ) for the sake of the community (6:17). Thus the solemn speech of God is the ultimate proof of the community's confession, for it is God's oath to the community. The readers would have been aware of the significance of oaths as supporting arguments. Here one may compare Philo's frequent appeal to oaths.

---

45. Olbricht, "Anticipating," 539.

46. Cf. Thurén, "Is There Biblical Argumentation?" *Rhetorical Argumentation in Biblical Texts*, 90. "Seen from a normative point of view, much of religious reasoning is problematic indeed. Many chains of thought could be directly classified as fallacies. But this is not due to lacking logical ability, or to the age of the texts, but to their ideological and religious character." Thurén adds, "The appeal to Scripture is typical of early Christian reasoning." While this proof may not be persuasive to those outside this subculture, it is effective to those who recognize it. "And if the audience believes that there is an existing, active God, and that the speaker reliably represents God's opinions, what could be a stronger proof than to refer to those opinions" (ibid., 91).

47. The context indicates that the κύριος in 7:21; 8:8 is God. For God as κύριος, see also 8:2, 11; 10:30; 12:5–6, 14; 13:6. The Son is κύριος in 2:3; 7:14.

The Claim on the Readers (2:1–4)

Argumenta in Hebrews provide the basis for the claim on the readers (cf. 3:7—4:11; 5:11—6:8; 10:19–31). Δεῖ in 2:1 indicates the relationship between the argument and the claim. Consistent with the *synkrisis*, the author makes the *a fortiori* argument to support his claim. The *a fortiori argument* is one of the common features in Hebrews. The author employs the first-class conditional sentence here (cf. 12:25–27) to speak of the consequences of disobedience. One may compare also the argument in 10:26–31 (without the conditional sentence). *Synkrisis* is the basis for a special claim on the readers. We may compare the statement of Quintilian:

> At times, again, we may advance a parallel to make something which we desire to exaggerate seem greater than ever, as Cicero does in the pro Cluentio, where, after telling a story of a woman of Miletus who took a bribe from the reversionary heirs to prevent the birth of her expected child, he cries, "How much greater is the punishment deserved by Oppianicus for the same offence! For that woman, by doing violence to her own body did but torture herself, whereas he procured the same result by applying violence and torture to the body of another."[48] (*Inst.* 8.4.11)

The appeal to fear is a common mode of argumentation in Hebrews (6:4–6; 10:26–31; 12:25–29). Based on the *synkrisis*, the author indicates that the greater salvation bears the greater responsibility and results in greater punishment for those who disregard their greater possession. The appeal to fear is a common means of persuasion in antiquity. It is what the rhetoricians call *deinosis*, the attempt to shock the audience into listening to the speaker's message.[49] Aristotle discusses the appeal to fear in *Rhetoric* 2.5.1:

---

48. Cited in Lausberg, *Handbook of Literary Rhetoric*, § 404. Cf. Quintilian (*Inst. Or.* 5.11.9. "While examples may at times . . . apply in their entirety, at times we shall argue from the greater to the lesser or from the less to the greater. 'Cities have been overthrown by the violation of the marriage bond. What punishment then will meet the case of adultery?' 'Flute players have been recalled by the state to the city which they had left. How much more then is it just that the leading citizens who have rendered good services to their country should be recalled from that exile to which they have been driven by envy.'" Cf. also *Inst. Or.* 8.4.13, "Did that illustrious citizen, the pontifex maximus, Publius Scipio, acting merely in his private capacity, kill Tiberius Gracchus when he introduced by slight changes for the worse that did not seriously impair the constitution of the state, and shall we as consuls suffer Cataline to live, whose aim was to lay waste the whole world with fire and sword?" Quintilian adds, "One thing is magnified in order to effect a corresponding augmentation elsewhere, and it is by reasoning that our hearers are then led on from the first point to the second which we desire to emphasize" (8.4.15.).

49. Lausberg, *Handbook of Literary Rhetoric*, §257.3; Quintilian, *Inst.* 6.2.24.

Let fear be defined as a painful or troubled feeling caused by the impression of an imminent evil that causes destruction or pain; for men do not fear all evils, for instance, becoming unjust or slow witted (βραδύς) but only such as involve great pain or destruction (φθαρτικοῦ ἢ λυπηροῦ). (trans. Freese LCL)[50]

Refutatio (2:5–18)

The Scripture citation in 2:6–8a appears at first to be a continuation of the appeal to Scripture in 1:5–13. However, after indicating that "all things have been subjected under his feet" (2:8a), the author addresses the critical issue faced by the community in the statement in 2:8b, "We do not yet see all things in subjection to him," which expresses an objection to the claims that the author has made in 1:1—2:4. That is, the author's task is to refute this objection and persuade the community in view of the dissonance between the Christian confession and their own experience. The remainder of the chapter is a refutation of that objection. In 2:9 he offers a thesis that he will demonstrate in 2:10–18. "Crowned with glory and honor" is a restatement of the initial confession (cf. 1:4), which the author clarifies with information not developed in chapter 1: The suffering of death was the prerequisite for the crowning with glory and honor. Before the author can continue with the confirmation of his basic thesis (chapter 1), he must first address objections that are derived from the experience of the listeners. In 2:10–18 the authors offers the refutation.

Refutatio, the demonstration of the invalidity of the opponent's position,[51] was a major topic among rhetorical theorists. Aristotle (*Rhet.* 3.13.14–15) and Quintilian (*Inst. Or.* 3.9.1) list the *refutatio* (Greek ἀνασκευή also λύσις) among the proofs, while the *Auctor ad Herennium* (1.10, 18) and Cicero (*Inv.* 1.42, 78) regard it as a separate part of the speech.[52] It was included among the progymnasmata.[53] Normally, it appeared after the proofs, but it could appear elsewhere in the argument.[54] The author meets the

---

50. See Nongbri, "A Touch of Condemnation in a Word of Exhortation," 275

51. Lausberg, *Handbook of Literary Rhetoric*, §404. Cf. Nicolaus, *Progymnasmata* 6, "Refutation is a statement in rebuttal of something that has been credibly stated and confirmation is the opposite." Hermogenes 5, "Refutation (ἀνασκευή) is an overturning of something that has been proposed, and confirmation (κατασκευή) is the opposite." According to Apthonius 5 (101), "Those engaged in refutation should first state the false claim of those who advance it, then add an exposition of the subject."

52. J. Martin, *Antike Rhetorik*, 125.

53. Lausberg, *Handbook of Literary Rhetoric*, §262.

54. See Hellholm, "Amplificatio in the Macro-Structure of Rom," 134: Hermogenes

challenge of the interlocutor with an explanation of the dissonance between the confession and the reality.

Γάρ in 2:10 points to the justification for the assumption that solidarity in suffering is the prerequisite for glory and honor. The author argues in 2:10 that "it was fitting" (ἔπρεπεν γὰρ αὐτῷ), which forms an inclusio with ὤφειλεν in 2:17. At both the beginning and the end of the unit, the author argues on the basis of appropriateness and necessity, appealing to a principle that he assumes will be persuasive to the readers. That is, in 2:10, 17 the author appeals to necessity to argue that the suffering and solidarity of the Son with humankind is the precondition for the exaltation.

Here one finds the most distinctive features of the author's argumentation. In 2:10 and 7:26 the author argues from what is fitting (πρέπειν). Closely related to the argument from what is fitting is the argument that "it is necessary" (7:12, 27; 8:3; 9:16, 23) and the statement that "it is impossible" (ἀδύνατον, 6:4, 18; 10:4; 11:6). The sacrifice of Jesus was both "fitting" (2:10; 7:26) and "necessary" (9:16, 23) because it is "impossible" for the blood of bulls and goats to take away sins (10:4). This claim points to an understanding of a generic principle that the author assumes will be convincing to the readers.

The author's connection to Greco-Roman rhetoric is most transparent at this point, for the appeal to the possible, the necessary, and the fitting were basic to ancient argumentation. For example, the author of *Rhetoric ad Alexandrum* lists the three species of rhetoric, and then divides them into subcategories (exhortation, dissuasion, encomium, vituperation, accusation, defense and investigation [1421b 8–11]). These abstract rhetorical categories aim at proving the following: in exhortation, that the cause presented is just (δίκαιον), legitimate (νόμιμον), convenient (συμφέρον), noble (καλόν), agreeable (ἡδύ), accessible (ῥάδιον), possible (δυνατόν), and necessary (ἀναγκαῖον); and in dissuasion, the opposite.[55] Rhetorical theorists frequently listed the necessary, the fitting, and the possible among the appropriate arguments of deliberative speech.[56] Aristotle reflects not only on the possible (δυνατόν), but also on the impossible (ἀδύνατον) in

---

states that some rhetoricians put the counter proposal (antithesis) before its refutation (*lysis*), while Demosthenes is inconsistence since "at times . . . he refutes the argument of his opponent before he offers his own proposals." Aristotle, who treats the refutatio in the chapter dealing with the dispositio within the probatio section, emphasizes the strategic order of the confirmatio and the refutatio respectively (*Rhet* 3.13.14–15).

55. Alexandre, *Rhetorical Argumentation*, 55. See the discussion in Löhr, "Reflections of Rhetorical Terminology in Hebrews," 204–9.

56. See Lausberg, *Handbook of Literary Rhetoric*, § 375 for different versions of suitable arguments, the κεφάλαια. Hermogenes, *Prog.* 6, τῷ νομίμῳ, τῷ δικαίῳ, τῷ συμφέροντι, τῷ δυνατῳ, τῷ πρέποντι.

the context of common topics of the three genera of speech. According to Aristotle, the topos of the possible is most appropriate for deliberative speech (*Rhet.* 2.18.5 [1392a]).

Whereas Aristotle restricts himself to enumerating several examples of logical and natural possibility, he says of the impossible (ἀδύνατον, 2.19.15 [1392b]): "Concerning the impossible, it is clear that there is a supply of arguments to be derived from the opposite of what has been said about the possible" (LCL). The distinction between possible and impossible is fundamental to each orator.

The appeal to what is fitting, necessary, and impossible to support the Christian confession would not have been convincing to the ancient listeners outside the Christian community. Indeed, a common topic in philosophical discussions was the subject of what was "fitting for God."[57] The claim that the incarnation and suffering of Christ were "fitting for God" is contrary to Greek thought.[58] However, the author assumes that his readers do not question the basic Christian confession. Hence, he assumes that the argument will be effective.

In further support of the author's *refutatio* is the statement in 2:11, which also states a general principle. Γάρ in 2:11 suggests that the statement is in support of 2:10: "For the one who sanctifies and those who are being sanctified are of one." This statement is a maxim (Greek γνώμη; Latin *sententia*), which the author presents as a general truth that provides the basis for the argument in 2:12–18. Students were taught that supporting a thesis with a maxim was an appropriate argumentation pattern.[59] The *Progymnasmata* of Theon, for example, advocates the confirmation of a thesis by a maxim: "We will get the introductions of theses by confirming the thesis with a maxim, a proverb, a chreia, a useful saying, a story, an encomium, or a denunciation of the subject matter which the investigation concerns."[60]

Once more the author employs one of his favorite modes of argumentation. One may observe the numerous maxims that appear as the basis of for the argument. These maxims appear to point to what is generally true from observation and are closely related to what is fitting, necessary, and impossible. Some of the maxims are based on commonplace observation

---

57. See ch. 3, "The Appropriate, the Necessary, and the Impossible: Faith and Reason in Hebrews."

58. Thompson, "The Appropriate, the Necessary, and the Impossible," 305. "The claim of Hebrews that the sacrifice of Christ was 'fitting for God' is a remarkable tour de force in the ancient context, where the association of God with human suffering would have been abhorrent." See also Attridge, *Hebrews*, 82.

59. Ramsaran, *Liberating Words*, 10.

60. Ramsaran, *Liberating Words*, 10.

(cf. 3:3; 5:13-14), while others appeal to recognized wisdom. It is "beyond dispute," for example, that an oath is for confirmation (cf. 6:16) and that "it is impossible for God to lie" (6:18). No one would question that "the word of God is living and active" (4:12) and that "it is appointed for men once to die and after that the judgment" (9:27). Many of the author's contemporaries would agree that "it is impossible for the blood of bulls and goats to take away sins" (cf. 10:4).

Other maxims are disputable, but the author apparently assumes that they are generally true. For example, despite his claims, it is not "beyond dispute that the lesser is blessed by the greater" (7:7), for exceptions to this claim are present in Scripture. Similarly, the statement that "where there is a διαθήκη, there is of necessity the death of the testator" (9:16) is not always true. Other maxims appear to be the author's creation, which he offers as a basis for the argument. Three times, for example, the author introduces an argument with the introductory "Every priest . . ." (5:1; 8:3; 10:11), in which he summarizes the priestly task in a brief statement.[61] These are not full descriptions of the task of the high priest, however, but the features that are important to the argument.

The statements that "it was necessary for the copies of the things in heaven to be cleansed with these" (9:23) and "it is impossible to restore to repentance" those who fall away (6:4) are probably the author's creation. The author has thus combined commonplace observations with his own maxims to create a cumulative effect. The effectiveness of these maxims on the reader depends on his ethos.[62]

These maxims commonly function as the premise of the argument.[63] The author begins with the general principle (i.e., that "every priest is appointed" or that "the one who sanctifies and those who are sanctified are one") and applies it to Jesus. In 2:10-18, for example, the maxim "the one who sanctifies and those who are sanctified are of one" is the premise for the discussion of the solidarity of the human Jesus with the people (2:11b-18). As the argument indicates, ἐξ ἑνός is a term for the family solidarity of the seed of Abraham (cf. 2:16).[64] The author refutes the readers' objection (2:8b) with the claim of the solidarity of the Son with the people.

---

61. 5:1, "Every priest is appointed to offer gifts and sacrifices for sins"; 8:3, "Every priest is appointed to offer gifts and sacrifices for sins"; 10:11, "Every priest stood."

62. Ramsaran, *Liberating Words*, 9.

63. Aristotle defines the maxim (γνώμη) as a declaration concerning a general matter related to human action or as the major premise or conclusions of a rhetorical syllogism (*Rhet.* 2.21).

64. Swetnam, "Ἐξ ἑνός in Hebrews 2,11," 521-22. Cf. Philo, *conf.* 147.

The maxim played an important role in ancient rhetoric. The maxim was an individual's spoken expression of recognized wisdom based on general observations and applied to particular circumstances of the moment.[65] The *sententia* is an "infinite" insofar as it is not restricted to an individual case. The truth of the gnomic maxim was generally thought to be universal and indisputable.[66] The infinite character and demonstrative function of the *sententia* are due to the fact that it is regarded, in the social milieu of its range of validity and application, as a piece of wisdom with the same authority as a legal judgment or a written law, applicable to many concrete.

Confirmatio and Exempla (3:1—4:13)

After the *refutatio* in 2:5-18, the author amplifies the original thesis (1:1-4) with a parallel *synkrisis*. The comparison of Moses the servant (3:5) to Jesus the Son (3:6) recapitulates the comparison between the servants (angels) and the Son in 1:5-13 and indicates that, while both Moses and Jesus were faithful (πιστός), the Son is superior to the servant. Inasmuch as Num 12:7 (Heb 3:2) was a basic text indicating that Moses is God's spokesman, the author may also be implying a *synkrisis* between God's word in the past and the ultimate word in the Son (cf. 1:1-2). With the transitional phrase, "We are his house, if we hold firm to the boasting of hope" (3:6b), the author proceeds to the claim that he makes on the readers, once more appealing to scriptural support (cf. 1:5-13). The citation of Ps 95:7-11 in Heb 3:7-11 functions at more than one level. At one level it extends the *synkrisis* of Moses and Jesus into the next generation to imply a contrast between Joshua and Jesus—and between the wilderness generation and the church—in order to demonstrate that only Jesus ushers the people into the ultimate rest. At another level, the passage restates the warning in 2:1-4. The passage also functions as a negative example (ὑπόδειγμα) for the listeners (4:11). Israel's failure is an *exemplum* for the church.

The *exemplum* is a pervasive feature of the argument of Hebrews. Scripture serves as a storehouse for *exempla*. The author argues from observations in nature (cf. 6:7-9) and from individuals in Scripture. Within the symmetrical structure of the homily, the *exemplum* in 3:1—4:13 has a counterpart in 10:32—12:11. In 3:7—4:11 Israel in the wilderness is the example of ἀπιστία (3:12, 19; 4:2), while the latter is composed of examples of πίστις. Elsewhere, Esau is the negative example (12:15-17), while Abraham is the

---

65. Ramsaran, "Living and Dying, Living is Dying (Phil. 1:21)," 327; Ramsaran, *Liberating Words*, 10.

66. Ramsaran, "Living as Dying, Living is Dying (Phil. 1:21)," 327.

positive example (6:12–13). Indeed, the author challenges the readers to be μιμηταί of faithful people who inherited the promises (6:12).

The argument from example is a common feature both in ancient and modern rhetoric.[67] According to Quintilian (*Inst. Or.* 5.11.6), "The most important of the proofs of this class is that which is most appropriately called *exemplum*, that is to say the adducing of some past action real or assured which may serve to persuade the audience of the truth of the point we are trying to make." The historical *exemplum* is the most common (Quintilian, *Inst. Or.* 5.11.1): "The third kind of proof, which is drawn into the service of the case from without, is styled a *paradeigma* by the Greeks, who apply the term to all comparisons of like with like but more especially to historical parallels" (*Inst. Or.* 5.11.1). Quintilian adds that

> It will also be found useful when we are speaking of what is likely to happen to refer to historical parallels: for instance if the orator asserts that Dionysius is asking for a bodyguard that with their armed assistance he may establish himself as a tyrant, he may address the parallel case of Pisistratus who secured the supreme power by similar means.[68]

Argument and Persuasion in Hebrews 5–13

The author introduces the major argumentative strategies of Hebrews 1:1—4:13 and then amplifies them in the *probatio* in 4:14—10:31 and the *peroratio* in 10:32—13:25, as I have demonstrated in the previous section. The author bases his appeal to the readers on *synkrisis* (5:1–10; 7:1–23; 8:1—10:18), maxims, the argument from impossibility and necessity (6:4–6; 10:1–4; 9:23), and *exempla* (ch. 11). Only in a few instances does he introduce argumentative strategies drawn from ancient rhetorical practice that he has not used previously. In 7:1–3, for example, he argues on the basis of the etymology of the name of Melchizedek. The argument from etymology was commonplace among Philo and the teachers of rhetoric.

According to Plato, "Whoever knows names also knows the things they represent" (*Cratylus* 435d), for he believed that words communicate the essence of things.[69] According to Cicero (*Topica* 8.36), "In debate many arguments are elicited from a word through etymology."[70] Quintilian gives

---

67. Lausberg, *Handbook of Literary Rhetoric*, § 412.
68. *Inst. Or.* 5.11.8
69. Alexandre, *Rhetorical Argumentation*, 38.
70. See also *Academica* 1.8.30–33; *De Or.* 2.39.162–65.

an extended discussion on the use and misuse of etymology, indicating that the analysis of the derivation of words is often useful as a means of definition (*Inst. Or.* 1.6.28–31).[71] Philo makes frequent use of the argument from etymology, often in connection with proper names.[72] For example, he gives the etymology of Jubal (*Post. Cain* 100; cf. Gen 4:21), Abram (*Leg. All.* 3:83; cf. Gen 12:1), Hagar (*Congr.* 20; cf. Gen 16:1). The derivation of words is the basis also when he discusses abstract concepts, such as sense perception (αἴσθησις, *Deus* 42) and violence (βίαιον, *Deus* 103). He devotes an extended section in *de Plantatione* to the derivation of numerous words (149–59).

One may also observe the use of the rhetorical term κεφάλαιον . . . τοιοῦτον ἔχομεν in 8:1, which summarizes the arguments of the preceding chapters, especially chapter 7, and introduces the extended development of this theme in 8:1—10:18.[73] Rhetorical theorists reflected on the main arguments of a speech. The τελικὰ κεφάλαια as a system of arguments particularly suitable for the deliberative speech. Hermogenes (*Prog.* 6, 11), Aphthonius (*Prog.* 10), and Nicolaus (*Prog.* 42, 72, 77, 78) enumerated the τελικὰ κεφάλαια in very similar terms. Thus the author of Hebrews employs technical rhetorical terminology to describe the "main argument" of the homily.

Conclusion

The argument of Hebrews would not have been persuasive to the general population of a Greco-Roman city, for the author proceeded from assumptions about God, Scripture, and the Christ event that were not widely accepted. However, the argumentative strategies were commonplace in Greco-Roman literature. The repeated use of *synkrisis* as a framework for the homily and the comparison based on the two levels of reality were in common use among rhetoricians and philosophers. The refutation of the objections of the listeners (2:8–18) was a vital part of the ancient argument. While ancient readers would not have agreed with the author's understanding of the appropriate, the necessary, and the impossible, they would have recognized the legitimacy of the appeal to those categories. The appeal to examples of the past and the argument from etymology were also common modes of argumentation. Thus the author of Hebrews not only demonstrates accepted rhetorical practice not only in the style and arrangement of the homily but also in the mode of argumentation.

---

71. See the discussion in Lausberg, *Handbook of Literary Rhetoric*, § 466.
72. Conley, "Philo of Alexandria."
73. Löhr, "Rhetorical Terminology," 202.

CHAPTER 5

WHAT HAS MIDDLE PLATONISM TO DO WITH HEBREWS

In the second century, Celsus, a Middle Platonist known to us only through Origen's *Contra Celsum*, launched a major attack on Christian belief. Celsus, who was well acquainted with various Christian groups, saw irreconcilable differences between Platonism and Christianity. He had harsh words against the doctrines of creation (*C. Cels.* 8.49) and resurrection and ridiculed the Christian insistence on faith rather than knowledge (*C. Cels.* 1. 9). He gave an extended critique of the doctrine of the incarnation, insisting that such a change would be contrary to the nature of the immutable God (*C. Cels.* 4.2, 14). Christian writers recognized some of the same conflicts between Christianity and Platonism, maintaining that the doctrines of creation, incarnation, and eschatological triumph were incompatible with the Platonic views of God and the world. Nevertheless, while Christians recognized the conflict between their credo and Platonism, they also employed Platonic language and categories in varying degrees to explain Christian beliefs.[1] The Apostolic Fathers,[2] the Apologists,[3] and the later Christian tradition all employed Platonic categories to articulate their convictions while holding to beliefs that were in conflict with the Platonic

---

1. Originally published in *Reading the Epistle to the Hebrews: A Resource for Students*, edited by Eric F. Mason and Kevin B. McCruden, 31–52. Atlanta: Society of Biblical Literature, 2011.
Meijering, "Wie Platonisierten Christen?" 17.

2. Wyller, "Plato," 697.

3. They described the deity with the terms borrowed from Middle Platonism, agreeing that God cannot undergo change. According to Athenagoras (*Leg. pro Christ.* 10), God is "uncreated, eternal, invisible, impassible, infinite." Similarly, Justin expresses his belief in the transcendence of God in Platonic terms (*Apol.* 2.9; See Andressen, "Justin und der mittlere Platonismus," 159–95.

tradition. Platonic categories were the common property not only of the elite but of all educated people.[4]

The refined language of the Epistle to the Hebrews leaves no doubt that the author belonged to the educated circles among whom the tenets of Platonism were commonplace. Moreover, scholars have recognized the similarities between the Platonic language of Philo of Alexandria and Hebrews, especially in the description of the heavenly tabernacle in Heb 8:1–5. The author cites the instructions to Moses, "See that you make everything according to the archetype shown you on the mountain" (8:5; Exod 25:40). The heavenly archetype is the "true tent" in heaven (8:2), while the one on earth is a "copy and shadow." The language evokes Plato's theory of ideas (*Resp.* 514–17; *Laws* 1.643c), according to which earthly matters are shadows of heavenly archetypes. Philo gave a Platonic interpretation to Exod 25:40 (*QE* 2.52; *Alleg. Interp.* 3.100–102; *Planting* 26–27; *Moses* 2.71–75), and the later church fathers also read the passage with Platonic lenses (Origen, *Hom. Exod.* 9.2: Eusebius, *PE* 12.19.1–9).

To what extent was the author a Platonist? His interaction with Platonism has been one of the most disputed issues in the scholarship in the last century. Numerous scholars have observed that his affirmation of the Christian credo was incompatible with Platonism and denied any significant connection between the author and Philo.[5] The belief in the divine work in creation (1:2; 2:10; 11:3) and the explicit references to the preexistent Son who was "a little while lower than the angels" (2:9) and lived in the flesh (5:7–8) before his exaltation (cf. 1:3, 13) are contrary to Platonic teachings. The traditional Jewish belief in the two ages, which is also incompatible with Platonism, is a consistent feature of the homily. God has spoken "in these last days" (1:2), and believers have "tasted the powers of the coming age" (6:5; cf. 9:9–10). They anticipate the final apocalyptic shaking of the heavens and the earth (12:26–28).

The eschatological features of Hebrews do not preclude the presence of Platonic thought, however, for patristic writers offer abundant evidence that Jewish eschatological expectations and Platonic metaphysics, despite their apparent incompatibility, commonly existed alongside each other. Justin and Clement of Alexandria, for example, affirmed a Christian eschatology while expressing themselves in the language of Platonism.[6] Thus the pur-

---

4. Backhaus, "Per Christum in Deum," 262.

5. Mackie, *Eschatology and Exhortation in the Epistle to the Hebrews*, 83–104.

6. Thompson, "*Ephapax*: The One and the Many in Hebrews," 580. Justin speaks frequently of the second advent (*Dial.* 31.1–3; 110.2–4; 111.1; 118.1; 121.3) and insists that the "great and terrible day" (*Dial.* 49.2) is coming soon (*Dial.* 32.4). Christ will "appear in Jerusalem" (*Dial.* 85.7) and destroy all his enemies (*Dial.* 121.3), including the "man

pose of the article is to determine the extent to which Platonism played a role in the argument of Hebrews.

Philo and Middle Platonism

Since Hugo Grotius first identified parallels between Hebrews and the works of Philo, numerous works have examined the relationships between them, noting their common use of Platonic language. Philo was, however, a major representative of a larger movement, Middle Platonism, which emerged in the first century BCE after the Platonic tradition turned from the skepticism of the Academy to a renewed interest in metaphysics.[7] While several names of Middle Platonists are known to us, few works have remained. Philo (ca. 20 BCE-ca. 50 CE) and Plutarch of Chaeroneia (ca. CE 45-124), both of whom have left a substantial body of literature, are major sources of our knowledge of this school of thought. Philo applied the Middle Platonic framework to the allegorical interpretation of Scripture, while Plutarch applied it to Greek myths. Thus our understanding of the intellectual climate of Hebrews requires that we compare this homily, not only with Philo but also with those who shared Philo's approach to religious traditions.

While Middle Platonists shared common ground with other philosophical schools, the distinguishing feature and dominant concern of Middle Platonists was the transcendence of God, who was commonly identified as the One, the existence of the ideas, and the immortality of the soul.[8] The corollary to the transcendence of God was the chasm separating God and the incorporeal world of ideas from the material world and human weakness. Middle Platonists described this duality as the distinction between Being and becoming. True Being in the intelligible world exists in timeless eternity (*aiōn*), while the perceptible world is subject to constant becoming (*genesis*). The latter is subject to change, never remaining in the same state (Philo, *Creation* 12). Philo indicates that everything in creation must change, while immutability is the property of God (*Leg.* 2.33). The supreme God is "motherless," "unbegotten," and "abiding" (*Creation* 100; cf. *Vit. Mos.*

---

of sin" (*Dial.* 32.4). Although Clement of Alexandria tried to harmonize apocalyptic with Greek cosmology, he maintained a hope for the end, speaking of "the resurrection for which we hope; when, at the end of the world, the angels receive into the celestial abodes those who repent" (*Quis div.* 42). After the second coming of Christ, all of the righteous will be taken up into heaven (*Ecl.* 56-67). For the eschatology of Justin and Clement of Alexandria, see Daley, *The Hope of the Early Church*, 20-22, 44-47.

7. Middle Platonism is the designation for the Platonic tradition in the era from 80 BCE until CE 220. Klauck, *Alte Welt und neuer Glaube*, 59.

8. Dillon, *Middle Platonists*, 48-49.

2.12). Plutarch asks, "What is real Being? It is the eternal and unbegotten and imperishable, without beginning and without end, to which [a length of] time, not even one, brings change" (392 E). In *The E at Delphi*, he comments on the E at the entrance of the temple of Apollo, suggesting that E signifies the Greek "You are" (*ei*), the appropriate address to God, who is unchanging and uncontaminated by matter (*E Delph.* 392f) while humankind inhabits the world of becoming and is subject to change, decay, and mortality. "Everything of a mortal nature is at some stage between coming into existence and passing away" (*E Delph.* 392b). Thus Plutarch says that the antithesis to "you are" (*ei*) is "know thyself" (*gnōthi sauton*). He explains that the address "you are" is an utterance addressed in awe to the God who exists through all eternity, while "know thyself" is a reminder to mortals of their own weaknesses (*E Delph.* 394c).

Consistent with their distinction between the two realms of reality, Middle Platonists distinguish between the One, which transcends the universe, and the Indefinite Dyad, the principle of duality, which is infinitely divisible. The One belongs to the intelligible world, while the latter can be seen throughout nature.[9] Middle Platonists identify the transcendent God with the One, who stands above the principle of multiplicity that is associated with the realm of becoming. Whereas God is one and unmixed (Philo, *Abr.* 122), humans belong to the world of becoming that is characterized by multiplicity. Indeed, Philo frequently employs words for multiplicity to describe the inferiority of things that belong to the material world (*Plant.* 44; *Somn.* 2.14). Plutarch's distinction between being and becoming/eternity and time corresponds to his distinction between the one and the many. God is stable and unitary, and the human, subject to becoming, is in a state of constant change and therefore lacks unity.[10] God is One, and humankind is many and always in a state of birth and decay (*E. Delph.* 392).

The major challenge for Middle Platonists was to overcome the radical separation between the transcendent deity and the material world.[11] In order to preserve the transcendence of the divine Being, they claimed an intermediate principle that mediated between the first principle and the material world.[12] Philo claims that God created the world through the *logos* (*Sacr.* 8), who serves the deity by providing links between God and everything else (*Deus* 57). He uses the same language to describe wisdom (*sophia, Conf.* 146–47). Similarly, Plutarch identifies such a figure with Isis,

9. Dillon, *The Middle Platonists*, 46.
10. Whittaker, "Plato, Platonism, and Christianity," 56.
11. Backhaus, "Per Christum in Deum," 263.
12. Cox, *By the Same Word*, 43.

who mediates between the transcendent and material realms.[13] Beneath this intermediate being the Platonic cosmos was filled with subordinate intermediate beings. Philo describes the angels who exist below the transcendent God, while Plutarch speaks of a cosmos populated by daemons (see below).

The bridging of the chasm between the two realms became the challenge of Middle Platonism. The possibility of knowledge of God became the starting point of Middle Platonic philosophy.[14] Human knowledge of God comes by perception. Human knowledge of God comes by perception. God is immutable, and humans are inherently unstable. The task is for humans to overcome the instability of their existence and to know God.

This philosophical framework was welcome in Alexandrian Judaism and in its heir, Alexandrian Christianity. The emphasis on transcendence was the central feature that made Middle Platonism popular to Jews of the Diaspora, providing the means for combining this principle with their traditional belief in the sovereignty of God.[15] Just as Middle Platonism preserved the transcendence of God by positing an intermediary principle, Alexandrian Judaism incorporated intermediaries into their cosmology. Philo spoke of both wisdom (*sophia*) and word (*logos* also means reason).

Hebrews and Middle Platonism

Like Philo and Plutarch, the author of Hebrews is the interpreter of religious traditions. He addresses second-generation believers who are discouraged because they have not seen the eschatological triumph of God and are weary from a long journey that has not reached its goal. After declaring of the Son, "He has put all things under his feet" (2:8), he acknowledges, "We do not yet see all things in subjection to him" (2:8b), expressing the frustrations of readers whose experience conflicts with their confession. The passage of time and the experience of marginalization (cf. 10:32–35) have led the readers to ask if the commitment is worth the price that is being paid. Indeed, the unstable situation of the readers is evident in the concern that they "drift away" (2:1), "fall away" (3:12; cf. 6:4–6), or be "carried away" (13:9) and the description of them as "refugees" (6:18). The author's challenge is to rebuild their symbolic world and provide an anchor that is stable and firm (6:19) in the midst of the instability of their existence. The entry of Christ into the heavenly world is the anchor that the community can now grasp (6:18). Indeed, the exaltation of Christ, expressed in the words of Ps 110, provides

13. Dillon, *The Middle Platonists*, 46.
14. Andresen, "Antike und Christentum," 161.
15. Cox, *By the Same Word*, 30.

the unifying thread (cf. 1:3, 13; 6:20; 7:3, 23-24; 8:1; 10:12) for declaring the transcendence of the Christ who sat down at the right hand of God. Having entered the transcendent reality, he opens the way for believers to follow (cf. 2:10; 4:14-16; 6:20; 10:19-23). Although this reality is unseen at the present (2:8b; 11:1), the promise of fulfillment remains for believers (cf. 4:1).

Closely related to the emphasis on the transcendent reality is the author's consistent use of comparison (Greek *synkrisis*), a common rhetorical device among ancient orators. Interpreters have observed that Hebrews is a series of comparisons between the Christ event and the people and institutions of the Old Testament. Indeed, the author employs "better" (*kreittōn*) thirteen times in the homily in addition to other comparisons. These comparisons in Hebrews do not reflect a polemic against the Old Testament or Judaism but are rhetorical devices that demonstrate the greatness of the work of Christ, as Aristotle indicates in describing the importance of *synkrisis* in speeches in praise of a distinguished person (*Rhet.* 1.9.38-39):

> And you must compare him with illustrious personages, for it affords ground for amplification and is noble, if he can be proved better than men of worth. Amplification is with good reason ranked as one of the forms of praise, since it consists in superiority, and superiority is one of the things that are noble.

In contrast to the ancient orator's use of *synkrisis*, the distinguishing feature of this rhetorical device in Hebrews is its use in the comparison of beings and realities that belong to two levels of reality. That is, transcendent beings and realities are better than earthly counterparts. Christ is "better" than the angels (1:4) as a result of his exaltation, and the order of Melchizedek to which he was appointed at the exaltation (cf. 5:6, 10; 6:20) is greater than the Aaronic priesthood (7:7). Because he offers better sacrifices (9:23) in a greater tabernacle (9:11-14), believers have a greater covenant (7:22; 8:6), a greater hope (7:19; cf. 10:34), and greater promises (8:5; 11:40) than their earthly counterparts. Believers have not come to Mount Sinai, which "may be touched" (12:18) but to the heavenly Mount Zion (12:22). Believers, therefore, belong to a reality that is not perceptible to the senses, for it is both invisible (11:1, 27) and untouchable (12:18). The author describes the transcendent world by a variety of terms. It is the promised rest (4:3, 9), the heavenly sanctuary (8:1-5; 9:1-14, 23), the heavenly city, homeland, and unshakable kingdom. He compares them with the counterparts on earth.

Similar comparisons appear in the works of Philo and Plutarch. Plutarch says that "For that which really is and is perceptible and good is superior (*kreittōn*) to destruction and change" (*Isis and Osiris* 373). Similarly, Philo commonly compares the heavenly with the earthly insisting that the heavenly reality is better (cf. *Creation* 140; *Heir* 89; *Joseph* 147). Philo describes God as "greater than the good, more venerable than the Monad, purer than the unit" (*Rewards and Punishments* 40). The mind of the universe is "supremely pure and undefiled, superior to excellence and superior to knowledge, and even superior to the good itself and the fair itself" (*Creation* 8).

Christ and the Angels

The opening words of Hebrews establish the major themes of the homily as the author summarizes in poetic form the path of the preexistent Son from his primordial state to his earthly existence ("when he made purification for sins") and subsequent exaltation to "the right hand of the majesty on high" (1:3). As the Scriptural proofs indicate in 1:5-13, the author's primary focus is on the exaltation. In this initial allusion to Ps 110:1, he introduces the theme of the transcendence of the Son and high priest (cf. 4:14-16; 6:20; 8:1—10:18), anticipating his consistent distinction between this creation and the heavenly world (cf. 9:11, 23; 12:18, 22). With the claim that the Son has become "greater than the angels" (1:4), he suggests that angels do not share in the Son's exalted status, introducing the first *synkrisis* between the transcendent one and the objects of comparison. "Better" (*kreittōn*) is used here, as elsewhere, to suggest the spatial contrast between the heavenly and the earthly, inferior reality (see 9:11-14, 23; 10:34).

The author demonstrates the superiority of the Son to the angels in the catena of citations in 1:5-13, carefully arranging the passages to support his claim. Drawing on OT imagery, the author cites two well-known messianic texts (Ps 2:7; 2 Sam 7:14) to affirm that the exaltation is also the coronation of Jesus as Son (1:5; cf. 5:5-6, 10) when all of the angels worship him (1:6). This claim is of special importance to the author, for whom it is axiomatic that the inferior pays homage to the superior (7:4-8).[16]

Having cited three passages to demonstrate that the Son is better than the angels (1:5-6), the author now provides the basis for the argument (1:7-12). The sequence of the citations indicates how the exaltation makes the Son better than the angels. The contrasting statements to the angels (1:7) and to the Son (1:8-9) suggests their fundamental difference. Whereas God "makes the angels into winds" (cf. Ps 104:4), he says to the son, "Your throne, O God, is forever and ever" (cf. Ps 44:7 LXX). Unlike the rabbis who cited Ps 104:4 to demonstrate the transcendence of God or the might of the angels, the contrast with the eternity of the Son (1:8)

---

16. Thompson, *The Beginnings of Christian Philosophy*, 132.

indicates that angels, unlike the Son, are changeable. Because they are a part of creation, they are inferior to the Son.

The place of angels within creation is analogous to the role of intermediate beings in the thought of Middle Platonists, for whom the radical separation of the deity from the material worlds necessitated the existence of the daemons to mediate with the realm of the senses.[17] Plutarch speaks of those beings who live on the boundary between gods and men who are subject to human emotions and involuntary changes (*Obsolescence of Oracles* 416). They are a "ministering class, midway between gods and men" (*Isis and Osiris* 361; cf. "ministering spirits" in Heb 1:14). The angels in Philo have a similar role (*Giants* 16) as the proper inhabitants of the air (*Giants* 16). In his interpretation of the story of Jacob's ladder he indicates that angels "ascend and descend" (*Dreams* 1.33) throughout the universe, and they are subject to change (*Giants* 17).

The author reinforces the distinction between the eternal Son and the changeable angels in the extended citation in 1:10–12 (cf. Ps 102:26–28), which originally described God's sovereignty over creation. Once more a passage originally addressed to God becomes God's address to the Son. The words, "You are from the beginning, you established the earth, the works of your hands are the heavens," recall the description of the role of the preexistent Son at the creation in 1:2–3. The chiastic structure of the psalm in 1:11–12 introduces the sharp contrast between the Son and the created order. In contrast to the creation, which is subject to destruction, aging, and change (1:11a, c–12ab), the Son abides (*diameneis*, 11:b) and is the same (*ho autos*, 1:12c). The fact that both angels and the creation are subject to change suggests that angels belong to the creation. The Son, however, is exalted above the creation, and thus he is not subject to destruction or aging. He abides and is the same.

By using this Ps 102:26–28 as an exaltation text, the author has introduced the two levels of reality into the argument. This distinction is reminiscent of the Platonic view, according to which "becoming" (*genesis*) is the characteristic of this creation, while eternal being is characteristic of the intelligible world and the deity. One may compare Philo's argument that this world is subject to destruction (*Alleg. Laws* 3.101) in contrast to those things above the creation that are abiding (*monimoi*) and sure (*bebaioi*) and eternal (*aidioi*).

Two phrases in the citation are especially significant for the argument of Hebrews. In the first place, the affirmation "But you abide (*su de diameneis*)" contrasts the eternity of the exalted Son with the transitory nature of

---

17. Dillon, *The Middle Platonists*, 216.

the creation. That Christ remains is of central importance to Hebrews (cf. 7:3, 24; 13:8).[18] The author also speaks of a transcendent possession that "abides" (*menei*, 10:34; 12:27; 13:14). The frequent use of *menein* in theologically significant passages indicates that the author has chosen Ps 102 because it coheres with the theme of the eternity of the exalted one and the transitory nature of the material world.

The claim that only the exalted Christ abides (*diamenei*) corresponds to the Platonic view of the intelligible world and the deity. For Plato the ideal world as abides (*Tim.* 37D). According to Philo, God stands the same, remaining (*menōn*) immutable (*Dreams* 2.201), and individuals find their stability only in him. He quotes approvingly the words of Philolaus: "There is, he says, a supreme ruler of all things, God, ever One, abiding, without motion, like unto himself, different from all others" (*Creation* 100). Similarly, Plutarch maintains that the deity is commonly called the monad because God abides (*menei*, *Concerning Talkativeness* 507a). For both writers the verb connotes the immutability of God.

In the second place, the divine voice says to the exalted Christ, "You are the same (*ho autos*), and your years will never end" (1:12c). Here also the author attributes to Christ the quality that Philo and Plutarch ascribe to the deity. Philo says that God remains the same (*ho autos*), while the heavenly bodies are in constant motion (*Posterity* 19–20). In commenting on the appropriate way address God with the word "you are" (*ei*) is to acknowledge that only true Being remains the same (*ho autos*, *E Delph.* 392e), while the rest of the creation is subject to change. Thus, while the author of Hebrews employs the psalm in a contrast to declare that the exalted Christ is *ho autos*, Middle Platonists employed this designation alongside other terms for the immutability of the deity.

The author anticipated the church fathers in reading Ps 102:26–28 with the lenses of Middle Platonism. In commenting on this psalm, Eusebius argues that Plutarch's claim that "you are" is the appropriate way to address God is actually a commentary on the words of Exod 3:14 ("I am the one who is") Ps 102:28 ("you are the same").

Christ and the Priesthood of Aaron: 4:14—10:31

The exaltation also provides the framework for the central section of Hebrews (4:14—10:31), which begins with the affirmation that the exalted Son is also the "high priest who passed through the heavens" (4:14) and concludes with the claim that he entered behind the curtain into the heavenly

---

18. Thompson, *Beginnings*, 138.

sanctuary (10:19–23). While the author proceeds from his portrayal of Jesus as Son to his work as high priest, he maintains the focus on Christ as the exalted one. According to 4:14—5:10, Jesus first sympathized with human weakness (4:15) and suffering (5:7–8) before he was appointed high priest according to the order of Melchizedek at the exaltation. After a paraenetic interlude (5:11—6:12), the author reaffirms that the exaltation was also the appointment to the priesthood of Melchizedek (6:19–20). As the reference to the exaltation indicates, this priesthood is transcendent. The exalted high priest serves in a heavenly tabernacle where he offered the ultimate sacrifice. The distinction between the two spheres of reality is evident in the author's *synkrisis* in describing the sanctuary.

made by the Lord	made by man (8:2)
Archetype	copy and shadow (8:5)
greater and more perfect tent (9:11)	worldly (*kosmikos*, 9:1)
not made by hands (9:11, 24)	[implied: made by hands] (9:11, 24)

Similarly, the author distinguishes between the animal sacrifices offered on earth and the sacrifice of Christ, who offered himself in heaven (9:1–14). The former cleanse only the flesh but the latter cleanse the conscience (9:9–10). The entire presentation is built on the *synkrisis*, declaring the superiority of the heavenly over the earthly. The author does not merely contrast the old with the new but demonstrates the superiority of the transcendent reality to the earthly system. Thus the author's argument in 7:1—10:18 rests on the ontological dualism by which he contrasts the work of the high priest in the heavenly sanctuary with the high priests of the earthly sanctuary.[19]

As the author indicates in 6:19–20, the heavenly high priesthood of Melchizedek (ch. 7) is the anchor for the wavering readers. Citing Gen 14:18–20 and Ps 110:4, the two OT passages that mention this mysterious figure, the author elaborates on the nature of this priesthood to demonstrate that he is "like the Son of God" (7:3). After the brief description of the etymology of Melchizedek's name and the brief summary of the encounter between Abraham and Melchizedek (7:1–2), the author describes the major attributes of Melchizedek in four parallel lines (7:3). When the author describes Melchizedek as "without father (*apatōr*), without mother (*amētōr*), without genealogy (*agenealogētos*)" and "without beginning of days or end of life" in the first two lines, he is not merely employing the common rabbinic

---

19. Thompson, "*Ephapax*," 569.

argument from the silence of Scripture but developing an important theme, as the fourth line indicates (7:3d). Here the author cites Ps 110:4, which declares that this priesthood is "forever" (*eis ton aiōna*). The previous use of this phrase (cf. 1:8; 6:20) indicates its significance for the author, who adds to it "he abides" (*menei*). The three lines that precede 7:3d may be understood as an interpretation of the claim that "he abides forever."

Ancient readers would have recognized that one who is "without father" and "without mother" is a divine being. Philo refers to the "motherless and virgin Nike" (*Opif.* 100). He maintains that the number 7 is the image of the supreme God and is "motherless," "unbegotten," and "abiding." In *De vita Mosis*, Philo describes the creation of the Sabbath, claiming it was in the first place motherless, exempt from female parentage, begotten by the Father alone, without beginning, brought to the birth, yet not carried in the womb. Secondly, he saw not only these, that she was all lovely and motherless, but that she was also ever virgin, neither born of a mother nor a mother herself, neither bred from corruption nor doomed to suffer corruption (2.12).

The reference to Melchizedek as "without father, without mother, without genealogy" also employs the negative theology (later known as *via negativa*) of Middle Platonists, who maintained that one can most appropriately describe God using negation,[20] denying of God a series of qualities in such a way as to show the deity's superiority to them.[21] Plutarch speaks of deities who are unbegotten (*agennētos*, Is. Os.359cd; *Table-Talk* 718; *Dinner of the Seven Wise Men* 153), uncreated, (*agenētos*, *E. Delph.* 392), and incorruptible (*aphthartos*, Is. Os.359c, 373d). Negative theology became especially important to patristic writers.[22]

The statement that Melchizedek is "without beginning of days or end of life" also echoes the philosophical description of the deity, indicating that the divine (*apatōr, amētōr*) is eternal. The phrase has its clearest analogies in philosophical descriptions of the deity. Plutarch says true Being "has no beginning nor is it destined to come to an end" (*E. Delph.* 393a; cf. 392e; *Isis and Osiris* 359c). The author elaborates on the phrase with the citation of Ps 110:4, "He abides a priest forever." As in 1:5–13, understands the exaltation to mean that Christ, in the heavenly world, abides (cf. *diamenei*, 1:11). *Menei*, used in 7:3 for the order of Melchizedek, is used regularly in Hebrews for heavenly realities (cf. 10:34; 12:27; 13:14). This description is analogous to Philo's depiction of God as the one who abides (*Somn.* 2.221). Thus, just

---

20. Dillon, *Middle Platonists*, 284; Neyrey, 441.
21. Dillon, *Middle Platonists*, 107.
22. Neyrey, "'Without Beginning of Days or End of Life,'" 441.

as *menein* is used in Platonism for the immutability of the deity, it is used in Hebrews for the immutability of Christ.[23]

The eternity of the high priest becomes the dominant theme in Hebrews 7, which is an elaboration on the abiding priesthood (7:3) in the form of a *synkrisis*. In 7:4-10 the author indicates the superiority of the priesthood of Melchizedek to the Levitical order, contrasting "the one who lives" with "dying men" (7:8). The author develops this contrast further, focusing on the psalm's use of the term "order" (*taxis*) and comparing the "order of Aaron" (7:11) with the "order of Melchizedek" (7:11). Not only does the announcement of the latter indicate a change from one to the other, but the latter is ontologically superior. This comparison of two orders of priesthood reiterates the earlier comparison between the exalted Son and the angels (1:4-13), indicating in both instances that the transcendent one abides ([*dia*]*menei*) while angels and earthly priests belong to the realm that is subject to change, destruction, and death. The former is "fleshly" (*sarkinē*), while the latter possesses an "indestructible life" (7:16) because of the exaltation. The treatment of Melchizedek reaches the culmination in the comparison between those priests who were not able to abide (*paramenein*) in contrast to the one who abides forever (*menei eis ton aiōna*, 7:23-24).

The comparison between the eternal order (*taxis*) of the priesthood of Melchizedek with the impermanent order of Aaron is reminiscent of the distinction between the celestial and the earthly orders (*taxeis*) in Philo and among Middle Platonist writers. Philo speaks of the "category (*taxis*) of the incorporeal and intelligible" (*Opif.* 34) and of the transcendent order (*Praem.* 42). The priesthood according to the order of Melchizedek is not only superior because it is later in time; it is qualitatively and metaphysically superior. The Levitical priesthood belongs to the sphere of the flesh and of death (cf. 7:8), while the priesthood of Melchizedek belongs to the heavenly and unchangeable sphere. Just as the exalted Son is greater than the angels and creation (1:6-12) because he alone is immutable and abiding, the exalted high priest is greater than mortal high priests.

This *synkrisis* corresponds to a fundamental principle of Middle Platonism: the distinction between the eternity of the transcendent realm and the change and impermanent character of the creation (cf. *Is. Os.* 369d). Indeed, Plutarch contrasts true Being, which is eternal, without beginning or end" (cf. Heb 7:3) with matter, a "receptacle . . . of birth and decay" (*E. Delph.* 392f).

A significant feature of the dualistic framework of Hebrews is the distinction between the finality of the work of Christ in the heavenly sanctuary

---

23. Thompson, *Beginnings*, 121.

and the incompleteness of the sacrificial ministry on the earth. Consistent with the contrast between the "many and various ways" in which God spoke to the fathers and the ultimate revelation in the Son (1:1–2), a primary focus of 7:1—10:18 is repeated use of *hapax* (or *ephapax*) for the work of Christ. The term, which can have the simple meaning "once," is used in Hebrews for a single event that is "once for all" in contrast to multiple occurrences.[24] The importance of this focus on the "once for all" quality of the Christ event is evident in the fact that the term is used more in Hebrews than in all other NT books combined. This distinction is implicit in the use of the reference to the descendants of Levi and the one man in 7:5 and 7:20–21. It becomes explicit in the use of the "many" and the one high priest in 7:23–24. Here the many belong to the sphere of death (cf. 7:8, 23), signifying the imperfection of the Levitical order.[25] In contrast to the many high priests of the earthly sphere, who are prevented by death from remaining, the work of the exalted high priest is *ephapax*. The author's distinction is rooted in the metaphysical distinction between two levels of reality The distinction between the one and the many is the context for the claim that the sacrifice of Christ was *ephapax* (7:27) in contrast to sacrifices offered "each day." The author elaborates on the significance of *ephapax* in the parallel statement in 7:27, summarizing the argument of chapter 7 with the contrast between "those who are subject to weakness" and the one who was "made perfect forever" (*eis ton aiōna teteleiōmenon*). With the singular event of the exaltation, the priest according to the order of Melchizedek entered into eternity and abides forever.

This contrast between the one and the many extends into the description of the cultus in 9:1—10:18 as the author continues to contrast the two levels of reality. In the earthly sanctuary (9:1) that is "made with hands" (9:11, 24), priests offer sacrifices continually (*dia pantos*, 9:6) in the outer court (9:7). Christ entered into the sanctuary "not made with hands" (9:12) to offer a sacrifice that was *ephapax* (9:12). The author clarifies his point in 9:25, indicating that an earthly sacrifice must be offered again and again (*pollakis*), whereas the sacrifice of Christ is *hapax* (9:26). With the repetition of "each year" (10:1, 3) and "each day" (10:11) to describe sacrifices offered many times (*pollakis*, 10:11), he concludes the central section of the homily with the contrast to the one who offered a single sacrifice "for all time" (*eis to diēnekes*, cf. 7:3). Alluding to Ps 110:1, he claims the finality of the work of Christ by contrasting those who stood offering sacrifices with the one who sat down at the right hand of God (10:12). This contrast is the basis for the conclusion of this central section and the claim that "by a single sacrifice he

---

24. BDAG 97.
25. Weiss, *Der Brief an die Hebräer*, 415; Grässer, *An die Hebräer*, 2.258.

has perfected for all time (*mia gar prosphora teteleiōen eis to diēnekes*) those who are sanctified" (10:14). At the conclusion, therefore, the author explicitly contrasts the one and the many. Only the priestly activity that belongs to the heavenly world is forever.

The author's consistent use of this distinction between the one and the many, which is unique in the NT, raises the question of the intellectual framework in which the argument works. The author's vertical dualism invites a comparison with his Platonic contemporaries, for whom the distinction between the one and the many was fundamental. Philo, for example, insists that God created the world in six days (*Opif.* 13). However, "God once for all (*hapax*) made a final use of six days for the completion of the world and had no further need of time-periods" (*Decal.* 99). Thus Philo's distinction between the "once" and the successive time periods is consistent with the delineation between time and eternity. The high priest, who enters the sanctuary once each year, symbolizes the entry into the unseen. No one may enter but one who is free from all defects, not wasting himself with any passion great or small but endowed with a nature sound and complete and perfect in every respect. To him it is permitted to enter once a year and behold the sights that are forbidden to others, because in him alone of all resides the winged and heavenly yearning for those forms of good that are incorporeal and imperishable. (*Ebr.* 136). Similarly, according to *De gigantibus*, the high priest Reason (*ho archiereus logos*) is permitted to resort to the sacred doctrines only "once a year" (*Gig.* 52), signifying the stability that accompanies the contemplation of the "Indivisible Unity." On the other hand, the many never find stability because only those people who have disrobed themselves of all created things may come near to God. Thus Philo interprets the cultic activity of the high priest within a cosmological dualism that distinguishes between the two levels of reality.

Plutarch also distinguishes the one and the many, associating the former with the intelligible world and the latter with the material world. This distinction is evident in his treatment of Isis and Osiris. The heavenly Osiris represents the one, while Isis represents the many, as symbolized in their robes, for the robes of Isis are variegated in color, while the robes of Osiris have only one color (*Is. Os.* 382c). The variety in the colors of Isis's robe indicates her association with matter and the many, while the singular color in the robe of Osiris represents the purity of the one. Therefore, when they have once (*hapax*) taken off the robe of Osiris, they guard it and ensure that it remains untouched, while they use the robe of Isis many times over. Plutarch explains in *Is. Os.* 382d, for in use those things that are perceptible and ready at hand afford many disclosures of themselves and opportunities to view them as they are changed about in various ways. But the appreciation of the conceptual, the pure, and the simple, shining through the soul like a flash of lightning, affords an opportunity to touch and see but once (*hapax*).

Plutarch's distinction between the one and the many reflects his dualism between Being and becoming. He expresses Osiris's association with the intelligible world of timelessness with the contrast between the event that is *hapax* and those which are repeated numerous times. The former points to the intelligible world, while the latter describes events in the material world. One may compare Plutarch's claim in *E Delph.*, noted above, according to which, "He, being One, has with only one 'now' completely filled 'for ever'" (*E Delph.* 393a–b). Plutarch's use of *hapax* indicates a moment when linear time becomes concentrated in one unsurpassed moment when the cycle of events is transcended by timelessness.[26]

The distinction between the one and the many in the works of Philo and Plutarch provide the background for the comparison in Hebrews between the many priests and sacrifices and the ultimate sacrifice of the exalted Christ. While the references to a historical event distinguish Hebrews from the Middle Platonists, he nevertheless works within the two levels of reality to affirm that the work of Christ is *ephapax* and beyond multiplicity in a way that is analogous to the ontology of the Middle Platonists. The assurance of the transcendence and eternity of the Christian possession serves the author's paraenetic purpose of providing stability for insecure believers.

Seeing the Invisible One: Hebrews 11

The appropriate response to the work of Christ in the transcendent sanctuary is "the full assurance of faith" (*plērophoria pisteōs*, 10:22) rather than the lack of faith (*apistia*) exhibited by Israel (3:12, 19; 4:2). Both the description of ancient Israel's lack of faith and the extended section in 10:32—12:11 indicates that faith is inseparable from endurance in Hebrews. The author says to the readers, "You endured sufferings" (10:32, *hypemeinate pathēmatōn*) in the early days, and "You need endurance" (*hypomonē*) before giving the positive examples of faith in chapter 11. All of the exemplars of faith endured deprivations similar to those of the readers. Thus faith, like the Hebrew equivalent *amn*, involves standing firm under all circumstances.

---

26. Wilfried, *Ein unerschütterliches Reich*.

Endurance is only one dimension of faith, however, as the working definition indicates in 11:1. In contrast to Paul, the author does not speak of faith in Christ, for Jesus is himself the pioneer of faith (*tēs pisteōs archēgos*, 12:2). The parallel phrases "assurance (*hypostasis*) of things hoped for" and "conviction (*elegchos*) of things not seen" point to the second dimension of faith. *Hypostasis*, which means literally "to stand under,"[27] is used metaphorically in philosophical literature and in Hebrews (cf. 1:3; 3:14) for reality, equating reality with a firm place to stand. Thus faith involves taking one's stand, not on the visible realities, but "on things hoped for." Similarly, *elegchos* means "proof" or "conviction," and in Heb 11:1 means "a proving (or conviction about) unseen things."[28] "Things hoped for" and "things not seen" is the author's equivalent of the earlier "not made by hands, not of this creation" (9:11) and the subsequent "what can (not) be touched" (12:18) and "what cannot be shaken" (12:27–28). Faith, therefore, is finding a place to stand in the invisible, transcendent reality. The author encourages readers who do not see the world in subjection to the Son (2:8b) to recognize that reality is not to be found in the visible world.

The author offers numerous equivalents for "things unseen" in his portrayal of the heroes of faith. The heroes sought an inheritance (11:8), a "city having foundations whose maker and builder is God" (11:10, 16), a homeland (11:14), a promise (11:9, 13), and a reward (11:26), but, like the readers, never saw the transcendent reality. However, they had special powers of perception to recognize the reality of the unseen world, as the references to knowing and seeing indicate. In the first place, they know of the reality of the unseen. "We know that the worlds were created by the word of God, so that what is seen was made from things that are not visible" (11:3). The readers themselves were able to endure the confiscation of their property because they knew that they had an abiding possession (10:34). In the second place, the heroes had the capacity to see the unseen. They saw the heavenly homeland from a distance (11:13). Moses "looked to the reward" (11:26) and left Egypt, not fearing the edict of the king, for "he endured as seeing the invisible one" (11:27).

The images of knowing and seeing invisible realities are commonplace in the literature of Middle Platonism. In describing God's role in creating the intelligible world as a pattern for the world of the senses, Philo describes the former as "a world discernible only by their mind" and the latter "the world which our senses can perceive" (*Opif.* 19). Although the heavenly city is invisible for Philo, it is perceptible to the one who has the special capacity

---

27. Grässer, *Der Glaube im Hebräerbrief*, 48.
28. BDAG 315.

to see the invisible (*Post. Cain* 15; *Immut.* 3; *Plant.* 17; *Praem.* 27). He speaks of the apprehensions of reality gained by the "soul's eye" (*Mig. Ab.* 39; cf. *Heir* 89). Similarly, Alcinous describes the deity as ineffable and graspable only by the intellect (*Epit.* 10.4).

According to Heb 11, the knowledge that reality is not in the phenomenal world makes one a stranger to this world.[29] The author transforms the story of Abraham as a literal "stranger and alien" (Gen 23:4), declaring that the patriarch and his family were "strangers and aliens on the earth" (11:13). The author emphasizes Abraham's alien existence, indicating that he "went out," not knowing where he was going (11:8), sojourned as an alien (*allotrios*), and lived in tents (11:9). Similarly, Moses, in looking beyond temporary pleasure and the treasures of Egypt to the invisible one (11:25-27), chose to suffer with his people. At the conclusion of the list of heroes the author describes faithful people who "wandered in deserts and mountains, and in caves and holes in the ground," declaring that the world was not "worthy" of them (11:38). Their actual home, as the author insists, is not on earth but a "city that has foundations, whose maker and builder is God" (11:10; cf. 11:16) and a heavenly homeland (11:14, 16). Thus they were strangers in an ontological and not in a sociological sense.[30] Having an invisible homeland in heaven made them strangers on earth. This portrayal of faith is consistent with the author's earlier view that believers are on a journey toward the heavenly rest (3:7—4:11), and that the exalted Christ has opened the way (2:20; 6:20; 10:19-23).

A familiar theme in Middle Platonism is the alien existence of those whose homeland is in the invisible world. According to Philo, the wise are appropriately called sojourners (*paroikountes*). The heavenly region, the place of their citizenship, is their native land; the earthly region is a foreign country in which they live as sojourners (*Conf. Ling.* 75-78; cf. *Q. Gen.* 4.74; *Somn.* 1.181). Those who migrate from their homes place their faith in God (*Her.* 99). According to *de Congress.* 84-87, our task is to recognize our duty to hate the habits and customs of the lands in which we live, which are symbolized as Egypt and Canaan.[31] Jacob's temporary residence with Laban is symbolic of the soul's expectations of a city (*Somn.* 1. 46 1).

The idea that one is a stranger on earth has deep roots in the philosophic tradition.[32] (Plutarch's essay *De Exilo* describes the situation of literal exiles before concluding with reflections about exile as a metaphor

---

29. Ernst Käsemann, *Wandering People of God*, 22-24.
30. Backhaus, "Das Land der Verheißung," 175.
31. Thompson, *Beginnings of Christian Philosophy*, 60.
32. Feldmeier, *Die Christen als Fremde*, 27-38.

for human existence. He cites the ancient words of Empedocles, "All of us . . . are sojourners here and strangers and exiles" (*Exil.* 607d). Because the soul has come from elsewhere, one may say that "the soul is an exile and a wanderer" (607e).

The portrayal of the object of faith as "seeing the invisible one" (11:27; cf. 11:1) is an appropriate pastoral response to readers who "do not see everything in subjection to the Son" (2:8b). In the list of heroes the author reminds the readers of others who did not see God's handiwork on earth but endured marginalization because of their capacity to see the transcendent homeland. Although the author does not incorporate a complete Platonic ontology, he employs those aspects of Middle Platonism that advance his purpose, maintaining that the reality on which believers should rely is the unseen world.

Eschatology and Ontology: Hebrews 12:14–29

This reality is not only unseen, as the recapitulation of the homily in 12:14–19 indicates. The author presents Esau as the negative alternative to the heroes in chapter 11 (12:16–17). Unlike Moses, who chose the unseen reality over the temporary pleasures of sin (11:26), Esau chose the temporary—a single meal—over the eternal. The author encourages the readers not to be like Esau, adapting the familiar contrast between Mount Sinai and Mount Zion from Jewish literature. The parallel "you have not come to what may be touched, . . . you have come to Mount Zion, the city of the living God, the heavenly Jerusalem" (12:18, 22) once more contrasts material and transcendent realities. The description of Mount Sinai as "what may be touched" may reflect the use of Exod 19:12–13, which promises death to anyone who touches the mountain. The author of Hebrews, however, characterizes the entire Sinai theophany as tangible, suggesting that believers have approached the untouchable transcendent realm, the city which the ancient faithful people saw only in the distance. This comparison corresponds to the Platonic distinction between the sense-perceptible and intelligible realities. For Plato, that which is touchable belongs to the sphere of sense perception (*Phaedo* 99e; *Tim.* 28b, 31b). Indeed, God is described in other Hellenistic literature as "untouchable" (*apsēlaphētos*).[33] Christians, in contrast to ancient Israel, have approached the transcendent city.

This dualistic distinction between two realms leads the author to contrast the word (12:19) on earth (12:25) that the Israelites heard from Sinai with the voice that believers now hear from heaven (12:24–25). Citing Hag

---

33. See Thompson, *Beginnings of Christian Philosophy*, 45, for texts.

2:6, the author recalls the promise of an eschatological earthquake, a familiar theme in apocalyptic literature, in which God will "shake not only the earth but also the heaven" (12:26). In the interpretation in 12:27, the author departs from the usual apocalyptic expectation, contrasting the heavens and the earth that will be shaken with those things that cannot be shaken and indicating that the latter will abide. He further characterizes those things that will be shaken as "made." Thus he distinguishes between two levels of reality. The "heavens and the earth" that will be shaken belong to the material world. One may compare Philo's use of the term *saleuein*, which was used primarily for things in the earthly sphere (*de Post. Cain* 22–23; *Somn.* 2.221, 37). For the author, that which is shakable belongs to the world of sense perception. "He knows two worlds already possessing full reality, one of which is material, and therefore shakable; the other is not material, and is unshakable. When the material world appears, only the world that is presently unseen (11:1) and untouchable (12:18) remains."[34] The author has thus maintained an apocalyptic tradition but has interpreted it in Platonic terms, focusing on the stability of the heavenly world. Anticipating the Christian Middle Platonists who followed him, he brought together apocalyptic thought and Platonic ontology.

Conclusion

What does Middle Platonism have to do with Hebrews? Just as we now recognize that Judaism and Hellenism did not exist in separate worlds, we have abundant evidence that Jewish eschatology and Platonic ontology could exist alongside one another and intersect in a variety of ways. The author of Hebrews demonstrates neither a profound knowledge of Platonism nor a belief in all of the major tenets of its point of view. However, like the Christian theologians who came after him, he employed Platonic assumptions for his own pastoral purposes. Responding to the readers' loss of confidence in the eschatological hope, the author provides stability for their existence by reassuring them of the eternal and transcendent Christ (1:10–12; 7:3, 23–24), who alone is the anchor for their insecure existence (6:19–20). With his focus on what is eternal rather than transitory, he appeals to the major theme of Middle Platonism. While he maintains the traditional Jewish eschatological hope, he shifts the emphasis to the stable, invisible, and untouchable reality that provides certainty for wavering people. With Philo, he maintains that wavering humans can find security in proximity to one who is immutable.

34. Thompson, *Beginnings of Christian Philosophy*, 50.

CHAPTER 6

EPHAPAX: THE ONE AND THE MANY IN HEBREWS

The alliterative πολυμερῶς καὶ πολυτρόπως, with which the Epistle to the Hebrews begins, illustrates the author's skillful use of language and employment of the conventions of elevated speech that are present in other Hellenistic texts. The use of alliteration with the initial π was characteristic of rhetorical refinement[1] and was common at the beginning of a speech.[2] However, one may ask whether more than rhetorical flourish is present in the phrase. Inasmuch as Heb 1:1–4 is the "overture" introducing a sequence of arguments based on *synkrisis*, the contrast between the "many and various ways" that God has spoken in the past (πάλαι) with God's speaking in a son "in these last days" suggests a qualitative distinction between the provisional and the final. In contrast to the multiple modes of speech by the prophets, God's speech in a son is once-for-all. Indeed, the comparison to God's speech in a son in the last days suggests a comparison between the many and the one.[3]

1. Originally published in *New Testament Studies* 53 (2007) 566–81.
Plutarch, *de Def. Or.* 23, πολύχυτον καὶ πολύτρεπτον; Maximus of Tyre (*Diss.* 1.2a) describes harmonies that are "complex and versatile" (πολυφόνως τε καὶ πολυτρόπως) and music "of many different sounds in many different forms" (12b, πολυμεροῦς ταύτης καὶ πολυτρόπου). Cf. 7.2 d, τὸ σῶμα πολυμερὲς καὶ πολύφωνον. On Philo's use of alliteration with π, see *De Ebr.* 170; *Vit Mos.* 1.117; *Somn.* 1.134; 1.221; *Flacc.* 46. Schröger, *Der Verfasser des Hebräerbriefes als Schriftausleger*, 301. See also Josephus, *Ant.* 10.42, for the description of God: ὅτι ποικίλη τέ ἐστι καὶ πολύτροπος. On Plutarch, cf. Almqvist, *Plutarch und das Neue Testament*, 128.

2. Cf. Luke 1:1, πολλοί . . . περὶ τῶν ἐν ἡμῖν πραγμάτων; Sir. 1:1, πολλῶν καὶ μεγάλων ἡμῖν διὰ τοῦ νόμου καὶ τῶν προφητῶν. For references to speeches beginning with πολλοί, see Bauer, "Πολλοί Luk 1,1" 263–66.

3. For a discussion of the issue of continuity and discontinuity reflected in 1.1–2, see Smillie, "Contrast or Continuity in Hebrews 1.1–2," 543–60. Smillie argues that the absence of the language of comparison, which is pervasive in the rest of the homily, indicates that the author intends no contrast between God's speaking in the past and

The author's focus on this qualitative distinction between the one and the many is also suggested by his repeated use of ἅπαξ (or ἐφάπαξ) in the later argument. The term, which can have the simple meaning "once," is used in Hebrews for a single occurrence that is "once for all"[4] in contrast to multiple occurrences.[5] The importance of this focus on the "once for all" quality of the Christ event is evident in the fact that the term is used more in Hebrews than in all other NT books combined. A fundamental aspect of his argumentation is the claim that Christ offered himself ἐφάπαξ (7:27) and entered into the sanctuary ἐφάπαξ (9:12; 10:10; ἅπαξ, 9:26). In contrast to the unique work of Christ are the many (πλείονες) Levitical priests (7:27) who offer sacrifices "many times" (πολλάκις, 10:11; cf. 9:25-26). Moreover, Christians have once (ἅπαξ) been enlightened in an event that is unrepeatable. Thus the author's argument reflects his own inner logic and a set of assumptions that will be persuasive if they are shared by the audience. This contrast between the one and the many is a distinctive feature of Hebrews.

Both the pervasiveness of this theme in Hebrews and its relative absence elsewhere in the NT raise significant questions that have not been addressed in previous literature. Although the commentators have noted the importance of (ἐφ)ἅπαξ in this homily, no one has given a comprehensive analysis of the role of this theme within the total argument or indicated why the author expects the contrast between the one and the many to be persuasive to the audience.[6] Since arguments are effective when they appeal to the premises shared by the speaker and the recipients and possess a level of coherence,[7] we will illuminate this argument in Hebrews when we observe its logical structure and premises and recognize the place of these assumptions in ancient discourse. Consequently, my task is twofold. In the first place, I

God's speaking in the last days, but affirms continuity between the two revelations. His larger concern is to demonstrate that Hebrews is not anti-Semitic. This distinction is, however, misplaced, as the author's employment of *synkrisis* indicates. In many instances, the function of *synkrisis* is to show the greatness of the object of praise by comparing the person with other people of great stature. Aristotle (*Rhet.* 1.9. 38) offers advice on how to praise one's subject: "And you must compare him with illustrious personages, for it affords ground for amplification and is noble, if he can be proved better than men of worth."

4. BDAG, 97.

5. Spicq, *Theological Lexicon of the New Testament*, 139.

6. See Perelman and Olbrechts-Tyteca, *The New Rhetoric* 26-27, for the distinction between argumentation and persuasion. Since what is persuasive to one audience may be ridiculous to another, persuasion appeals to shared premises. See also Thurén, "On Studying Ethical Argumentation and Persuasion," 464-78.

7. See Alexandre, *Rhetorical Argumentation*; Perelman and Olbrechts-Tyteca, *The New Rhetoric*, 23: "In argumentation, the important thing is not knowing what the speaker regards as true or important, but knowing the views of those he is addressing."

shall analyze the place of this theme within the larger context of Hebrews to determine how the argument works in its basic structure. In the second place, I shall compare the author's argument with analogous motifs in the literature of the period in order to ascertain the kind of audience that would have shared the author's basic assumptions about the one and the many. Since Philo and the author of Hebrews converge at numerous other points that may reflect assumptions drawn from Middle Platonism,[8] Philo is an appropriate basis for comparison of the two authors on the subject of the one and the many. Plutarch offers another important comparative source, since he offers a window into Hellenistic thought at the precise moment when Christianity encountered Greek philosophy in the late first and early second century. Furthermore, inasmuch as both Philo and Plutarch address the issue in their attempts to interpret inherited narratives from their respective religious traditions in an extended corpus, a comparison of these two authors with Hebrews offers considerable potential for illuminating our understanding of the intellectual world of the author of Hebrews.

I. The Context in Hebrews

The author's claim for the ἐφάπαξ work of Christ appears exclusively within the central section of the book (7:1—10:18), which is intended to provide the basis for the readers to "hold fast to the confession" (4:14; 10:28). This section is introduced with the claim for the exaltation, which the author announces with the perfect participle (διεληλυθότα [τοὺς οὐρανούς], 4:14), aorist participle (τελειωθείς, 5:10), and aorist verb (εἰσῆλθεν [the heavenly sanctuary], 6:20; 9:12; cf. 6:19; 9:24; 10:19), indicating the decisive nature of the event. Thus the remainder of 7:1—10:18 assumes the exaltation as a basis for the author's comparison of two levels of reality. In chapter 7, the exalted high priest is qualitatively superior to the mortal priests who belong to the sphere of the flesh (7:16), and in 8:1-6, the high priest who serves in the heavenly sanctuary is superior to those who only serve in the earthly copy. In chapter 9, the author contrasts the perfect sacrifice in the heavenly sanctuary with the ineffectual sacrifices of the earthly copy (9:1–14). The author does not merely contrast the old with the new but demonstrates the superiority of the transcendent reality to the earthly system. Thus the author's argument in 7:1—10:18 rests on the ontological dualism by which he contrasts the

---

8. The relationship the author of Hebrews and the Middle Platonism of Philo has been a matter of debate. For the claim that Hebrews was influenced by Middle Platonism, see Thompson, *The Beginnings of Christian Philosophy*, 152; Eisele, *Ein unerschütterliches Reich*; Busch, "Der mitleidende Hohopriester," 19–30.

work of the high priest in the heavenly sanctuary with the high priests of the earthly sanctuary.[9] With this claim for the transcendent reality in 7:1—10:18, he attempts to rebuild the community's symbolic world.

Psalm 110:1, 4 provides the frame for the argument of the central section (cf: 7:3; 10:12-14).[10] The passage is significant not only because of its reference to Melchizedek but also because of the presence of εἰς τὸν αἰῶνα, to which the author adds μένει in 7:3 and substitutes εἰς τὸ διηνεκές, the phrase he employs also in 10:12, 14. The significance of εἰς τὸν αἰῶνα in Ps 110:4 first becomes evident in Heb 7 when the author interprets τάξις in the psalm as a reference to two types of priesthood, which are contrasted in ontological terms as heavenly and earthly. This usage of τάξις corresponds to Philo's distinction between levels of reality that he describes as τάξεις.[11] Since the τάξις of Melchizedek is exalted, it abides forever. The author's description of this priesthood in 7:3 as "without father" (ἀπάτωρ) and "without mother" (ἀμήτωρ) corresponds to Hellenistic descriptions of deity,[12] and the phrase "having neither beginning of days nor end of life" (μήτε ἀρχὴν ἡμερῶν μήτε ζωῆς τέλος ἔχων) was used in philosophical literature for the deity.[13] The last phrase in 7:3, a paraphrase of Ps 110:4, becomes the leitmotif of the entire central section of Hebrews, as the inclusio with Heb 10:14 suggests. The claim that this priesthood μένει εἰς τὸν διηνεκές becomes the basis for the contrast between the one and the many.

The comparison of the eternal high priest with the mortal priesthood of Aaron is based on the words εἰς τὸν αἰῶνα in Ps 110:4. The Aaronic priests are "dying men" in contrast to the one who lives (7:8). The earthly high priest belongs to the sphere of the flesh, while the exalted high priest has an "indestructible life" (7:16). The Aaronic high priest is prevented by death from abiding, while the exalted high priest abides forever (7:23-24). Thus

---

9. See Sterling, "Ontology versus Eschatology," 190-211.

10. See Kurianal, *Jesus Our High Priest* for the claim that Ps 110:4 provides the structure for the first half of the central section in 5:1—7:23.

11. Philo, *Opif.* 34, "In the category of the incorporeal and intelligible" (ἐν τῇ τάξει τῶν ἀσωμάτων καὶ νοητῶν). Cf. *De Somn.* I.229-31.

12. Cf. Plato, *Symposium* 180d; on the usage by Philo, see below, p. [***]. Plutarch depicts the gods as "unborn" (ἀγέννητοι, *Is. Os.* 359c). Justin (*Dial.* 5.1) and Athenagoras (*Leg.* 4) use ἀγέννητος for God. For further discussion, see Neyrey, "'Without Beginning of Days or End of Life' (Hebrews 7.3)"; Thompson, *Beginnings of Christian Philosophy*, 119.

13. Aristotle (*de Caelo* 1.9.283 b 26) maintains that the world is eternal, adding: αρχὴν μὲν καὶ τελευτὴν οὐκ ἔχων τοῦ παντὸς αἰῶνος. See also Cicero, *Nat. D.* I.24.38; I.17.20. Plutarch, *Is. Os.* 359C; *E Delph.* 392. Plutarch is discussed in greater detail on page [***]. See also Thompson, *Beginnings of Christian Philosophy*, 120; Neyrey, "Without Beginning," 444.

the author employs Ps 110:4 to compare priests who belong to two spheres of reality, maintaining that the heavenly priest abides forever.

A corollary of this comparison is the distinction between the one and the many. This distinction is implicit in the use of the plural οἱ μέν . . . ὁ δέ in 7:5 and 7:20–21. It becomes explicit in the use of οἱ . . . πλείονες . . . ὁ δέ in 7:23–24. Here the many belong to the sphere of death (cf. 7:8, 23), signifying the imperfection of the Levitical order.[14] In 7:23 he repeats the contrast between the many (πλείονες) who die with the one (ὁ δέ) who lives. Only the latter is able to save his people εἰς τὸ παντελές (7:25). The distinction between the one and the many is the context for the claim that the sacrifice of Christ was ἐφάπαξ (7:27) in contrast to sacrifices offered "each day." The author elaborates on the significance of ἐφάπαξ in the parallel statement in 7:27, summarizing the argument of chapter 7 with the contrast between "those who are subject to weakness" and the one who was "made perfect forever" (εἰς τὸν αἰῶνα τετελειωμένον). The latter is equivalent to ἐφάπαξ. With the singular event of the exaltation, the priest according to the order of Melchizedek entered into eternity and abides forever. E. Grässer correctly noted, "Multiplicity and repetition are thus characteristic of mortality and earthly imperfection (9:1–10; 10:1–2, 11), while oneness and uniqueness are characteristic of the transcendent-eternal" (7:27; 9:12, 26; 10:10, 12).[15] In contrast to the many high priests of the earthly sphere who are prevented by death from remaining, the work of the exalted high priest is ἐφάπαξ. The author's distinction is rooted in the metaphysical distinction between two levels of reality.[16]

This contrast between the one and the many extends into the description of the cultus in 9:1—10:18 as the author continues to contrast the two levels of reality. In the earthly sanctuary (9:1) that is "made with hands" (9:11, 24), priests offer sacrifices continually (διὰ παντός, 9:6) in the outer court (9:7). Christ entered into the sanctuary "not made with hands" (9:12) to offer a sacrifice that was ἐφάπαξ (9:12). The author clarifies his point in 9:25, indicating that an earthly sacrifice must be offered πολλάκις—"each year"—whereas the sacrifice of Christ is ἅπαξ (9:26). The author amplifies this argument in 10:1–18. With the repetition of "each year" (10:1, 3) and "each day" (10:11) to describe sacrifices offered many times (πολλάκις, 10:11), he concludes the central section of the homily with the contrast to

---

14. Weiss, *Der Brief an die Hebräer* 415. See also Grässer, *An die Hebräer*, 2.258.

15. Grässer, *An die Hebräer*, 2.58 ("Vielheit und Wiederholung sind also Kennzeichen der Todverfallenheit und irdischen Unvollkommenheit (9:1–10; 10:1–2, 11), while Einzigkeit und Einmaligkeit den Charakter des Jenseitig-Ewigen haben").

16. Laub, *Bekenntnis und Auslegung*, 229; Thompson, *Beginnings of Christian Philosophy*, 126.

the one who offered a single sacrifice (μίαν θυσίαν) "for all time" (εἰς τὸ διηνεκές). Alluding to Ps 110:1, he claims the finality of the work of Christ by contrasting those who stood offering sacrifices with the one who sat down at the right hand of God (10:12). This contrast is the basis for the conclusion of this central section and the claim that "by a single sacrifice he has perfected for all time (μιᾷ γὰρ προσφορᾷ τετελείωκεν εἰς τὸ διηνεκές) those who are sanctified" (10:14). At the conclusion, therefore, the author explicitly contrasts the one and the many. Only the priestly activity that belongs to the heavenly world is forever.

The once-for-all sacrifice of Christ in the heavenly sanctuary has consequences for believers, as the exhortations that frame this unit (6:4–11; 10:26–31) indicate. The claim that those who have "once (ἅπαξ) been enlightened" cannot be restored to repentance (6:4) is consistent with the logic of the author's argument in the central theological section in 7:1—10:18. Inasmuch as the Christ event is ἐφάπαξ, the salvation event is unrepeatable (ἅπαξ) for believers, for whom "there is no more sacrifice for sins" (10:26). The author warns the community that the rejection of the ultimate sacrificial event will result in ultimate consequences.

This distinction between the one and the many is to be seen within the logic and thought world of Hebrews. The many priests and sacrifices belong to the created order. The final ἐφάπαξ moment is the singular saving event of the sacrifice and exaltation of Christ, who becomes the priest εἰς τὸν αἰῶνα. The author's consistent use of this distinction between the one and the many, which is unique in the NT, raises the question of the intellectual framework in which the argument works. The author's vertical dualism invites a comparison with his Platonic contemporaries.

II. The One and the Many in Middle Platonism

The relationship between the one and the many is a theme that is developed in Middle Platonism within the framework of the metaphysics inherited and adapted from Plato. In their attempt to explain the origins or causes of all existence, Middle Platonists adapted the Platonic idea of the two first principles (God and matter) into three principles: God (νοῦς) as the ultimate cause, the ideas as the paradigmatic cause, and matter as the material cause.[17] All of reality may be divided into the two realms of the intelligible and the perceptible world. The former is characterized by Being, while the latter is characterized by becoming. True Being in the intelligible world exists

---

17. Baltes, "Middle Platonism," 858–63. See also Runia, "Was Philo a Middle Platonist?" 112–40.

in timeless eternity (αἰών), while the perceptible world is subject to constant becoming (γένεσις). Consistent with this dualism, Middle Platonists distinguish between the One, which transcends the universe, and the Indefinite Dyad, the principle of duality, which is infinitely divisible. The One belongs to the intelligible world, while the latter can be seen throughout nature.[18] Middle Platonists identify the transcendent God with the One.

II.1 Philo of Alexandria

As a Jew who was a Jew loyal to the Scripture and heavily dependent on the first principles of Middle Platonism, Philo integrates the Bible's depiction of God's relationship to the world into the Platonic tradition. Thus Philo indicates that everything in creation must change, while immutability is the property of God (*Leg.* II.33). Philo's focus on the immutability of God is evident in the passages in which he interprets the references to God's standing as an indication of God's immutability. In *Somn.* II.219–23, Philo interprets Pharaoh's statement "In my dream I was standing on the banks of the Nile" (Gen 41:17), commenting that only God and the friends of God are unswerving and stable (*Leg.* II.219). He interprets God's speech to Moses, "Here I stand there before thou wast, on the rock in Horeb" (Exod 17:6), indicating that the true meaning is that God stands "ever the same immutable" (ἑστὼς ἐν ὁμοίῳ καὶ μένων ἄτρεπτος). Similarly, the statement that "they saw the place where the God of Israel stood" (Exod 24:10) suggests that God's standing is an indication of his immutability (*De Somn.* II.222).[19]

In his interpretation of the creation narrative, Philo employs the categories of Middle Platonism.[20] He says that Moses

> understood that it was most essential that among the things that exist there be an active cause and a passive object, and that the former is the mind of the universe, supremely pure and undefiled, superior to excellence and superior to knowledge, and even superior to the good itself and the fair itself, whereas the passive object was without its own source of life and movement. (*Opif.* 8)

God is the supreme mind (νοῦς) who first created the intelligible world (νοητὸς κόσμος, *Opif.* 16) as a pattern for the visible world (ὁρατὸν κόσμον). The world of ideas belongs to the intelligible world that is eternal and unchanging, while the world of the senses is described as becoming

---

18. Dillon, *The Middle Platonists*, 3.
19. Maas, *Unveränderlichkeit*, 104.
20. Runia, "Was Philo a Middle Platonist?" 137.

(γένεσις) because it is subject to change and never remaining in the same state (*Opif.* 12).

Philo identifies the personal God of Judaism with the Platonic supreme principle, often describing God as the "One" (*Opif.* 171), the Monad (*Leg.* II.3; *Her.* 183; *Cher.* 87),[21] and the truly Existent (ὁ ὢν ὄντως, *Opif.* 172; *Decal.* 8; *Spec.* I.28). As Philo's frequent references to God as the "One" suggest, the contrast between the one and the many has a significant role in his metaphysic. Philo comments on the statement that "it is not good that the man should be alone" (Gen 2:18), concluding that only God, "being One, is alone and unique" (*Leg.* II.1). He adds, "God is alone, a Unity, in the sense that His nature is simple not composite, whereas each one of us and of all other created beings is made up of many things" (*Leg.* II.2). Philo concludes that the "One" and the "Monad" are the only standard for determining the category to which God belongs, indicating that God is prior to the universe, and that "number is subsequent to the universe" (*Leg.* II.3). Elsewhere, however, Philo describes God as "greater than the good, more venerable than the monad, purer than the unit" (*Praem.* 40). To deny that God is unoriginate and incorruptible (ἀγένητον καὶ ἄτρεπτον) is to wrong oneself, for one must believe that "He is One and incorruptible and unchangeable" (ἕνα καὶ ἄφθαρτον καὶ ἄτρεπτον, *Leg.* I.51).

As the transcendent One, God stands above the principle of multiplicity that is associated with the realm of becoming. Whereas the monad is the image of the first cause, the dyad of matter is "passive and divisible" (*Spec.* III.180). Therefore, one who worships the dyad rather than the monad "holds matter in higher esteem than God." Whereas God is one and unmixed (cf. *Abr.* 122), humans belong to the world of becoming that is characterized by multiplicity. Indeed, Philo frequently employs words for multiplicity to describe the inferiority of things that belong to the material world.[22]

Philo recalls that Hannah is the mother of one child, citing the words of 1 Sam 2:5, "The barren hath borne seven, but she that had many children languished." Philo concludes that the One is equivalent to 7, the ideal number. Samuel, as an only child, is born "in accordance with the One and the Monad, the truly existent" (τὴν μονάδα, τὸ ὄντως ὄν, *Deus* 12; cf. *Her.* 187). Here the One is God, while the many represent the burdens of a life not turned toward God.

In *Opif.* 100, Philo again equates the number 7 with the One:

---

21. Dillon, "The Nature of God in the 'Quod Deus,'" 217–27.

22. Philo uses ποικίλος and πολυτρόπως for the imperfection of the material world. See *Ebr.* 36; *Plant.* 44; *Somn.* II.14. See Dey, *The Intermediary World and Patterns of Perfection in Philo and Hebrews*, 129–30.

> It is in the nature of 7 alone, as I have said, neither to beget nor to be begotten. For this reason other philosophers liken this number to the motherless (ἀμήτορι) and virgin Nikè (i.e., Athena), who is said to have appeared out of the head of Zeus, while the Pythagoreans liken it to the ruler of all things: for that which neither begets nor is begotten remains motionless; for creation takes place in movement, since there is movement both in that which begets and that which is begotten. There is only one thing that neither causes motion nor experiences it, the original Ruler and Sovereign. Of him 7 may be fitly said to be a symbol (εἰκών). Evidence of what I say is supplied by Philolaus in these words: "There is, he says, a supreme ruler of all things, God, ever One, abiding, without motion, like unto himself, different from all others."

The number 7 is the εἰκών of the supreme God and is "motherless," "unbegotten," and "abiding." Similarly, in *De vita Mosis*, Philo describes the creation of the Sabbath, claiming it was

> in the first place motherless, exempt from female parentage, begotten by the Father alone, without beginning, brought to the birth, yet not carried in the womb. Secondly, he saw not only these, that she was all lovely and motherless, but that she was also ever virgin, neither born of a mother nor a mother herself, neither bred from corruption nor doomed to suffer corruption. (2.12)

One may compare in *Leg.* I.15, where Philo concludes that 7 is the first number after the perfect number 6, and identical with the number 1. According to *Spec.* I.170, the seventh day is equal to eternity.[23]

For Philo, the one belongs to the intelligible world of Being, while the many are associated with the physical world of becoming. Philo expresses interest in the words of Ps 61:1, "The Lord spake once (ἅπαξ), I have heard these two things." He adds, "For 'once' is like the unmixed, for the unmixed is a monad and the monad is unmixed, whereas twice is like the mixed, for the mixed is not single, since it admits both combination and separation" (*Deus* 82).

Philo insists, against many of his contemporaries, that God created the world in six days (*Opif.* 13). However, "God once for all (ἅπαξ) made a final use of six days for the completion of the world and had no further need of time-periods" (*Decal.* 99). Thus Philo's distinction between the "once" and the successive time periods is consistent with the delineation

---

23. For Philo's indebtedness to arithmological literature, see Runia, *Philo of Alexandria*, 274–75.

between time and eternity. God is "One and incorruptible and unchangeable" (*Leg.* 1.51). Since God is the "ageless God," Philo insists that people be taught to understand nothing with God is ancient or past, but that everything is timeless (*Sacr.* 76). God has no future, and God's life is not in time, but in eternity. In eternity "there is no past nor future, but only present existence" (*Deus* 32; cf. Plato, *Tim.* 37D).

Philo's distinction between time and eternity is evident in his allegorical treatment of the temporal references in the Torah. For example, when he recalls the promise of Isaac's birth to Sarah "next year" (Gen 17:21; *Mut.* 267), he adds that "in the other year" (Gen 17:21) does not refer to "an interval of time which is measured by the revolutions of sun and moon, but by something truly mysterious, strange and new" that is beyond the realm of sense perception, but has its place in "the incorporeal and intelligible, and to it belongs the model and archetype of time, eternity or aeon" (cf. Plato, *Tim.* 37d).

Like the author of Hebrews, Philo finds great significance in the high priest's sacrifice on the Day of Atonement, giving special attention to the Torah's command that the high priest not enter the most holy place "at any time" (Lev 16:2), but only "once in the year" (Lev 16:34). According to *Legat.* 306, the high priest enters the shrine "once a year, not twice" because God wanted to protect the shrine. The tabernacle and all of its contents, according to *Ebr.* 136, are unseen, and no one is permitted to touch them. The only exception is made for the one who is

> free from all defects, not wasting himself with any passion great or small but endowed with a nature sound and complete and perfect in every respect. To him it is permitted to enter once a year and behold the sights which are forbidden to others, because in him alone of all resides the winged and heavenly yearning for those forms of good which are incorporeal and imperishable.

Similarly, according to *De gigantibus*, the high priest Reason (ὁ ἀρχιερεὺς λόγος) is permitted to resort to the sacred doctrines only "once a year" (*Gig.* 52), signifying the stability that accompanies the contemplation of the "Indivisible Unity." On the other hand, the many never find stability because only those people who have disrobed themselves of all created things may come near to God. Thus Philo interprets the cultic activity of the high priest within a cosmological dualism that distinguishes between the two levels of reality. The high priest's entry into the sanctuary occurs only "once a year" in the transcendent sanctuary.

Just as the stability that accompanies access to God is the highest joy of the soul, abandonment by God is the worst fate that the individual can experience, as the story of Cain indicates. Cain's cry, "My punishment is greater than I can bear" (Gen 4:13), signifies the consequence of being cast out by God. "But the soul that has once (ἅπαξ) been dismissed from hearth and home as irreconcilable, has been expelled for all eternity, and can never return to her ancient abode" (*Det.* 149). Philo's conclusion is consistent with his claim for the irrevocability of God's words.

Philo's dependence on Plato's *Timaeus* reflects his place in the Platonic distinction between time and eternity. Philo argues consistently that the One belongs to the intelligible world and is eternal, in contrast to the many. Eternity is "without mother" and one, while time belongs to the world of becoming, birth, and death. Philo's use of ἅπαξ reflects his distinction between the one and the many and his distinction between the immutability of God and the instability of the creation.

II.2 Plutarch

As one who was both a Platonic philosopher and priest at Delphi, Plutarch also discussed the one and the many within the framework of Platonic dualism. Plutarch's view of God the supreme being corresponds to Platonic views, as his essay *The E at Delphi* (*E Delph.*) indicates. Here Ammonius, apparently representing Plutarch's view,[24] claims that the E inscribed at the temple of Delphi is to be interpreted as, "You are" (εἶ), the only address that is appropriate for true being. He offers a Platonic explanation when he asks "What is Being?" (ὄντως ὄν), and then answers, "It is that which is eternal, without beginning and without end, to which no length of time brings change" (*E Delph.* 392). To address God with the word εἶ is to acknowledge that only true being remains the same (ὁ αὐτός, *E Delph.* 392e). He is unchanging and uncontaminated by matter (*E Delph.* 392f).

The distinction between Being and becoming is fundamental to Plutarch's ontology. While only the eternal God is true Being and can be addressed with the words, "You are," humankind inhabits the world of becoming and is subject to change, decay, and mortality. "Everything of a mortal nature is at some stage between coming into existence and passing away" (*E Delph.* 392b). Thus Plutarch says that the antithesis to "you are" (εἶ) is "know thyself" (γνῶθι σαυτόν). Plutarch explains that the address "you are" is an utterance addressed in awe to the God who exists through all eternity, while "know thyself" is a reminder to mortals of their own weaknesses (*E Delph.* 394c).

---

24. Dillon, *Middle Platonists*, 199.

The distinction between being and becoming corresponds to Plutarch's description of time and eternity. Plutarch maintains that time is something that is set in motion, and that it is associated with matter. It is a receptacle of birth and decay, for whom the familiar "afterwards" and "before," "shall be" and "has been" are a confession of Not Being (*E. Delph.* 392F). Since these temporal words can be ascribed only to nonbeing, Plutarch insists that it is inappropriate to say that the deity "was" or "will be" because these words are associated with "that which by its nature has no permanence in Being" (*E Delph.*393).

> But God is (if there be need to say so), and He exists for no fixed time, but for the everlasting ages which are immovable, timeless, and undeviating, in which there is no earlier nor later, no future nor past, no older nor younger; but He, being One has with only one "Now" completely filled "Forever" (ἐνὶ τῷ ἐνὶ τῷ νῦν τὸ ἀεὶ πεπλήρωκε); and only when Being is after His pattern is it in reality Being, not having been nor about to be, nor has it had a beginning nor is it destined to come to an end. Under these conditions, therefore, we ought, as we pay Him reference, to greet Him and to address Him with the words, "Thou art"; or even, I vow, as did some of the men of old, "That art One" (*E Delph.* 393a–b).

Plutarch's ἐνὶ τῷ νῦν corresponds to the (ἐφ)άπαξ in Hebrews. Both concepts describe a type of timelessness insofar as they concentrate linear time in a qualitative transcendent point in time and thus bring to an end the succession of time periods in the unity of one moment.[25] Only the highest Being can possess this time point of eternity.

Plutarch's distinction between being and becoming/eternity and time corresponds to his distinction between the one and the many. God is stable and unitary, and the human, subject to becoming, is in a state of constant change and therefore lacks unity.[26] Thus the contrast between Being and becoming is also the contrast between the one and the many. God is one, and humankind is many.[27] Plutarch indicates on several occasions that God is one and abiding in contrast to everything in the material world. In *E Delph.* (393b) Plutarch says, "In fact the Deity is not Many," unlike those who are a heterogeneous collection of hundreds of factors combined in a haphazard way. "But Being must have Unity, even as Unity must have Being." He

---

25. Eisele, *Ein unerschütterliches Reich*, 420.
26. Whittaker, "Plutarch, Platonism, and Christianity," 56.
27. Whittaker, "Plutarch, Platonism, and Christianity," 56.

maintains that Apollo's name is well suited for the deity, for his name means "denying the Many and abjuring multiplicity."

Plutarch's dualistic distinction between Being and becoming becomes the hermeneutical principle for his reading of the myth of Isis and Osiris.[28] As a good Platonist, Plutarch indicates that creation (γένεσις) is the image of Being in matter (οὐσίας ἐν ὕλῃ); what is created (τὸ γιγνόμενον) is a picture of reality (μίμημα τοῦ ὄντος, 372a). This world is neither eternal nor imperishable but is the world of becoming: "being ever reborn, contrives to remain always young and never subject to destruction in the changes and cycles of events." When Plutarch transfers this ontology to the myth, he describes Isis and Osiris as beings who were translated from demigods (ἐκ δαιμόνιων) into gods (361e, 362e). The soul of Osiris is the intelligible world and "the ruler of all that is good" (*Is. Os.* 371). Like the deity in *E Delph.* 392f, he is "unpolluted and pure from all matter that is subject to destruction and death" (382f) and the leader and king of the unseen world (383a) as well as the ruler and king of the intelligible world (*Is. Os.* 383f). The soul of Osiris is not explicitly said to be the Ideas but more specifically "that which really is and is intelligible and good," the apparent equivalent of God in the speech of Ammonius in *E Delph*. His divine consort, Isis, is the material principle in nature, who gives birth to Horus, "the image of the perceptible world" (εἰκόνα τοῦ νοητοῦ κόσμου αἰσθητὸν ὄντα, 373b).[29] Isis and Osiris, along with Horus, are engaged in a cosmic conflict with Seth-Typhon, who represents everything that is destructive in the visible world (*E Delph.* 369a). The yearning of Isis for the good is the story of the human soul's search for "the knowledge of Him who is the First, the Lord of All, the Ideal One" (ἡ τοῦ πρώτου καὶ κυρίου καὶ νοητοῦ γνῶσις (*Is. Os.* 352a).

The relationship between the one and the many is most evident in Plutarch's interpretation of the robes of Isis and Osiris. Osiris represents the one and Isis represents the many, as the contrast in their robes indicates, for the robes of Isis are variegated in color, while the robes of Osiris have only one color (*Is. Os.* 382c). The variety of colors in the robe of Isis signifies that "her power is concerned with matter which becomes everything and receives everything, light and darkness, day and night, fire and water, life and death, beginning and end" (*Is. Os.* 382c). The single robe of Osiris, on the other hand, indicates that whatever is primary and conceptual is without admixture. Therefore, when they have once (ἅπαξ) taken off the robe of

---

28. Bianchi, "Plutarch und der Dualismus"; Brenk, "An Imperial Heritage: The Religious Spirit of Plutarch."

29. Griffiths, *Plutarch's De Iside et Osiride*, 562.

Osiris, they guard it and ensure that it remains untouched, while they use the robe of Isis many times over. Plutarch explains in *Is. Os.* 382d:

> for in use those things that are perceptible and ready at hand afford many disclosures of themselves and opportunities to view them as they are changed about in various ways. But the appreciation of the conceptual, the pure, and the simple, shining through the soul like a flash of lightning, affords an opportunity to touch and see but once (ἅπαξ).

Plutarch concludes from this account that Plato and Aristotle call this part of philosophy the *epoptic*, for it describes the highest knowledge. In Platonic terms, it is the knowledge of the bodiless and divine ideas, that is, of the highest idea, which is identical with God and the good, the ἐποπτή.[30] It is the acquisition of knowledge that is so complete that it is once for all (ἅπαξ).

Plutarch's distinction between the one and the many reflects his dualism between Being and becoming. He expresses Osiris's association with the intelligible world of timelessness with the contrast between the event that is ἅπαξ and those which are repeated numerous times. The former points to the intelligible world, while the latter describes events in the material world. One may compare Plutarch's claim in *E Delph.*, noted above, according to which, "He, being One, has with only one 'now' completely filled for ever" (*E Delph.* 393a-b: εἷς ὢν ἑνὶ τῷ νῦν τὸ ἀεὶ πεπλήρωκε)". Plutarch's use of ἅπαξ indicates a moment when linear time becomes concentrated in one unsurpassed moment when the cycle of events is transcended by timelessness.[31]

Plutarch consistently connects God's immutability with God's oneness, distinguishing these characteristics from the constant change and multiplicity in creation. This relationship between God's immutability and oneness is evident when Plutarch indicates that "the monad does not pass out of its own boundaries but remains once and for all one (ἀλλ' ἅπαξ τὸ ἕν μένει)" and concludes that the monad (μονάς) derives its name from μένειν: "for which reason it is called a monad" (*De Garrul.* 507a). Plutarch's immutable and abiding deity exists in timelessness, far removed from the instability of the created world.

---

30. Hopfner, *Plutarch über Isis und Osiris*, 279.
31. Eisele, *Ein unerschütterliches Reich*, 420.

III. Hebrews and Middle Platonism

The distinction between the one and the many in Middle Platonism illuminates the argument of Hebrews, indicating the author's indebtedness to philosophical reflection about the nature of the deity and reality. The author's portrayal of the order of Melchizedek as "abiding," "without mother" and "without father" is rooted in the philosophical tradition, as the comparison with Philo and Plutarch demonstrates. His argument in 7:1—10:18 is coherent in its insistence that multiplicity and repetition are characteristic of the phenomenal world ("this creation," 9:12; cf. 7:16) while eternity belongs to the heavenly world. Because the heavenly high priest is eternal, his work is ἐφάπαξ. In placing this distinction of the one and the many within the metaphysical dualism of the two spheres of reality, the author reflects assumptions that are also present in Philo's claim that the deity is above the principle of multiplicity (cf. *Spec.* III.180; *Abr.* 122; *Leg.* II.2; *Deus* 82). Just as Philo argues that the God who "once" (ἅπαξ) created the world no longer needed time periods (*Decal.* 99), the author concludes that the sacrifice ἐφάπαξ needs no repetition, for the exalted high priest has entered eternity. Although the author does not develop this theme as thoroughly as Philo does, a dependence on a common thought world between the two writers best accounts for the consistent appeal to this theme in Hebrews.

Plutarch also illuminates the author's description of the cultic work of Christ, which is perfected forever. The contrast between the finality of the epoptic vision in the cult of Isis corresponds to the finality of the work of Christ. Just as the many-colored robe of Isis signifies her association with "life and death, beginning and end" in the perceptible world (*Is. Os.* 382C), the repeated sacrifices of Hebrews indicate the incompleteness of the ministry in the earthly sanctuary. Just as the robe of the heavenly Osiris is disclosed once (ἅπαξ), the sacrifice of Christ is ἐφάπαξ (10:10).

The author's claim that it is impossible (ἀδύνατον) to renew to repentance "those who have once (ἅπαξ) been enlightened" is not only consistent with his argument about the once-for-all sacrifice of Christ but also corresponds to Philo's claim (*Det.* 149) that "the soul that has once (ἅπαξ) been dismissed from hearth and home... can never return to her ancient abode" (εἰς τὸν ἀρχαῖον οἶκον ἐπανελθεῖν ἀδυνατοῦσα). Both writers assume that the forfeiture of the transcendent salvation results in the impossibility of restoration to a relationship with God.

One need not conclude that the author is a thoroughgoing Middle Platonist to recognize that his use of this consistent argument reflects an awareness of the Platonic tradition. Indeed, the author's claim that God has spoken "in these last days" (1:1) in a singular event within the created world indicates his distance from the Platonic tradition. He is loyal to a Christian tradition, according to which Christ came into the world (cf. 10:5) for a "little while" (2:9), offered himself as a sacrifice (2:17–18), and was exalted (1:3; 6:19–20). The voice that once spoke in Jesus Christ (1:1) will speak once more (12:26–27) in a final act, removing the heavens and the earth.[32] With a plot that extends from creation to the coming of Christ and the formation of the community of faith as the culmination of Israel's story, this narrative stands in tension with the ontological dualism that pervades the author's argument. This tension is not unique to the author, for the same tension existed among the church fathers, who held both to the claim for God's acts within history inherited from the tradition and to the language of Platonic ontology. Indeed, one of the greatest challenges of the church fathers was to affirm both the credo and the Platonic idea of the immutability of God.[33] Justin and Clement of Alexandria, for example, affirmed a Christian eschatology while expressing themselves in the language of Platonism.[34] As children of an era shaped by Platonism, the church fathers found in Platonism the language to interpret their Christian belief.[35]

Although the author is not as consistent in his appeal to Platonic assumptions as Philo and Plutarch, his argument is internally coherent in its insistence that the work of the exalted Christ is ἐφάπαξ in contrast to the multiple priests and sacrifices of the physical world. This argument for the finality of the work of Christ, therefore, reflects his reliance on the ontological assumptions that he shared with Middle Platonists. Thus, although he departs from Middle Platonism in his conviction that "God has spoken" (1:1) in a specific event, he anticipates the work of others who employ Platonic categories to explain their faith.

32. On the basic plot of Hebrews, see Schenck, *Understanding the Book of Hebrews*, 10–11.

33. Meijering, "Wie Platonisierten Christen?" 15–28, 18.

34. On Justin's Middle Platonism, see Andresen, "Justin und der mittlere Platonismus," 159–95. See also Edwards, "On the Platonic Schooling of Justin Martyr," 17–34. Justin employs Platonic language to speak of the transcendence of God, appealing to *Tim.* 28c (*2 Apol.* 10.6), which had a significant impact on Justin's view of God (for the Platonic language for the attributes of God, see also *1 Apol.* 26.5; *Dial.* 7.3; 16.4; 34.8; 48.2). At the same time, Justin holds firmly to traditional Christian eschatology, speaking frequently of the second advent (*Dial.* 31.1–3; 110.2–4; 111.1; 118.1, 121.3) and insisting that the "great and terrible day" (*Dial.* 49.2) is coming soon (*Dial.* 32.4). Christ will "appear in Jerusalem" (*Dial.* 85.7) and destroy all his enemies (*Dial.* 121.3), including the "man of sin" (*Dial.* 32.4). Although Clement of Alexandria tried to harmonize apocalyptic with Greek cosmology, he maintained a hope for the end, speaking of "the resurrection for which we hope; when, at the end of the world, the angels . . . receive into the celestial abodes those who repent" (*Quis div.* 42), and describes the events that follow the second coming of Christ, when all of the righteous will be taken up into heaven (*Ecl.* 56–67). For the eschatology of Justin and Clement of Alexandria, see Daley, *The Hope of the Early Church*, 20–22, 44–47.

35. Meijering, "Wie Platonisierten Christen?" 27.

CHAPTER 7

"STRANGERS ON THE EARTH"

PHILOSOPHICAL PERSPECTIVE ON THE PROMISE IN HEBREWS

The acknowledgment that "now we do not yet see all things subjected to him" (2:8c) is a critical turn in the argument of Hebrews, for it calls into question all that the author has said until this point. The opening words of the homily proclaimed that God had broken the silence, speaking to the listeners ("to us," 1:2) through the incarnation, death, and exaltation of the Son (1:1–4). Anticipating the argument of the entire homily, the author gives special emphasis to the exaltation as the occasion of the Son's inheritance of a new name and appointment as God's Son (1:4–5). God has also spoken to the Son through the Scriptures (1:5–13), confirming the Son's eternal, cosmic rule (1:7–13). Linking two psalms that share a common phrase in a christological reading (Ps 110:1; 8:5–7), the author proclaims both that God will "place all enemies under his feet" (1:13; cf. Ps 110:1) and that God has "placed all things under his feet" (2:8a; Ps 8:7). Indeed, he reinforces the latter claim, affirming that "he left nothing that is not in subjection to him" (2:8b).

The tension between the two psalms corresponds to the crisis experienced by the readers, whose voice may be heard in the objection, "Now we do not yet see all things in subjection" (2:8c).[1] Although they have heard of the eschatological victory "in these last days" (1:2; cf. 6:4), they do not consciously share in it, for they live between the "now" (νῦν, 2:8c; cf. 8:6) and the "not yet" (οὔπω, 2:8c).[2] The author has mentioned their place in this cosmic victory—even angels serve them (1:14)—but what they have heard conflicts with what they see. At the moment the heavenly world is

---

1. Originally published in *Restoration Quarterly* 57 (2015) 193–212. Hans-Friedrich Weiss, *Der Brief an die Hebräer*, 198.

2. Schenck, *Cosmology and Eschatology in Hebrews*, 59–60.

remote from them, and the promises remain unfulfilled. The enthronement of the Son does not correspond to the realities on earth.[3] What they see is fear of death (2:14–17), marginalization (10:32–34; 13:3), and suffering (12:4–11). The continuing inability to see the salvation weakens the faith of the addressees, giving the impression that they are helpless before all powers.[4] Because the end of their suffering is not in sight, they are in danger of drifting away (2:1; cf. 3:12; 6:4) rather than remaining steadfast until the end (cf. 3:12; 6:4, 9–11).

Although their dilemma grows out of disappointment with the claims of triumph in their confession, it is not unlike the common problem faced by others in antiquity who struggled with the remoteness of the transcendent world from their own lives. One of the major challenges of Middle Platonism, for example, was to overcome the distance separating the transcendent God from the physical world and humanity.[5] God is the eternal and unchanging Being, but humans belong to an ever-changing reality that provides no stability for their lives.[6] Both the author of Hebrews and the Middle Platonists addressed the problem of providing certainty within the context of disorienting realities.

My task in this chapter is to demonstrate that the author meets that challenge, using the resources of rhetoric and philosophy to reinterpret the tradition handed on from the first generation of those who followed Christ (cf. 2:1–4) while offering a new reading of the Scriptures. He shares with the early Christian tradition the conviction that the church lives between the last days (1:2; cf. 6:4) inaugurated in the Christ event and the final day (Heb 10:25; cf. 9:27; 12:27–28). The central category for responding to the problem of the "not yet" is the promise, which the author reshapes with the categories of Hellenistic philosophy. While his belief in the incarnation and the end of the created world indicates that he is not a consistent Platonist, he nevertheless employs the language of Middle Platonism to accomplish his task.

---

3. Grässer, *An die Hebräer*, 1.20. See also März, ". . . Nur für kurze Zeit under die Engel gestellt (Hebr 2,7)," 49.

4. März, ". . . Nur fur kurze Zeit under die Engel gestellt (Hebr 2,7)," 49.

5. Backhaus, "Per Christum in Deum" 263. Backhaus, "Das Land der Verheißung," 173.

6. Ferrari, "Der Gott Plutarchs und der Gott Platons," 15.

The Rhetoric of Hebrews: The Message of the Promise

The author follows the common practice of rhetoricians who first named the *stasis* of the case before proceeding with the argument.[7] According to Quintilian, the *basis* (Greek *stasis*) is the kind of question that arises from the first conflict between parties (*Inst.* 3.6.5). He adds that "every question is based on assertion by one party and denial by another" (*Inst.* 3.6.7). The *stasis* of this "word of exhortation" (13:22) is the conflict between the christological claims (1:1–14; 2:5–8) and the listeners' response in 2:8c.

Quintilian maintains that the task of the speaker is to maintain a focus on the *stasis* throughout the argument, never introducing irrelevant issues into the case at hand (*Inst.* 3.6.3). The author's consistent reference to the promise and its synonyms suggests the coherence of his argument. Forms of ἐπαγ- appear throughout the homily—more frequently than in any other book of the NT.[8] Synonyms for ἐπαγ-, which are also prominent in the homily, include ἐλπίς (3:6; 6:11, 18; 7:19; 10:23; cf. ἐλπιζομένων in 11:1), God's oath (cf. forms of ὀμνύειν in 3:11, 18; 6:13; 7:20–21), the inheritance (κληρονομία, 9:15; 11:8) of salvation (1:14; 6:12), and the reward (μισθαποδοσία, 10:35; cf. 11:6), as well as other images (cf. 4:3, 8–9; 10:34; 11:8–16). Consistent with the author's acknowledgment that "we do not yet see all things in subjection to him," he never indicates that the promises have been fulfilled. In contrast to Acts and the Pauline letters, Hebrews presents the promise as a goal that lies in the future and a reality that is still unseen.[9] Although ἐπαγγελία is never used in the LXX in a theological sense,[10] it is the comprehensive term in Hebrews for the eschatological hope.[11]

To place the eschatology of Hebrews within the narrative of Jewish expectation leaves unanswered questions about the author's interpretation of the promise, for ancient writers envisioned God's promise to Israel in a

---

7. Koester, *Hebrews*, 221.

8. Cf. ἐπαγγελία in 4:1; 6:12, 15, 17; 7:6; 8:6; 9:15; 10:36; 11:9, 13, 17, 33, 39; ἐπαγγέλλεσθαι in 6:13; 10:23; 12:26. Elsewhere in the NT it appears prominently in Acts (eight times), Romans (seven times), and Galatians (nine times). It appears eighteen times in Hebrews as compared to twenty-two times in the Pauline corpus, and only seventeen times in the entire LXX. See Sand, ἐπαγγελία, *EDNT* 2.14.

9. The speakers of Acts claim that the story of Christ is the fulfillment of the promises to Israel (1:4; 2:33, 39; 7:17; 13:23, 32; 23:2; cf. Luke 24:49). According to Paul, the promise to Abraham of countless descendants has become a reality with the inclusion of the gentiles (Rom 4:17; Gal 3:16–17; cf. Rom 15:8–9). He affirms that "all of the promises have their 'yes' in Christ" (2 Cor 1:20).

10. Schniewind and Friedrich, ἐπαγγελία, *TDNT* 2.579.

11. Schenck, *Cosmology and Eschatology in Hebrews*, 60.

variety of ways. Thus, as the scholarship of the past generation has shown, one can no longer demarcate sharply between Jewish eschatology and Platonic ontology because these perspectives intersected in a variety of ways. N. Walter has described the variety of expressions of Jewish eschatology within the Second Temple period, distinguishing between apocalyptic and Hellenistic eschatology.[12] While these two perspectives did not exist in isolation, they are nevertheless distinguishable. Apocalyptic expectation commonly included the hope for a future event that would result in the restoration of Israel in the land or in a new creation.[13] Hellenistic Jewish texts speak of an individual hope rather than one of a future event and national restoration.[14] Early Christian Platonists maintained *both* Platonic ontology *and* Jewish eschatology.[15] Thus one does not need to choose between Jewish eschatology and Platonic ontology in the interpretation of Hebrews.

The Promise as the *Grundgedanke* of Hebrews

Interpreters have observed that numerous *inclusios* provide the structural signals indicating the coherence of the argument of Hebrews and the

---

12. Walter, "'Hellenistische Eschatologie' im Frühjudentum," 331-47.

13. In the Psalms of Solomon, for example, the writer laments that Israel was expelled from the inheritance (9:1) and prays that the "righteous will inherit the promise of the land" (12:6; 11:7, 9). In the Testament of Joseph, the patriarch prophesies that Egypt will oppress Israel, but that the Lord will lead the people to the land, "the promise made to your fathers" (20:1). Other texts speak of a catastrophic event that will result in a new heaven and new earth (cf. Syr. Bar. 57:2).

14. Hellenistic elements are evident in these passages. In the Testament of Job, the "holy land" is identical with the "world of the unchangeable," the home already prepared for Job. In Joseph and Aseneth (8:11), Joseph prays that Aseneth will enter into God's "rest" and live in God's "eternal life for ever (and) ever." Both 2 and 4 Maccabees anticipate eternal life with God for the martyrs, although neither refers to an earthly historical event. According to 4 Maccabees, the ancestors live in eternity with God (7:19; 13:17; 16:25; 17:18), and martyrdom is the "path to immortality" (14:5-6; cf. 16:13), although nothing specific is said about how they proceed to immortality. Ps.-Phocylides speaks of the immortality of the soul (115). According to the Wisdom of Solomon, one expects the immortality of the soul as the reward for the righteous (3:4; 4:14; 15:3). The souls of the righteous are in God's hand, and nothing touches them (3:1). The life of the pious is already anchored in the heavenly world, and they have hope for immortality (3:4) and can expect eternal life and God's reward (5:16-17; 8:17-18). Thus the thought of individual recompense and the certainty that the pious have eternal life is more important in this circle than how one conceives of the transition to heavenly existence. See Wolter, "'Hellenistische Eschatologie,'" 340.

15. See Thompson, "*Ephapax*: The One and the Many in Hebrews," 580-81. Both Justin and Clement of Alexandria combined Platonic ontology with the traditional view of the end of the world.

author's constant focus on the *stasis*. The readers' challenge to the author's claim, "We do not yet see all things in subjection to him" (2:8c) forms an *inclusio* with the working definition of faith as the ἐλπιζομένων ὑπόστασις, πραγμάτων ἔλεγχος βλεπομένων (11:1).[16] It is only one of numerous *inclusios* that provide the frame for the homily or units within it.[17] Thus, although the homily has numerous alternations in subject matter and literary genre, the structural signals point to a coherent argument with three major divisions. The first major unit, marked by an *inclusio* on the word of God (1:1–2; 4:12–13), introduces the problem confronting the community: the dissonance between what it has heard and what it sees as it travels through the wilderness. The author responds with the promise of entering God's rest (4:1–2). As the *inclusio* marking the central section indicates (4:14–16; 10:19–25), the cultic section provides the stable reality that the wavering community can now grasp (cf. κατεχεῖν in 4:14; 10:23; cf. κρατεῖν in 6:18): the guarantee of God's promise (cf. 6:13–20; 7:19; 9:15).[18] Building on the first two sections, the final division (10:32—13:25) is a renewed challenge for the community to hear the divine promise and an answer to the original dilemma posed by the gap between the community's confession and the reality it sees. F. J. Schierse captures the emphasis on the promise, designating the three sections as 1) the community and the word of the promise (1:1—4:13), 2) the community and the work of the promise (4:14—10:31), and 3) the community and the goal of the promise (10:32—13:25).[19]

---

16. Brawley, "Discoursive Structure and the Unseen in Hebrews 2:8 and 11:1," 86–89.

17. The opening words, "God has spoken . . ." (1:1) correspond to the divine voice that addresses the community near the end of the homily (12:25), promising to shake the heavens and the earth at the end (12:26–27). The contrast between the transient creation and the eternal Son (1:8–12) corresponds to the contrast between the material creation and the abiding and unshakable reality (12:27–28). Nauck, "Zum Aufbau des Hebräerbriefes," 199–206. Albert Vanhoye and others have observed the correspondence between the portrayal of the unfaithful ancestors (3:1—4:11) and the faithful ancestors in ch. 11. See Vanhoye, *La structure littéraire de l'Epître aux Hébreux*, 153–58.

18. Although the *inclusio* that frames the central section is widely recognized, the division between the conclusion of the central section and the beginning of the final section is debated. The presence of the theme of ὑπομονή/ὑπομένειν in 10:32–39 and 12:1–13 (cf. 10:32, 36; 12:1, 2, 7) as the frame for the list of heroes of faith suggests that the final section begins in 10:32. See also Rose, *Die Wolke der Zeugen*, 30–33.

19. Schierse, *Verheißung und Heilsvollendung*, 207–9. While I agree with Schierse's division of the argument into subunits, I offer alternative titles for the subdivisions: 1) the promise that remains, 2) the promise guaranteed, and 3) the promise as "things hoped for" and "things unseen."

The Promise That Remains (1:1—4:13)

The first major section of Hebrews functions as a *narratio*, introducing the themes that the author will develop in the subsequent sections. The *inclusio* of 1:1-2 and 4:12-13 focuses the attention of the readers on the word of God that now addresses the community. God not only has spoken in the Christ event (1:1-3; cf. forms of λέγειν in 1:5, 6, 7; 2:6) but now speaks directly to the community through Psalm 95 (3:7-15; 4:7). God's oath to ancient Israel, "They shall not enter my rest" (3:11; cf. Ps 95:11), is now a promise to the listeners, the inheritance of salvation (cf. 1:14) that remains unseen.

Both ancient Israel and the listeners received the same word of promise (cf. 4:1-2). Because of Israel's failure to enter the κατάπαυσις, believers stand before a "promise that is still open" (4:1). In contrast to earlier Christian tradition, the promise in Hebrews has not become a reality, for it remains open to the listeners. It is both the promise that is "left over" (καταλειπομένης ἐπαγγελίας) and the sabbath that remains (ἀπολείπει, 4:6, 9) for the people of God. Thus the author responds to the community's cognitive dissonance with the assurance that what it does not see remains open as a promise.

Κατάπαυσις is a polyvalent term in Jewish tradition. In the Pentateuch, the promise of the land is the inheritance (κληρονομία) and the place of rest (κατάπαυσις, cf. Deut 12:9-10; 25:19; Jos 21:43) from Israel's enemies. In Isaiah, the temple is the place of God's rest (Isa 66:2; cf. 1 Chr 23:25; 28:2). In Jewish apocalyptic literature, it is the destiny of the faithful.[20] As the argument from Scripture indicates in Heb 4:3-9, the promise is a participation in God's primordial rest (4:3-9), not the earthly promised land. This use of the *gezera shewa* connecting κατάπαυσις in Ps 94 LXX with καταπαύειν in Gen 2:2 evokes the language of Philo and Middle Platonists, who employed the terminology of rest to speak of the immutability of God and the transcendent world. Philo, like the author of Hebrews, identifies the Sabbath (Exod 20:10) with God's rest, indicating that rest (ἀνάπαυσις) belongs to God alone (*Cher.* 87-90; *Fug.* 173-74) and that the human goal is to participate in God's rest.[21]

The repeated use of εἰσέρχεσθαι in 3:7—4:11 offers insight into the author's understanding of the promise of rest. While Israel did not enter the transcendent rest (3:11, 18, 19), the author assures the readers, "we who believe enter (εἰσερχόμεθα) into the rest" (4:3), where they will rest as God rested (4:10). He concludes the section, "Let us take every effort

---

20. See Hofius, *Katapausis*, 74.
21. See Backhaus, "Das Land der Verheißung," 178.

to enter (εἰσελθεῖν) into that rest" (4:11). Elsewhere the author speaks of the hope "entering behind the curtain" at the exaltation of Christ (6:19) and of the occasion when the exalted high priest "entered" (εἰσῆλθεν) into the heavenly sanctuary (9:12, 24). To enter God's rest, therefore, is to enter the transcendent sanctuary, the place of God's rest. Like the author of Joseph and Aseneth, he envisions the promise as a place into which one enters (cf. Jos. Asen. 8:11). The nature of this promise becomes evident in the author's elaboration of the Christian confession in chapter 1. The exalted Son sits at the right hand of God above the angels and the material world (1:3–13). In the claim that Jesus "sat down at the right hand of God" (1:3, 13), the author introduces the text (Ps 110:1) that dominates the homily (cf. 8:1; 6:20; 7:3, 23–24; 81; 10:12). The Son who has sat down at God's right hand (1:1, 13) has entered the heavenly sanctuary (8:1). The transcendent Son and high priest abides forever (1:8–12; 7:3, 16, 23–24), having completed his work (cf. 10:12), while counterparts belonging to the creation exist in the sphere of change and death (cf. 1:7; 7:23). After his descent below the angels, the Son is now crowned with glory and honor (2:9). As the ἀρχηγός (2:10), he opens the way to the heavenly κατάπαυσις. The promise is neither the land of Canaan nor the countless descendants, as in traditional Jewish thought, but the participation in God's transcendent rest. This rest is the equivalent to the place of the exaltation of Christ, for believers continue to follow the ἀρχηγός toward the destination. What the readers do not see is the fulfillment of the promise of participation in God's transcendent rest. The author makes no reference to traditional apocalyptic events in this section but to entering into God's primordial rest, where the exalted Lord has gone. Thus the author holds before those who cannot see the cosmic victory the promise of the transcendent rest. Their task in this situation is to live on in the wilderness in faith. According to Heb 2–4, those who do not see the world in subjection to the Son live as people in the wilderness on the way to the κατάπαυσις.

The Promise Guaranteed (4:14—10:31)

The *inclusio* of 4:14—10:31 indicates that the central cultic section of the homily has a paraenetic purpose: to encourage the readers to "hold on" (κατέχειν) to the confession (4:15; 10:23; cf. 6:18), knowing that "he who promises is faithful" (10:23). The references to the promise provide the frame for the cultic section (6:13–20; 10:23), indicating the author's continued focus, which becomes especially evident in the paraenesis that introduces the cultic section in 7:1—10:18. After the stern warning in 5:11—6:8, the author expresses confidence in the readers' faithfulness (6:9) and again urges them to maintain the "full assurance of hope until the end" (6:12). Echoing earlier exhortations (cf. 3:6, 14), he supports the paraenesis with the reflections on the promise in 6:9-20, using ἐπαγ- four times, ὀμνύειν/ὅρκος five times, and ἐλπίς two times within this brief unit. Having offered Israel as the example of ἀπιστία (3:12, 19; cf. 4:2), the author urges the readers to follow the positive example of "those who through πίστις and μακροθυμία inherit the promises" (6:12) but does not specify what promises the ancestors inherited.[22] The use of the present participle (κληρονομούντων) and the plural ἐπαγγελίαι suggests that he is stating a general principle that was true in the past and remains true for the listeners (cf. 4:1-2).[23]

Anticipating chapter 11, the author turns to Abraham in 6:13 to illustrate the general principle. For the second time in the homily, he associates God's oath with the promise (cf. 3:11; 4:2), suggesting that the ancestors and the listeners stand before the same unfulfilled promise (6:13; cf. 3:11). Although he cites God's promise to Abraham after the sacrifice of Isaac (Gen 22:17), he makes no reference to the original context. Moving from the plural ἐπαγγελίαι (6:12) to the singular, he says that Abraham obtained the promise (ἐπέτυχεν τὴν ἐπαγγελίας), drawing a parallel to the situation of the readers and suggesting that they too will inherit the promise only after they endure (cf. 10:36, ὑπομονή). Abraham, like the listeners, has received the irrevocable divine promise and is a model of the endurance necessary for those who do not see the fulfillment of the promise.

After another general statement in 6:16, the author applies the principle to the listeners in 6:17-20, leaving the story of Abraham behind. According to the general principle, which the author shares with Philo, "people swear by something greater, and beyond all dispute an oath is for confirmation (βεβαίωσις)."[24] This general principle applies to human interactions, especially to the courts, where βεβαίωσις is a legal term for the guarantee of an oath.[25] As the author's frequent use of forms of βεβαι- indicates (cf. 2:2-3; 3:6, 14; 6:16, 19; 9:17; 13:9), βεβαίωσις is the critical

---

22. Rose, "Verheißung und Erfüllung," 66.

23. As a general principle, the claim in 6:12 appears to contradict the later description of the ancestors who "died in faith, not having received the promise" (11:13; cf. 11:39). Attempts to resolve the contradiction have largely ignored that the focus of the passage is less on the content of the promise than on the fact that God swore, and that Abraham was a model of the πίστις and μακροθυμία required of the readers.

24. See the extended discussion of God's swearing "by himself" (cf. Gen 22:16) in Philo, *Leg. All.* 3.203-7; *Post. Cain* 92-94; *Sac.* 94; *Abr.* 273; *Spec. Leg.* 2.253. Unless otherwise noted, translations of Philo are from LCL.

25. BDAG, 173.

need for those who waver because of unfulfilled promises. Consequently, the oath is of critical importance to the author, as the three citations of divine oaths suggest (cf. 3:11; 6:14; 7:20–22).

As the application of the general principle in 6:17–20 indicates, those who need βεβαίωσις are "fugitives" (καταφυγόντες) in need of an anchor (6:18). Like Abraham, "the heirs of the promise" (6:17) have received the divine oath (6:17–20) as a guarantee.[26] If the oath in the court of law provides confirmation (6:16), the divine oath is especially (περρισσότερον) certain, for it is the evidence of the "unchangeability of God's will." Thus "through two unchangeable things," the "fugitives" may have "strong encouragement" (ἰσχυρὰν παράκλησιν) to grasp the hope that is set before them. They discover βεβαίωσις in the anchor of the soul that is firm and secure (ἀσφαλῆ καὶ βεβαίαν). Mixing the metaphors, the author describes the anchor as "entering behind the curtain" separating heaven and earth, where the forerunner has entered, becoming high priest forever after the order of Melchizedek" (6:20).

The anchor, a metaphor used nowhere else in Scripture, was a common image of hope.[27] The readers receive βεβαίωσις, not in the fulfillment of God's promises but in the divine oath that guarantees the promise. In the entry of the forerunner into the heavenly world, the listeners have received the irrevocable promise that they will ultimately enter into God's rest. While they do not see "all things in subjection to him," they have an anchor to grasp. The one who became high priest after the order of Melchizedek (κατὰ τὴν τάξιν Μελχισέδεκ ἀρχιερεὺς γενόμενος) in the past (6:20) is eternal (εἰς τὸν αἰῶνα). This assurance indicates that 7:1–10:18 is an elaboration of the promise that the disoriented readers can grasp as a result of the Christ event. This claim introduces the cultic section of 7:1–10:18, indicating that this elaboration of the community's confession is the promise of God.

Although 7:1–10:18 has been the focus of studies of both the Christology and soteriology of Hebrews, these topics cannot be separated from the crucial significance of the promise, which the author mentions three times in this section (7:6; 8:6; 9:15), in addition to the synonyms. The author establishes that believers have "better promises" (8:6) insofar as the death of Jesus establishes the conditions by which "those who have been called may

---

26. Μεσιτεύειν, a *hapax legomenon* in the NT, is a legal term, "to guarantee." BDAG, 634. The term anticipates the appellation of Jesus as μεσίτης in 7:1–10:18 (cf. 8:6; 9:15; 12:24).

27. Stobaeus records an aphorism of Socrates, according to which the securing of a boat with a weak anchor is the equivalent of basing one's hopes on a false understanding (Stobaeus, *Anthology* 3.2.45; cf. 4.46.22). See also Plutarch, *Exilio* 601–6; cf. Heliodorus, *Aethiopica* 7.24.4, "Hope is an anchor."

receive the promise of the eternal inheritance" (9:15). Thus both Christology and soteriology are the foundation for the reception of the promise.

Two *inclusios* shape the argument of 7:1—10:18, indicating the author's focus in this section. In the first *inclusio*, the exaltation of Christ (6:19-20; 10:11-12), expressed in the language of Ps 110:1 (cf. 8:1; 10:11-12), provides the setting for the argument, which consists of the ontological distinction between two levels of priesthood, cult, and sacrifice. The second *inclusio*, formed by εἰς τὸν αἰῶνα (6:20) and εἰς τὸ διηνεκές (10:14; cf. 7:3) and drawn from Ps 110:4,[28] suggests the importance of the eternity of the Son for the author's understanding of the promise in Hebrews. Existing above the world of mortality and incompleteness, the heavenly high priest abides forever. The phrase reiterates the earlier claim that the exalted Son is εἰς τὸν αἰῶνα (1:8; cf. Ps 44:7 LXX) and abides (διαμένεις, 1:11), in contrast to the mutable angels and the creation (1:7-12). Moreover, his sacrifice was εἰς τὸ διηνεκές (10:12-14). The author expresses little concern to speculate about the mysterious figure of Melchizedek in chapter 7 but focuses on the fact that he "abides forever" (μένει εἰς τὸ διηνεκές), unlike the Aaronic priests (cf. 7:16, 23-25, 28), who are prevented by death from remaining (7:23). While the priesthood of Aaron changed (7:12), the priest after the order of Melchizedek belongs to an "order" (τάξις, 7:11, 17) that is not subject to change. Because he is εἰς τὸν αἰῶνα, his sacrifice is (ἐφ)άπαξ (7:27; 9:26-27). That is, he was exalted above the sphere of time into the sphere of timelessness.

The author reinforces the eternity of the high priest, referring to the oath for the third time in the homily (cf. 3:11; 6:14) and continuing the focus on the oath in 6:17-20. The high priesthood of Melchizedek was "not without an oath" (ὁρκωμοσίας, 7:20). Citing Ps 110:4 fully, he focuses on the divine oath as the basis for the eternity of the Son (7:20-22): "The Lord has sworn and will not change his mind: You are a priest εἰς τὸν αἰῶνα." God's promise is irrevocable (cf. 6:17, ἀμετάθετος). Indeed, arguing from silence, he distinguishes between "the word of the oath" (7:28) and the law, suggesting that the latter was not accompanied by an oath. Unlike the Levitical priesthood, which was subject to change (7:11-19), the word in Jesus Christ is the "word of the oath" (7:28). The promise has not been fulfilled, but God has given his oath in the death and exaltation of Christ.

In addition to the interchangeable terms oath and promise, the author introduces διαθήκη, which is scarcely distinguishable from the oath and promise. Christ became both the "surety (ἔγγυος) of a better covenant" (7:22) and the mediator (μεσίτης) of a better covenant (8:6; 9:15; cf. 12:24),

---

28. The author renders the LXX εἰς τὸν αἰῶνα into the more elegant εἰς τὸ διηνεκές in 7:3; 10:12.

which is established on better promises (8:6). The terms ἔγγυος and μεσίτης are legal terms for the guarantee of the promise,[29] continuing the legal terminology employed in the claim that God "guaranteed" (ἐμεσίτευσεν)[30] the oath and promise in the work of Christ. The author interprets the new covenant (Jer 31:31–34) in cultic terms, with a special emphasis on the promise, "I will remember their sins no more" (8:12; 10:17). This promise is developed in 9:1—10:18, which describes the finality and eternity of the sacrifice of Christ. Like the oath and the promise, the διαθήκη requires a guarantee of the future. Thus, while the readers do not see the final triumph of God, the guaranteed promise is the secure anchor that they may hold. They have received the purification for sins in the past and the guarantee for the future. The community has access to the heavenly world in worship, even if it does not yet see the eschatological triumph.

The repeated use of κρείττων to describe the "better hope" (7:19), "better covenant" (7:22; 8:6), and "better promises" (8:6) corresponds to the consistent distinction between the two levels of reality, for the term is used to compare two levels of reality (cf. 1:4; 6:9; 11:16; 12:24). The "better promises" (8:6) belong to the transcendent world, which the exalted Christ has opened up to them.

After the description of the heavenly liturgy (9:1–14), the author concludes that the readers may "inherit the promises" (9:15). Thus the death of Christ is the presupposition for the availability of the promise. The content of God's promise is the believers' entry into the heavenly sanctuary, the corollary to the entry into God's rest. God's oath that the Son is eternal is also the guarantee of the promise to the community, for the entry of the high priest into the sanctuary opens the way for those who follow (cf. 10:19).

In the description of the promise in 4:14—10:31, the author assumes the eschatological view of the two ages, maintaining that the Christ event is an occasion within history that marks the turn of the ages (cf. 6:5). As in 1:1–2, God has spoken in the Christ event, promising that the exalted Lord is eternal. The author also anticipates the coming of the day (10:25) of the return of Christ (9:27–28). However, the author focuses on the exaltation of the Son to the transcendent world and the expectation that the readers will also enter. The content of the promise is that the Son is eternal and that believers will share in his eternity.

---

29. BDAG, 271, 634.
30. BDAG, 634.

The Promise as "Things Hoped for" and "Things Unseen" (10:32—13:25)

In the *peroratio*, which begins in 10:32, the author brings together the earlier arguments into a final exhortation that clarifies the problem of the unseen. The greatest concentration of references to the promise and its synonyms appears in the list of patriarchs in chapter 11, which the author introduces with his working definition of faith in 11:1.[31] The definition of faith as ἐλπιζομένων ὑπόστασις and ἔλεγχος οὐ βλεπομένων resumes the basic question of the homily (2:8b) and addresses the readers' most urgent concern: the problem of what remains unseen. Having anticipated chapter 11 with numerous references to faith (3:2, 5, 12, 19; 4:2; 6:12; 10:22, 39) as the appropriate response to the promise, the author defines πίστις in a way that looks back to the preceding argument and forward to the list of patriarchs in chapter 11. The definition is a window into the author's understanding of the promise.

The "things that are hoped for" and "things not seen" are the promises that stand before the community in the first ten chapters: the triumph of the Son (1:5–13), the entry into God's rest (4:1–11), and the ministry of the heavenly high priest in the heavenly sanctuary (7:1—10:18). Although the two expressions overlap, they are not precisely parallel, for "the things that are hoped for" are the promises that will be fulfilled in the future, while the "things not seen" are the eternal realities that exist in the transcendent world, which the author has described in 7:1—10:18. The latter phrase evokes the distinction among Platonists between the visible and invisible realities, which also influenced Jewish literature. Plato (*Resp.* 509D; cf. 7.524D; *Phaedo* 79A) speaks of the two realities, the visible (ὁρατόν) and the intelligible (νοητόν). Albinus (Alcinous) mentions the two components of reality from which the world is made (*Didask.* 13.1), ὁρατὸν καὶ ἁπτόν, ἡ δὲ ἀορατός τε καὶ ἀφανής. The same distinction appears in Wisdom, which describes the visible creation as τὰ βλεπόμενα (13:7). The author returns to the Platonic distinction in 11:27 in the description of God as the invisible one (ὁ ἀόρατος), using the term that never appears in the LXX but was common among Middle Platonists, including Philo, who employs the term ἀόρατος more than one hundred times to describe God, the soul, and the heavenly world. This distinction is evident in the contrast in 11:3 between what is visible (τὸ βλεπόμενον) and what is not visible (μὴ ἐκ φαινομένων). It also corresponds to the author's fondness for negatives to describe the transcendent world, which is "not made with hands" (9:11,

---

31. On the function of definitions in rhetorical discourse, see Rose, *Die Wolke der Zeugen*, 93-98.

24), "untouchable" (cf. 12:18, 22), and unshakable (12:27–28). This use of the α-privative for describing the deity and the intelligible world was a characteristic of Middle Platonism.[32]

While the definition of faith as ὑπόστασις and ἔλεγχος is a challenge to translators, both words emphasize the theme of the certainty and stability of the unseen reality. Ὑπόστασις, derived from ὑφίσταμαι (literally "stand under"), can mean reality (cf. 1:3; 3:14), realization,[33] foundation, or standing firm (German *feststehen*).[34] The context suggests that one cannot distinguish sharply among the proposed meanings, for the word suggests both the solid foundation and the act of taking a firm stand.[35] Indeed, the description of the listeners' early experience offers a commentary on the definition in 11:1. They had endured, "knowing" (γινώσκοντες) that they had "a better and abiding possession" (10:34) than the material goods that they had given up. This contrast suggests that the "better and abiding possession" is equivalent to "things hoped for" and "things unseen." "Knowing" suggests the meaning of "realization" for ὑπόστασις. However, the author continues the exhortation, contrasting faith (i.e., endurance) with shrinking back (11:39). This description suggests that faith involves taking a firm stand on the object of hope.

The description of faith as ἔλεγχος continues the author's focus on the certainty of "things not seen" (cf. 6:19–20).[36] Thus the author's response to the community's crisis is to insist that reality is not in visible and tangible things but in the unseen world. He employs Platonic assumptions for a pastoral purpose.

The author anticipates this working definition with examples of those who stood before the unseen promises. The ancestors in the wilderness failed to enter the promised heavenly κατάπαυσις because of ἀπιστία (3:12, 19). "Things hoped for" and "things not seen" include the promise of the heavenly κατάπαυσις and participation in God's primordial rest as well as the work of Christ in the sanctuary not made with hands. All that the author has described remains unseen. The listeners themselves endured abuse and the confiscation of their property because they knew that they had an abiding possession (10:32–34), the equivalent of "things hoped for" and "things not seen."

32. Dillon, *The Middle Platonists*, 284. Backhaus, "Per Christum in Deum," 263; Wolfson, "Albinus and Plotinus on Divine Attributes," 115–17.

33. BDAG, 1041.

34. Grässer, *An die Hebräer*, 3.95.

35. Rose, *Wolke der Zeugen*, 100–101.

36. BDAG, 315, indicates that ἔλεγχος refers to the evidence for the proof of something.

This working definition becomes the leitmotif in the description of heroes, all of whom shared the insecurity of the readers. The author employs a variety of words to describe "things hoped for" and "things unseen." As the general statement indicates, to have faith is to believe that God rewards those who seek him (11:6). Noah believed in "things not yet seen" (11:7) and became an heir (11:7). Abraham went out looking for an inheritance (κληρονομία) and sojourned in the land of promise with Isaac and Jacob (11:9), the "heirs of the promise" (11:10). The promise was the equivalent for the city (πόλις, 11:10, 16; cf. 12:22; 13:14) and homeland (πατρία, 11:14). Moses looked to the reward (11:26) and went out as "seeing the invisible" (11:27).

The patriarchs are the models for the readers, who also await a heavenly city (12:22; 13:14). The voice from heaven has promised (12:26) the shaking of heaven and earth, leaving only the abiding and unshakable reality, the equivalent to the city that "has foundations, whose maker and builder is God" (cf. 11:10), and God's primordial rest (cf. 4:4-9). The author reshapes the traditional eschatological expectation, assuming the two levels of reality that have been a major theme of the homily. Those things that have been made will pass away, but the transcendent reality remains for the readers to receive (12:28).[37] At the conclusion of the homily, the author urges the readers to "go out" (13:13) into the insecurity of the place outside the camp, following Jesus. Like Abraham (cf. 11:8), they go out to the homeless existence because they anticipate the abiding city. Abraham, the stranger in the world, is the model for believers.

Unfulfilled Promises and a People on the Way

Ernst Käsemann observed that the community's experience of unfulfilled promises results in an existence characterized by "Wanderschaft."[38] While a Greek equivalent of this term is not employed in Hebrews and it has no precise English equivalent, it is an appropriate image for the author's consistent description of the readers as people without a homeland. As the author indicated in the first ten chapters, those who do not see God's triumph follow their pioneer (ἀρχηγός, 2:10; 12:2) and forerunner (πρόδρομος, 6:20) through the wilderness of their present existence to the heavenly world, but they have not arrived (2:10-18; 6:18-20). They are "refugees" (καταφυγόντες, 6:18) looking for an anchor and are in danger of "drifting away" (cf. παραρυομεν, 2:1), as in rushing water.[39] Indeed, the entire setting

---

37. Eisele, *Ein unerschütterliches Reich*, 375.
38. Käsemann, *Das wandernde Gottesvolk*, 19.
39. On παραρρέω as an image of being swept away by flowing water, see BDAG, 770.

of the homily presupposes the wilderness experience, as the tabernacle imagery (9:1—10:18) and the comparison of the heavenly mountain with Sinai (12:18–19) suggest. The wilderness experience indicates the community's separation from the world in heaven that the author portrays. This imagery becomes especially important in the portrayal of the patriarchs, who are the models of living and dying with the unfulfilled promise (11:13–16, 39) of a homeland. The author's use of philosophical language becomes most evident in his interpretation of the problem of the unseen.

A Home for Refugees and Pilgrims

The corollary to the search for the invisible homeland is the existence of the patriarchs as migrants and outsiders, the most basic characteristic of the heroes in chapter 11.[40] In recalling that Abraham "sojourned" (παρῴκησεν, 11:9) and that the patriarchs were "strangers and sojourners" (ξένοι καὶ παρεπίδημοι, 11:13), the author echoes the LXX's description of Abraham as the nomad par excellence. The LXX consistently employs forms of παροικεῖν[41] to describe the nomadic existence of Abraham, Isaac, Jacob, and Moses (Gen 12:10; 17:8; 19:9; 20:1; 21:23, 34; 24:37; 26:3; 28:4; 32:5; 35:27; 36:7; 37:1; 47:4; Exod 2:22). Moses named his son Gershom because Moses was himself a πάροικος in the land (Exod 2:22). Indeed, the defining narratives of Israel involve the theme of the existence of Israel in a foreign land: the exodus from Egypt, the wilderness wanderings, and the exile.[42] The Israelites identified their history with "a wandering Aramaen" (Deut 26:5), who "sojourned" (παρῴκησεν) in Egypt. These narratives had a special significance for Israelites who lived outside the promised land.[43] Both 1 Peter and Hebrews follow this tradition, giving a positive interpretation to the patriarchs' existence as strangers and aliens for the sake of readers who were πάροικοι, not because they were literally noncitizens

---

40. Eisenbaum, *The Jewish Heroes of Christian History*, 184.
41. BDAG, 779, "to inhabit a place as a foreigner."
42. Backhaus, "Aufbruch ins Evangelium," 288.

43. Reinhard Feldmeier has shown that the narratives about strangers had a special significance for those who also lived as strangers. The accent on the patriarchs as strangers is a special theme of the Priestly document, which was written during the exile, when Israel appeared to be at an end as a nation. In retelling the story of Abraham, the writer emphasized that the patriarchs also were strangers looking for a promise. Jews who lived inside the land of promise did not accent this theme, while those who lived as minority communities gave a positive interpretation to the memory of Israel's ancestors as strangers. Feldmeier, "The 'Nation' of Strangers," 243.

but because they were alienated from their communities as a result of their confession (cf. 1 Pet 1:1, 17; 2:11).

After describing Noah as the outsider who "condemned the world" (11:7; cf. 11:38), the author of Hebrews devotes an extended section to Abraham, heightening the emphasis on his existence as a stranger.[44] Just as the κατάπαυσις in 4:1-11 was no longer the promised land expected by Israel, the κληρονομία (11:8) that Abraham seeks is no longer the κληρονομία in the land. His role as a stranger is evident in the repetition of the verbs ἐξελθεῖν/ἐξῆλθεν (11:8) and the reminder that the patriarchs lived in tents (11:9). Even in the land of promise, he was an alien (ἀλλοτρία, 11:9; cf. Philo, *Her.* 26). The same theme of alienation is evident in the description of Moses's suffering and departure from Egypt (11:25-26) and culminates in the summary of the patriarchs' existence in 11:38-39: They wandered around in mountains and caves and holes in the ground, and the world was not worthy of them.

The new dimension of the patriarchs' exile existence is that they were not only "strangers and resident aliens" (ξένοι καὶ παρεπίδημοι, 11:13; cf. Gen 23:4) but "strangers and aliens *on the earth*" (ἐπὶ τῆς γῆς, 11:13). Γῆ is not the promised land, as in Genesis, but the earth itself. They were thus not only outsiders in a sociological sense but in an ontological sense as well.[45] Thus they are illustrations of the working definition of faith in 11:1.[46] The believer never attains the fulfillment of the promise on earth but sees it only from afar (11:13; cf. Deut 34:4). Consequently, the ancestors died in faith, not receiving the promises (11:13, 39). For them, as for the readers of Hebrews, the fulfillment of the promise remains unseen.

The author's description of the patriarchs as strangers and resident aliens corresponds to his earlier description of the readers as "fugitives" (6:19) and his reference to their own marginalization (cf. 10:32-34), suggesting that the ancestors are the models for the readers' own approach to the problem of the unseen and unfulfilled promises. While the author's description of faithful people as fugitives, strangers, and resident aliens employs the vocabulary of Scripture, it also resonates with the philosophical literature that extends from the pre-Socratics to the Platonic tradition, where it is employed for the individual's separation from the transcendent world.[47] According to Democritus (frag. c7), "As people recognize that they have only

---

44. According to Gen 23:4 LXX, Abraham says, "I am a stranger and resident alien (ξένος καὶ παρεπίδημος) among you (μεθ ὑμῖν)."

45. Backhaus, "Das Land der Verheißung," 175.

46. Eisele, *Ein unerschütterliches Reich*, 383.

47. Feldmeier, *Die Christen als Fremde*, 29.

a brief lifetime in comparison to eternity, so they have a most beautiful life ... as in a foreign land (παρεπιδημία)." Empedocles, who was influenced by Pythagoras, describes his life as a flight and a vagabond existence (φυγὰς θεόθεν καὶ ἀλήτης) in which one is constantly on the way in a hostile, strange, environment because one belongs to a better world of the gods.[48] According to *Theatetus*, Socrates said, "Therefore we ought to flee (φυγεῖν) from earth to the dwelling place of the gods as fast as we can. This flight (φυγή) is to become like God in every way that we can" (176ab).

In the *Phaedo*, Socrates explains that his death is an ἀποδημία, a wandering from a strange land (61e; cf. 67c). According to Ps.-Plato, Socrates says, when called to the deathbed of Asiochos, "Life is only a temporary residence (παρεπιδημία)."[49] Aelius Aristides describes heaven as one's homeland (πατρίδα τὴν οὐρανόν). Similarly, Porphyry speaks of the individual's exile (ἀποδημία) from heaven (*Marc.* 5).

The description of the readers as fugitives (καταφυγόντες, 6:19) is reminiscent of a common theme in the philosophical literature. Several philosophers and other writers, including Plutarch of Chaeronea and Philo of Alexandria, wrote books or speeches with the title Περὶ φυγῆς.[50] Plutarch wrote *de Exilio* (περὶ φυγῆς) to encourage a friend who had been exiled. He insisted that "there is no such thing as a native land" (600E). Citing Empedocles's words, "I too a wanderer (φυγάς) and exile (ἀλήτης) from heaven" (607D), he added that "All of us ... are sojourners (μετανάστας) and strangers (ξένους) and exiles (φυγάδας)." Philo described life in the body as an exile from heaven, encouraging his reader, "Depart you here, from the earthly matter that surrounds you, escaping (ἐκφυγών) from that foulest prison, the body, and from its pleasures and desires that are like jailers with all your might and strength" (*Mig* 9). No place is really home, for the soul is in exile.

Plotinus employs the nautical metaphor to indicate this insecurity in his comments on the words of Odysseus (Homer, *Il.* 2.140), "Let us flee into the beloved homeland." Plotinus adds, "In what does this flight consist? We are in the sea like Odysseus ... in a flight from the sorcerer Circe or Calypso. ... There is our fatherland, from which we come and there is our father" (*On the Beautiful* 2.6.8.39). According to David Runia, the theme of Odysseus the wanderer, buffeted by the storms and tribulations of the earthly and bodily reality until he finds his way to his fatherland, the heavenly and spiritual realm,

---

48. Frg. 115; cited in Feldmeier, *Die Christen als Fremde*, 29.

49. Ps.-Plato, *Ax.* 365.

50. Runia, "The Theme of Flight and Exile," 1. In addition to Philo and Plutarch, Teles of Megara (long excerpt in Stob, *Flor.* 3.40.8); Dio, *Or.* 13; Favorinus of Arles (partly preserved as Vatic. Pap. 11 (see *DphA* 3.422).

is an important theme in Platonic philosophy.[51] Philo's knowledge of this tradition is evident in his advice that his reader should steer clear "of smoke and wave" (*Od.* 12.219) and run away from the ridiculous pursuits of mortal life as from that terrifying Charybdis, not touching it even with the tip of your toe (*Somn.* 2.270).[52] We do not have an explicit reference to such an allegory until much later (Numenius, as reported by Porphyry).[53]

The nautical imagery of human existence as life in a tumultuous river (cf. Heb 6:19–20) is also a common theme in the philosophical literature. Stobaeus cites an aphorism of Socrates, "To secure boat with weak anchor and to have hope on false judgment" (*Stob.* 3.2.4.5). Employing the imagery of flight and seafaring, Plutarch says that one must have good sense and reason, as a skipper needs an anchor that he may moor at any haven. Those who are hanging upon the future and longing for what they do not have are tossed about on hope as on a raft (606e; cf. Heb 6:19). Philo speaks of life's river (*Fug.* 49) and of the desire of all those who are beloved by God to fly from the "stormy waters of engrossing business with its perpetual turmoil of surge and billows and anchor in the calm safe shelter of virtue's roadsteads" (*Somn.* 2.225).

At the center of Philo's thought is the understanding of human existence as migration to the heavenly homeland.[54] Philo anticipated the author of Hebrews in appropriating the Greek concept of human existence as temporary residence into the retelling of the Genesis story. The soul of the wise individual follows the path "from the flesh to the spirit, from the material world with its darkness and passions to the light of the intelligible world, from slavery in Egypt to freedom in Canaan, land of virtue or city of God."[55] Commenting on the reminder that the Israelites are only aliens and tenants in the land owned by God (Lev 25:23), he adds that "each of us has come into this world (κόσμος) as into a foreign city, and in this city he does but sojourn (παροικεῖν) until he has exhausted his span of life" (*Cher.* 120), indicating that every created being is a sojourner and alien (*Cher.* 121).

A common theme in Philo's writings is that Abraham is the sojourner par excellence. In *De migratione Abrahami* Philo offers a radical interpretation of Abraham's departure from his land and kin. "Land" means "body" and "kinship" means "sense perception," both of which he must leave

---

51. Runia, "The Theme of Flight and Exile," 21. See also Lamberton, *Homer the Theologian*, 53.

52. Cited in Runia, "The Theme of Flight and Exile," 21.

53. Numenius, fr. 60 (=Porphyry, *De antro* 6).

54. Nikiprowetzky, *Le commentaire de l'Écriture chez Philon d'Alexandrie*, 239.

55. Nikiprowetzky, *Le commentaire de l'Écriture chez Philon d'Alexandrie*, 239; trans. in Runia, "The Theme of Flight and Exile," 21.

behind.[56] The language used for the body is very strong: "Depart you here, from the earthly matter that surrounds you, escaping (ἐκφυγών) from that foulest prison, the body, and from its pleasures and desires that are like jailers with all your might and strength" (*Migr.* 9). He returns to this theme elsewhere (*Her.* 267), arguing that God does not permit humankind to dwell in the body as if in a homeland, for God permits one to sojourn here, as in a foreign country. It is the fool who mistakes the body for the homeland and attempts to dwell rather than to sojourn (παροικεῖν).

In *De confusione linguarum*, Philo turns to Gen 11:2 as the basis for his comments on the importance of the temporary residence on earth for the people of faith. The wicked of Gen 11:2 live on the plain "as though it were their fatherland (ὡς ἐν πατρίδα)." They did not sojourn there as if on foreign soil but decided to stay permanently. By contrast, the wise are called sojourners (παροικοῦντες), for their life in the body is temporary. The heavenly region is their native land (πατρίς), and the earthly region is a foreign country in which they are sojourners (78). Thus Abraham, Isaac, and Jacob are called sojourners (76-82).[57] Like the author of Hebrews, Philo insists that the strangers in the land have a better city or country. Jacob's temporary residence with Laban is symbolic of the soul's expectation of a city (*Somn.* 1.46; cf. *Somn.* 1.46; 2.250). In *Her.* 26, Abraham asks, "Am I not a wanderer (μετανάστης) from my country, an outcast, an alien from my father's house. Do not all men call me excommunicate, exile, desolate and disenfranchised? Thou art my country (ἡ πατρίς)."

Philo contrasts Abraham and Cain, both of whom "went out" (Gen 4:16; 12:1-2), but in the opposite direction. Philo comments on Cain's exile, indicating that Cain went to the place called σαλός, or "tossing." He adds that the foolish man is subject to tossing and tumult, like the sea lashed by contrary winds when a storm is raging and never has quietness or calm (*Post. Cain* 22). He devotes an essay to stories of flight (φυγή) in which he speaks of the "torrent of life's river" and the need to find a safe haven in the house of wisdom rather than be overwhelmed by raging waters (*Fug.* 49-50).

Reinhard Feldmeier has noted the correlation between social alienation and the ontological description of the stranger and alien. Philo's frequent statements about the estrangement of the wise is occasioned considerably by the estrangement of the Jews in Alexandrian society.[58] Philo recalls the persecution of Jews among Alexandrian nationalists and Flaccus's comment that

---

56. See Runia, "The Theme of Flight and Exile," 13.
57. Thompson, *Beginnings of Christian Philosophy*, 59-60.
58. Feldmeier, *Christen als Fremde*, 68.

the Jews are "strangers and foreigners" (ξένοι καὶ ἐπήλυδες).[59] Philo offers a positive view of this condition by providing an ontological perspective, according to which the heroes of faith recognize their true homeland in heaven. Similarly, the author of Hebrews addresses the fundamental question of the readers by placing their own estrangement within a metaphysical context. His description of his readers as refugees (καταφυγόντες, 6:19) evokes the familiar image from philosophical literature. While his imagery of flight and homelessness does not carry all of the associations that these images had among the philosophers and the works of Philo, the author agrees with his contemporaries in describing human existence as a transient life on earth in anticipation of a transcendent homeland. To live without seeing the triumph of Christ belongs to the very nature of faith itself.

Epistemology, Faith, and the Promise

In his comment that faith is "the evidence of things not seen," the author returns to the basic issue facing the readers, who say, "We do not see everything in subjection to him." In chapter 11, he provides a solution to this problem, offering an epistemology by which they can experience the unseen reality. He anticipates this resolution in his description of the readers' past experience when they endured the loss of their property, knowing that they had a better and abiding possession (10:34). The elaboration on the definition of faith in 11:3 also points to the resolution: "By faith we know (νοοῦμεν) that the worlds were created by the word of God, so that what is seen was made from things that do not appear."[60] That is, faith has its own epistemology by which the believer knows what is real. The author's use of νοοῦμεν in 11:3 suggests that only in thinking do we recognize that behind the visible stands this invisible reality.[61] It concerns knowledge, which is made possible and mediated through faith. This epistemology is reminiscent of the Platonic argument that the invisible realities are known only by the νοῦς.[62]

The author describes this epistemology also with the imagery of seeing. For example, the patriarchs "died in faith, not having received the promise but having seen it from a distance" (11:13). The visual imagery is

---

59. *Flac.* 54; cited in Feldmeier, *Christen als Fremde*, 67.

60. The negative μή can refer to the entire clause or to ἐκ φαινομένων. Cf. BDF, 433 (3). The meaning remains the same in either case. Cf. Grässer, *An die Hebräer*, 3.109.

61. Eisele, *Ein unerschütterliches Reich*, 383.

62. Cf. Plato, *Tim.* 28A, 52, "invisible forms which it is the province of reason (νόησις) to contemplate." Cf. *Phaed.* 79A, "things that are always the same are grasped by reason."

most clearly stated in the description of Moses, who chose the afflictions of the Christ rather than the treasures of Egypt because "he saw the reward" (11:26). He then endured the loss of the security of Egypt, going out "as seeing the invisible one" (11:27). This statement is the author's commentary on the definition of faith as "evidence of things not seen" (11:1).[63] Not only do believers know a reality beyond the senses, but those who "do not see the world in subjection to him" can see invisible realities.

In light of the biblical theme that no one can see God and live (Deut 33:20),[64] the description of Moses "as seeing the invisible one" is noteworthy.[65] The language of "seeing the invisible (one)" resonates with the language of Platonic epistemology, which Philo also adapted into the biblical narrative. For Plato, the instrument for seeing the divine is the eye of the soul (*Rep.* 7. 533D), which is better than ten thousand eyes, for with it alone the truth is perceived (*Rep.* 7. 527). Plato speaks of that place beyond the heavens that reason can behold; all true knowledge is knowledge thereof. It is visible only to the mind (*Phaedr.* 247). Plato says, "We assume two kinds of existence, visible and invisible—things that are always the same can be grasped only by reason (*Phaedo* 79). He speaks specifically of the ascent of the soul to a vision of the existent (τὸ ὄν), which is visible only to the mind, the pilot of the soul (*Phaed.* 246e–247e, 249c). The vision of God becomes a common theme in the Platonic tradition.[66] According to Alcinous, "God is ineffable and comprehensible only by the intellect" (10.6).

Philo, who uses the term ἀόρατος more than one hundred times for God, employs the Platonic language for seeing God on numerous occasions. He describes what is beyond matter as "beyond sight" (*Post.* 15) and God as the one who cannot be seen (*Post.* 16). If even Moses was incapable of seeing God (*Mut.* 7–9), then only the most arrogant person "will boast of seeing the invisible God" (*QE* 2.37) because an ontological gulf separates humankind from God.[67] "By his very nature God is invisible and incomprehensible, and

63. Grässer, *An die Hebräer*, 3.124.

64. Biblical verses vary on the way they present the experience of seeing God. While some verses indicate that humans are not permitted to see God (cf. Exod 33:20), others indicate that God appeared to individuals. According to Gen 12:7 and 17:11, "And the Lord appeared to (was seen by) Abraham." According to Gen 32:25–33, Jacob says, "I have seen God face to face." Nowhere is God described as invisible. See Birnbaum, *The Place of Judaism in Philo's Thought*, 78.

65. The expression ὡς ὁρῶν indicates the paradoxical nature of faith (Grässer, *An die Hebräer*, 174). "Seeing the invisible" implies the use of other means of perception, as the parallels indicate. Cf. Marcus Aurelius, "Let us see (ὁρῶμεν), not with the eyes" (10:26). According to Aristotle, *de Mundo* 399a, the deity is described as ἀόρατος except to reason (λογισμός).

66. See Wolfson, "Albinus and Plotinus," 126–29.

67. Mackie, "Seeing God in Philo of Alexandria," 27.

thus the deity cannot be seen" by created beings (*Mut.* 9; *Post.* 168; *Conf.* 138), "for we have in us no organ by which we can envisage the Existent One, neither in sense . . . nor in mind" (*Mut.* 7; cf. also *Det.* 86–87).[68]

Despite the ontological chasm between God and humankind, Philo maintains that people of faith may see the invisible one. For example, Cain had no conception of the existent one, "having deliberately blinded the organ by which alone he could have seen him" (*Post.* 21). Philo contrasts Cain with the one "to whom it is given to gaze and soar beyond not only material but all immaterial things and to take God as his whole stay and support . . . and a faith unswerving (ἀκλινοῦς) and securely founded (βεβαιοτάτης, *Praem.* 30). He describes God's creation of one great city as a model for the creation, a "world discernible only by the mind" and the pattern for the world that our senses perceive" (*Opif.* 19). Through wisdom the soul sees God and his potencies (*Mut.* 3). Philo speaks of "invisible conceptions perceived only by the mind, of which the others are copies open to our senses" (*Ebr.* 132; *Abr.* 132). "When it sees the incomparable it does not yield to the counterpull of things like itself" (*Somn.* 2.227). Faith is the perpetual vision of the existent (*Praem.* 27). To believe in God is to disbelieve in all else, all that is created only to perish.

The people of faith, according to Philo, were able to see the invisible one. Abraham is the "virtuous person," whose spiritual eyes are awake and see (*QG* 4.2). His "mind" is able to "form an impression with more open eyes and more lucid vision." His "fully opened" mind then "runs toward the one" and he sees God as one who is clearly manifest, "directly visible" (4.4).[69] Moses entered into the darkness where God is, into the unseen, invisible, incorporeal, and archetypal essence of things. There "he beheld what is hidden from the sight of moral nature" (*Mos.* 1.158).

The transformation of the traditional hope for the fulfillment of the promise is evident in the focus on the ancestors as strangers on earth whose epistemology of faith involved "seeing the invisible one." This combination of themes indicates that the author's portrayal of faithful people of the past is derived not only from his reading of the LXX but also from the philosophical categories that he applies to the interpretation. This interpretation serves the pastoral purpose of interpreting the marginalization of those who do not see the triumph that they had expected. Like Jewish predecessors who also addressed the problem of marginalization, the author offers examples of other "fugitives" who did not find an answer on earth. To those who "do not see the world in subjection" (2:8), the author offers a new way of seeing.

---

68. Mackie, "Seeing God in Philo of Alexandria," 27.
69. Mackie, "Seeing God in Philo of Alexandria," 41.

CHAPTER 8

THE EPISTLE TO THE HEBREWS IN THE WORKS OF CLEMENT OF ALEXANDRIA

An Alexandrian tradition that extends from Philo to Clement of Alexandria is a well-established fact in scholarship. Clement had access to Philo's works through a school tradition in Alexandria,[1] and he often borrowed and reshaped exegetical traditions from his Alexandrian predecessor. Clement's intellectual heritage also included a Christian tradition that was mediated to him in Alexandria through the books that had gained authoritative status.[2] This heritage included the Epistle to the Hebrews, which Clement quotes on numerous occasions.[3] Indeed, as Franz Overbeck observed, Hebrews was first cited in the West (1 Clem. 36:2) but received canonical status first in the East, with the support of the Alexandrian church. He argued that the Alexandrian characteristics of Hebrews made it particularly acceptable to Clement and Origen.[4] Inasmuch as the Epistle to the Hebrews shares numerous connections with Philo and is cited frequently by Clement of Alexandria, the place of Hebrews within this tradition remains undetermined. Although Rowan Greer's study explored the exegesis of Hebrews from Origen to Cyril,[5] no one has examined the exegesis of Hebrews by Clement of Alexandria. Thus my task in this paper is to

---

1. Originally published in *Transmission and Reception: New Testament Text-Critical and Exegetical Studies*, edited by J. W. Childers and D. C. Parker, 239–54. Piscataway, NJ: Gorgias, 2006.
   Harding, "Christ as Greater than Moses in Clement of Alexandria's *Stromateis* I–II," 397.

2. Brooks, "Clement of Alexandria as a Witness to the Development of the New Testament Canon," 43.

3. See Mees, *Die Zitate aus dem Neuen Testament bei Clemens von Alexandrien*, 228–36.

4. Overbeck, *Zur Geschichte des Kanons*, 68–71.

5. Greer, *The Captain of our Salvation: A Study of the Patristic Exegesis of Hebrews*.

explore the place of Hebrews in this Alexandrian tradition. I shall examine Clement's use of Hebrews, giving special attention to the areas where Philo, Hebrews, and Clement share common interests.

Clement was well acquainted with the Epistle to the Hebrews, which he attributed to Paul (*Strom.* 6.8.62). According to Eusebius, Clement offered the following description of Hebrews in the *Hypotyposeis*, a work that is no longer extant:

> And as for the Epistle to the Hebrews, he says indeed that it is Paul's but that it was written for Hebrews in the Hebrew tongue, and that Luke, having carefully translated it, published it for the Greeks; hence, as a result of this translation, the same complexion of style is found in this Epistle and in the Acts: but that the [words] "Paul and apostle" were naturally not prefixed. For, says he, "in writing to Hebrews who had conceived a prejudice against him and were suspicious of him, he very wisely did not repel them at the beginning by putting his name."

Then he adds:

> But now, as the blessed elder used to say, since the Lord, being the apostle of the Almighty, was sent to the Hebrews, Paul, through modesty, since he had been sent to the Gentiles, does not inscribe himself as an apostle of the Hebrews, both to give due deference to the Lord and because he wrote to the Hebrews also out of his abundance, being a preacher and apostle to the Gentiles. (*HE* 6.14.1–4)[6]

The Prologue of Hebrews

Clement cites the prologue of Hebrews (1:1–4) on numerous occasions. Undoubtedly, the alliteration in the opening lines appealed to Clement, for he employed these words in a variety of contexts. For example, he describes the golden lamp of the tabernacle as the symbol of Christ, not in respect of form alone but in casting light "at sundry times and divers manners" (πολυτρόπως καὶ πολυμερῶς, *Strom.* 5.6.35).[7] In several passages, Clement cites the opening words to indicate the variety of revelation within Scripture. Christ is the "teacher of all created beings, the Fellow-counsellor of God," who is "from above"; hence, "in many ways and many times"

---

6. Translation is from LCL.

7. Translations from Clement are from Roberts and Donaldson, eds., *The Ante-Nicene Fathers*.

(πολυτρόπως καὶ πολυμερῶς, *Strom.* 6.7, 58) he "trains and perfects" his people. In *Strom.* 6.10.81, Clement says that "for having spoken at sundry times and in divers manners (πολυμερῶς . . . καὶ πολυτρόπως), it is not one way only that He is known." In *Strom.* 7.16.95, he refers to the variety ways in which God has spoken "by the prophets, the Gospel, and the blessed apostles 'in divers manners and at sundry times,' leading from the beginning of knowledge to the end."

Clement does not limit revelation to the canonical Scriptures. When he speaks of God's "manifold" wisdom, he includes secular science or art. He appeals to the prologue of Hebrews, interpreting πολυμερῶς καὶ πολυτρόπως as God's revelation in art, knowledge, faith, and prophecy (*Strom.* 1.4.27).

Clement also appealed to the christological language in the prologue of Hebrews. In *Strom.* 7.3.16, Clement employs images drawn from the Johannine literature and Hebrews to declare that Christ is the "true Onlybegotten, the express image (χαρακτήρ) of the glory of the universal King and Almighty Father (cf. Heb 1:3), who impressed on the Gnostic the seal of the perfect contemplation, according to His own image." In *Strom.* 7.10.58, Clement appeals to Hebrews to demonstrate that the Savior is God. "The apostle designates [the Son] as the express image (χαρακτήρ) of the glory of the Father." In *Strom.* 6.5.39, he describes the Son as "incomprehensible, everlasting, unmade, who made all things by the word of his power" (cf. Heb 1:3).

Clement's christological reflections echo the language of the prologue of Hebrews, which describes the Son as the χαρακτήρ of God's being. This term was not, however, limited to Hebrews. It is used by Philo in a variety of contexts. Philo uses the term both to denote the "impressions" made on the soul by God (cf. *Leg.* 2.95) and to describe the logos as the χαρακτήρ of the divine seal impressed upon the soul (*Fug.* 12; *Her.* 230; *Opif.* 18, 151).[8] Thus a natural progression exists from Philo's description of the χαρακτήρ of God in the logos to the christological use made by Hebrews and Clement.

Moses, the Wilderness, and the Promise of Rest

Philo, Hebrews, and Clement reflect on the role of Moses, citing Num 12:7, according to which Moses was "faithful in all [God's] house." In the original context, the passage indicates the intimate relationship to God that only Moses possessed as God's revealer. Philo appeals to the passage to show the glory of Moses. Indeed, Philo cites the passage alongside Exod 25:40,

---

8. See the discussion in Williamson, *Philo and the Epistle to the Hebrews,* 80.

another important passage in Hebrews (8:5). Both the author of Hebrews and Clement avoid the glorification of Moses in order not to diminish the exalted status of Christ. Such glorification of Moses may be known to both the author of Hebrews and Clement. However, both employ Num 12:7 as the basis for a comparison between Moses as servant and Christ the Son (Heb 3:5-6). Clement alludes to Num 12:7 when he says, "According to the apostle, 'the law was given through Moses, grace and truth through Jesus Christ' (cf. John 1:17), and gifts given through a faithful slave are not equal to those bestowed by a true son" (*Quis div.* 8.2.1).[9]

The introduction of the comparative faithfulness of Moses and Jesus in Heb 3:1-6 introduces the author to the description of the Israelites' ἀπιστία (cf. Heb 3:19; 4:2) that led to their forfeiture of the heavenly rest (κατάπαυσις). I have argued elsewhere that the author's interpretation of κατάπαυσις as the primordial rest of God is indebted to Philo, who identified God's rest with the Sabbath.[10] Although identification of rest with the Sabbath is based on Philo's interpretation of Genesis, it also reflects his use of the Pythagorean number speculation, according to which both the terms ἀνάπαυσις and ἑβδομάς were symbols of transcendence.[11]

Clement appeals to both Heb 3:7—4:11 and to Philo as the describes rest as the goal of the believer. He quotes Hebrews at length in *Prot.* 9.84.3-5, contemporizing the exhortation of the ancient psalm in the same way that the author of Hebrews had done earlier. Clement concludes that the Israelites learned by experience that "they could not be saved otherwise than by believing on Jesus" (*Prot.* 9.84.5). His identification of rest with the ultimate promise (*Paed.* 1.6.29) may suggest his acquaintance with Hebrews. Like the author of Hebrews, Clement finds significance in the fact that God rested on the seventh day (cf. Heb 4:4; *Strom.* 6.16.137-40). The goal of the believer, therefore is to share in God's rest, ascending beyond this creation.

Although Clement both cites and alludes to Heb 3:7—4:11 for his understanding of rest, his association of the number 7 and the Sabbath with an elaborate number symbolism is more indebted to Philo than to Hebrews. Hebrews shares the interest in the metaphysical significance of rest but does not engage in the extended analysis of the heavenly spheres that one finds in Philo and Clement.

---

9. Translation from LCL.
10. Thompson, *The Beginnings of Christian Philosophy*, 84. Cf. *Cher.* 87
11. Thompson, *The Beginnings of Christian Philosophy*, 85. See *Her.* 216; *Opif.* 100.

Milk and Meat and the Levels of Education

Ancient writers employed common images of childhood development to describe the process of intellectual maturation.[12] Metaphors of ingestion played a prominent role in distinguishing between the infant and the mature adult. The imagery of milk and solid food is a commonplace in the work of Philo of Alexandria. Philo writes: "But seeing that for babes (νηπίοις) milk is food but for grown men (τελείοις) wheat bread, there must also be milk-like foods for the soul in its childhood, which are the preliminary stages of school learning, and perfect foods for men, which are the instructions leading through prudence and temperance and virtue" (*Agr.* 9). This language comes to the clearest expression in *de Congressu quaerendae Eruditionis gratis*, where Philo argues that Hagar and Sarah represent the two levels of learning, the ἐγκύκλιος παιδεία and philosophy.[13] Philo describes the ἐγκύκλια as "the simple and milky foods of infancy" (*Congr.* 19). The imagery of food for intellectual advancement also appears in *Prob.* 160, where Philo describes the soul's advancement from the milk of childhood learning to the meat of philosophy (cf. *Agr.* 9).

Clement also employs the imagery of milk and solid food to describe the two levels of learning as he describes a specifically Christian *paideia*.[14] He pursues this theme most clearly in his *Paidagogus*, which he develops around the analogy between Christian formation and childhood development. He claims, "If we have been reborn to Christ, then the one who gives us this new birth nurses (ἐκτρέφει) us with his own milk—the Logos" (*Paid.* 1.6.49).

In using the analogy of milk and solid food for education, he cites 1 Cor 3:2 and Heb 5:12–14. Apparently because of the gnostic use of the first chapters of 1 Corinthians, Clement appeals more often to 1 Cor 3:2 to distinguish between the milk and solid food of education, although Heb 5:12–14 more adequately addresses the issue of education. He appeals to Heb 5:12–14 on three occasions, each in the *Stromateis*. In the first book of the *Stromateis* he contrasts the divine instruction with human philosophy, weaving together numerous passages that emphasize that contrast. In an extended passage, he brings together NT passages that contrast the children (those whose philosophy has not been) with adults. Children are the philosophers whose learning has not found culmination in Christ. Here he cites Heb 5:12–14.

---

12. Buell, *Making Christians*, 127.

13. Thompson, *Beginnings of Christian Philosophy*, 22.

14. Buel, *Making Christians*, 120.

Clement also employs Heb 5:12–14 to distinguish between levels of Christian education. In *Strom.* 5.10.62, he describes an instruction for the perfect. He focuses on the mysteries, arguing that knowledge does not belong to all, citing Heb 5:12–14 and 6:1 to distinguish between the levels of instruction. He also incorporates the distinction between children and adults in 1 Cor 3:2 and adds,

> If then the milk is said to belong to babes, and "meat" to be the food of the full-grown, milk will be understood to be the catechetical instruction—the first food, as it were, of the soul. And meat is the mystic contemplation. . . . For the knowledge of the divine essence is the meat and drink of the Divine Word.

Here Clement superimposes the educational metaphor of food from Heb 5:12–14 onto the imagery of milk and meat in 1 Cor 3:2. Whereas Hebrews indicts the entire community for its lack of progress in higher learning, Clement incorporates the Hebrews passage into his own theological vision, arguing that only the few will progress to the solid food of higher learning.

Thus, in the use of the language of nutrition to describe educational development, Philo, the author of Hebrews, and Clement share a common tradition that was widely known in Greek philosophical discussion. Although Clement employs Hebrews to advance his claim, Clement subverts the argument in Hebrews that the entire community should advance from milk to solid food, maintaining that solid food is only for the gnostic, who progresses into the higher studies.

The High Priest, the Levitical Cultus, and Christ

Jewish tradition reflected at length on the symbolic significance of the temple and the vestments of the high priest.[15] Both Philo and Josephus give a symbolic interpretation of the cultic passages of Exod 26–28. Thus when the author of Hebrews says, "Of these matters we cannot speak in detail" (9:6) after introducing the furniture of the tabernacle, he was undoubtedly referring to a tradition that described the cosmic symbolism of the cultus. Clement knows this tradition, as his extended discussion of the Levitical priesthood indicates.

---

15. See van den Hoek, *Clement of Alexandria and His Use of Philo*, 117. Runia, *Philo in Early Christian Literature*, 140. See also Bousset, *Jüdisch-christlicher Schulbetrieb in Alexandria und Rom*, 37–40.

Clement's knowledge of Hebrews is evident in his allusions to Heb 7:1—10:25. In several passages he alludes to phrases drawn from this cultic section of Hebrews without reference to its cultic context. For example, in *Strom.* 3.7.60, he says "It is good if for the sake of the kingdom of heaven a man emasculates himself from all desire, and 'purifies his conscience from dead works to serve the living God'" (cf. Heb 9:14).[16] He quotes Heb 8:10-12 in *Prot.* 11.89 (LCL) when he describes the benefits conferred by the coming of Christ. He describes the divine inheritance of the father, "deifying man by heavenly teaching, putting His laws into our minds, and writing them on our hearts" (cf. Heb 8:10; Jer 31:33). Clement adds the words from Heb 8:12 (cf. Jer 31:34), "I will be merciful to them . . . and will not remember their sins" (Heb 8:10-12). In his description of the marital relationship, he applies words spoken to the entire community in Hebrews to encourage that marriages be conducted "with a true heart, in full assurance of faith, having hearts sprinkled from an evil conscience, and the body washed with pure water, and holding the confession of hope; for He is faithful that promised" (*Strom.* 4.20.126; Heb 10:22-23). He appeals to Hebrews again in the same context, encouraging his readers to "follow peace with all men, and holiness, without which no man shall see the Lord" (*Strom.* 4.20.128; Heb 12:15). He contrasts Esau's surrender of his birthright (*Strom.* 4.20.129; Heb 12:16-17) with the ethical conduct in which "marriage is honorable in all, and the bed undefiled" (*Strom.* 4.20.129; Heb 13:4). When he describes the true philosophy, he speaks of the law as being but "the image and shadow of the truth" (*Strom* 6.7.58; cf. Heb 10:1). These passages are useful for Clement for their verbal echoes, but they do not reflect Clement's focus on the cultic section of Hebrews.

In other passages Clement may be influenced by Hebrews in his description of the Levitical cultus without actually citing the epistle. He demonstrates an interest in some of the same themes that are found in Hebrews. Like the author of Hebrews, he describes the cosmic significance of the entry of the high priest into the heavenly sanctuary that is found in Heb 9. He shares with Hebrews an interest in the cosmic symbolism of the tabernacle, appealing to Lev 16 (cf. Heb 9:1-14) for his interpretation. In *Strom.* 5, he interprets the high priest's change of clothes and washings (Lev 16:4-5). Using the words "wash," "take off," and "put on" as key images, he indicates that changing of clothes by the priest suggests the descent of Christ into the realm of the senses. This act symbolizes the gnostic, who has come to faith in Christ, has changed clothes, and entered into a new world.[17]

16. Translation in Oulton and Chadwick, *Alexandrian Christianity*, 67.
17. Van den Hoek, *Clement of Alexandria and His Use of Philo*, 143.

In *Exc.* 27.1.112, he offers a parallel interpretation of Lev 19:3-7, describing the priest's entry within the second veil of the tabernacle and his removal of the altar of incense.

> The priest on entering within the second veil removed the plate at the altar of incense, and entering himself in silence with the Name engraved upon his heart, indicating the laying aside of the body which has become pure like the golden plate and bright through purification, . . . the putting away as it were of the soul's body on which was stamped the lustre of piety, by which he was recognized by the Principalities and Powers as having put on the Name. Now he discards this body, the plate which had become light, within the second veil, that is in the rational sphere of the second complete veil of the universe, at the altar of incense, that is, with the angels who are the ministers of prayers carried aloft.[18]

Although Clement does not cite Hebrews specifically, his interpretation of the priest's entry behind the veil as the departure from earth corresponds to the interpretation in Heb 9:11-14. His reference to the acquisition of a name and the acknowledgment by the angels may also be an echo of Heb 1:1-4.

Clement's use of Lev 16 is also evident in his description of the cosmic veil separating heaven and earth. The entry of the high priest behind the veil symbolizes the archangel's entry into the highest realm (*Exc.* 38.2.140; cf. Heb 9:7). Similarly, Clement describes the furniture of the tabernacle in *Strom.* 5.5.33, explaining that the place between the inner veil, where the high priest alone could enter, was the middle most point of heaven and earth. Clement is probably echoing Hebrews when he says that "the Lord, having come alone into the intellectual world, enters by his sufferings, introduced into the knowledge of the Ineffable, ascending above every name which is known by sound."

Clement sees the vestments of the high priest as the symbol of the heavenly bodies and by extension the covenant (συνθήκη) between heaven and earth. This combination of priesthood and covenant might have been suggested by Heb 8:1-13, which brings together the new covenant of Jeremiah 31 within the context of the high priesthood of Christ.[19]

Philo wrote at length on the significance of the Levitical regulations.[20] Clement demonstrates a fascination with the cultic activities of the OT,

---

18. Translation in Casey, *The Excerpta ex Theodoto of Clement of Alexandria*.
19. Van den Hoek, *Clement of Alexandria and His Use of Philo*, 119.
20. See *Spec.* 1.66-100; *Somn.* 1.215; *Mos.* 2.71-135. *QE* 2.51-124. Shorter passages include *Leg.* 2.56; 3.119; *Cher.* 101-6; *Ebr.* 87; *Migr.* 102f; *Her.* 215f.; *Congr.* 117; *Fug.* 108ff; *Somn.* 1.214f; *Spec.* 296f.

including the significance of the tabernacle and the priest's role. In *Strom.* 5.5.32–40, Clement takes up these themes in a discussion of the symbolism of the cult. Although he takes these themes in his own direction, he follows a formal structure established by Philo of Alexandria.[21] Clement shares Philo's cosmological interest but develops his own direction with an emphasis on the history of salvation and the movement of Christ downwards in incarnation and the true gnostic's ascent on the mystic meaning of the tabernacle and furnishings.

In exploring the theme of the cult, Clement appeals to both Philo and Hebrews, placing his own stamp on the materials he has inherited. In *Protrepticus*, he speaks of "this Jesus, who is eternal, the one great high priest of the one God and of the father, prays for and exhorts them" (12.93 LCL). He refers to Melchizedek in several places, exhibiting a fascination with this mysterious figure that is also evident in Philo and Hebrews (6:20—7:28). In *Strom.* 2.5.21 he says that Christ "is the only high priest, who alone possesses the knowledge of the worship of God. He is Melchizedek, King of peace, the most fit of all to head the race of men." In *Strom.* 2.22.136, he speaks of "assimilations as far as possible in accordance with right reason is the end, and rest to perfect adoption by the Son, which ever glorifies the Father by the great high priest who has deigned to call us brethren and fellow-heirs" (cf. Heb 2:11). In the same context he cites Heb 6:20, identifying Christ as the "high priest after the order of Melchizedek" (*Strom.* 2.22.136). In *Strom.* 4.25.16 he recalls the story of Melchizedek with no specific christological reference, focusing on the bread and wine of the story as a symbol of the Eucharist.

Although Clement demonstrates a knowledge of Hebrews in his description of the symbolism of the Levitical cultus, he reflects little direct dependence on Hebrews in his exposition of the Levitical text. His symbolic interpretation is indebted largely to Philo. With his christological interpretation of the Levitical cultus, he follows a path that is parallel to that of Hebrews but rarely directly dependent on Heb 7:1—10:25. Inasmuch as Philo's works, Hebrews, and Clement's works reflect on a cosmic symbolism of the Levitical cultus, they reflect common interest. While one may speak of an Alexandrian tradition that focuses on the cosmic symbolism of the tabernacle, that tradition took a variety of forms.

---

21. Runia, *Philo in Early Christian Literature*, 140.

The Significance of Faith

Faith is a major topic for Clement, who must articulate a view of faith that distinguishes him both from the Greek denigration of faith and the gnostic's own interpretation.[22] Clement claims that the knowledge of God can be found only by faith.[23] He appealed to numerous passages in Paul, John, Plato, Aristotle, Theophrastus, Stoics, Epicurus, and others.[24] For Clement, faith included several aspects, and he appealed to Scripture to justify each of them.[25]

Faith as Preconception

Clement recognized that Greeks denigrated faith, but that it is what they recognize as a deliberate preconception or anticipation. Appealing to Heb 11 for his argument, Clement says, "But faith, which the Greeks disparage, deeming it futile and barbarous, is a voluntary preconception (πρόληψις), the assent of piety—the substance of things hoped for, the evidence of things not seen" (*Strom.* 2.2.8; cf. Heb 11:1). He adds, "For hereby . . . the elders obtained a good report" (cf. Heb 11:2) and then echoes Heb 11:6 when he says, "But without faith it is impossible to please God." For Clement, faith is a clear vision of the future, which links faith and hope.[26]

Clement associates faith with the preconception of the mind articulated by Epicurus and other ancient writers who argued that the discovery of truth requires hope and anticipation, which depend on faith. The ἄπιστος is hopeless in the search for truth.[27] As a preconception that precedes comprehension, faith is the anticipation that makes knowledge possible. Thus, although Clement pursues larger philosophical issues than are addressed in Hebrews, he finds the language of Heb 1:1 useful for establishing the equivalence between faith and hope.

Faith as Assent and Choice

In opposition to gnostics who claimed that faith is not a matter of free choice, Clement maintained that faith is a choice, a way of saying "yes" to

---

22. See Osborn, "Arguments for Faith in Clement of Alexandria," 1–2.
23. See Osborn, *The Philosophy of Clement of Alexandria*, 128.
24. Osborn, *The Philosophy of Clement of Alexandria*, 128.
25. Osborn, *The Philosophy of Clement of Alexandria*, 128.
26. Osborn, "Arguments for Faith in Clement of Alexandria," 7.
27. Osborn, "Arguments for Faith in Clement of Alexandria," 5.

God, as the Scriptural demand suggests.[28] Indeed, unbelief shows that faith is possible (*Strom*. 2.12.55). Clement appeals to Heb 11 to establish that faith is a choice (*Strom* 2.4.13), arguing that the great heroes of faith made a conscious choice to believe. He combines the accounts of the faithful from Heb 11, saying,

> "By faith Abel offered to God a fuller sacrifice than Cain, by which he received testimony that he was righteous, God giving testimony to him respecting his gifts; and by it he, being, dead, yet speaketh," and so forth, down to "than enjoy the pleasures of sin for a season." Faith having, therefore justified these before the law, made them heirs of the divine promise. Why then should I review and adduce any further testimonies of faith from the history of our lands? "For the time would fail me were I to tell of Gideon, Barak, Samson, Jephtha, David, and Samuel, and the prophets."

Faith and Martyrdom

Assent to God in faith leads one to be a *martus* throughout one's life.[29] Although Clement does not provide much information about persecution and martyrdom in Alexandria, he is one of the first Christian thinkers to offer reflections on the significance of martyrdom from a speculative point of view.[30] Clement demonstrates a knowledge of a variety of traditions as he articulates his own view of martyrdom. He places martyrdom in the larger context of the gnostic's search for perfection. In *Strom*. 4, Clement distinguishes perfection in faith from ordinary faith, and recalls the endurance of the martyrs as examples of penance and the ultimate purification.[31] After citing Paul as an example of patient endurance (Phil 4:11–13), Clement recalls the list of heroes from Heb 10–11.

Clement begins with the exhortation from Heb 10:32–39.

> "But call to mind the former days, in which, after ye were illuminated, ye endured a great fight of afflictions; partly, whilst ye were made a gazing stock, both by reproaches and afflictions; and partly, whilst ye became companions of them that were so used. For he had compassion on me in my bonds, and took

---

28. Osborn, "Arguments for Faith in Clement of Alexandria," 7.
29. Osborn, "Arguments for Faith in Clement of Alexandria," 7.
30. Van den Hoek, "Clement of Alexandria on Martyrdom," 327.
31. Van den Hoek, "Clement of Alexandria on Martyrdom," 327.

with joy the spoiling of your goods, knowing that you have a better and enduring substance. Cast not away therefore your confidence, which hath great recompense of reward. For ye have need of patience that, after doing the will of God, ye may obtain the promise. For yet a little while, and He that cometh will come, and will not tarry. Now the just shall live by faith; and if any man draw back, my soul shall have no pleasure in him. But we are not of them that draw back unto perdition but of them that believe to the saving of the soul." (*Strom.* 4.16.102; Heb 10:32–39).

Clement then recalls the examples given in Hebrews, recalling the end of Heb 11 and the beginning of Heb 12:

"They were stoned, they were tempted, were slain with the sword. They wandered about in sheep-skins and goat-skins, being destitute, afflicted, tormented, of whom the world was not worthy. They wandered in deserts, in mountains, in dens, and caves of the earth. And all having received a good report, through faith, received not the promise of God" (what is expressed by a parasiopesis is left to be understood, viz., "alone"). He adds accordingly, "God having provided some better things for us (for he was good), that they should not without us be made perfect. Wherefore also, having encompassing us such a cloud," holy and transparent, "of witnesses, laying aside every weight, and the sin which doth so easily beset us, let us run with patience the race set before us, looking unto Jesus, the author and finisher of our faith." (*Strom.* 4.16.102–3).

Among the heroes who are named in Heb 11, Clement mentions Moses, who esteemed "the reproach of Christ greater riches than the treasures of Egypt" and he "forsook Egypt, not fearing the wrath of the king, for he endured as seeing him who is invisible" (cf. Heb 11:26–27). Clement does not follow Heb 11 sequentially but returns to mention Enoch, Noah, and Rahab before adding to the list of faithful heroes in the OT.

Clement recalls the words of Clement of Rome, who had also made extensive use of Hebrews:

"Let us fix our eyes on those who have yielded perfect service to his magnificent glory. Let us take Enoch, who, being by his obedience found righteous, was translated; and Noah, who, having believed, was saved; and Abraham, who for his faith and hospitality was called the friend of God, and was the father of Isaac." "For hospitality and piety, Lot was saved from Sodom." "For faith and hospitality, Rahab the harlot was saved." From patience and faith they walked about in goatskins, and sheepskins, and folds of camels' hair, proclaiming the kingdom of Christ. (*Strom.* 4.17.105; cf. Heb 11:38; cf. 1 Clem. 12:1)

Clement's list of heroes is not limited to Heb 11. He fills in a gap in the list in Heb 11, adding Lot, Elijah, Elisha, Ezekiel, John, and David. In a style reminiscent of Hebrews' direct appeal to the audience, Clement urges his readers to accept deprivation, concluding that "the more we are subjected to peril, the more knowledge are we counted worthy of" (*Strom.* 4.17.110).

Faith as Seeing the Invisible

The declaration in Heb 11:1 that faith is the "evidence of things not seen" introduces the author's distinction between the two spheres of reality: the visible and the invisible worlds. This definition of faith anticipates a major theme of Heb 11. Thus, "what is seen was made from things that are not visible" (11:2). Nevertheless, the people of faith can see the invisible. They "saw" God's promises from a distance (11:13). Moses "looked" (ἀπέβλεψεν) to the reward (11:26) and "saw the invisible" (11:27).

Prior to Hebrews, Philo had described faith in similar terms. Abraham obeyed the voice to go to the promised land because he could see beyond the truths of the Chaldeans, who observed only visible existence (ὁρατὴν οὐσίαν) instead of the invisible world (*Abr.* 69). Abraham followed the pure beam and was established by the sight of the intelligible world (*Abr.* 70–71). Thus he was able to see the invisible (*Abr.* 74–79).[32] Although Isaac was old and could not see, according to Philo, he could fix his eyes on intelligible realities, allowing him to see the intelligible world.[33] Philo argues on numerous occasions that the wise person is able to see the invisible (cf. *Deus* 3; *Post.* 15).

Clement shares the view that the believer can see the invisible, and he extends the metaphor to argue that the believer must proceed beyond what may be perceived with the senses. The crowd may know only what they can experience with the five senses. Clement argues that we walk by faith, not by sight (*Strom.* 5.6.34; cf. 2 Cor 5:7). The one who hopes, like the one who believes, sees with his mind both mental objects and future things, for one can see the good, not with the eyes, but with the mind (*Strom.* 5.13.16).[34]

---

32. Thompson, *Beginnings of Christian Philosophy*, 59
33. Thompson, *Beginnings of Christian Philosophy*, 60.
34. Osborn, "Arguments for Faith in Clement of Alexandria," 9.

Faith as Pilgrimage

A common motif of Middle Platonism is that of human existence as a pilgrimage.[35] Philo insists that the people of faith are strangers and pilgrims. Abraham was the exemplar of the one who was a wanderer and an outcast from his father's house (cf. *Her.* 267). He was a stranger and sojourner whose home was in the intelligible world (*Abr.* 262–76; *Conf.* 75–82). Indeed, this pilgrimage was the central theme of Philo's thought. Hebrews 11 develops this theme at considerable length. In describing Abraham and his descendants as ξένοι καὶ παρεπίδημοί (11:13) the author echoes Philo.

Clement shares the theme of pilgrimage and develops it in his debates with Basilides and other gnostics. He distinguishes his view from that of Basilides, who maintains that people are naturally strangers on earth because they have a supramundane nature. "No one is a stranger to the world by nature, their essence being one, and God one. But the elect man dwells as a sojourner, knowing all things to be possessed and disposed of; and he makes use of the things which the Pythagoreans make out to be the threefold good things" (*Strom* 4.25.165). He insists that those who are numbered among God's people will have heaven as their country (*Prot.* 10.108 LCL). The one who is a stranger on earth "despises the things that others admire in it, and lives in it as though it were a desert, that he may not be constrained by locality but that his own free will may show him to be just" (*Strom.* 7.12.77). The gnostic does not taste the good things of this earth but is a "stranger and a pilgrim" (ξένος καὶ παρεπίδημος) with regard to the inheritances here.

Clement draws the ethical consequences of living as strangers, indicating the impact of the Christian's status as an alien on the common pursuits of life. He says, "We ought to behave as strangers and pilgrims (cf. Heb 11:13), if married as though we were not married (cf. 1 Cor 7:29), if possessing wealth as though we did not possess it, if procreating children as giving birth to mortals, as those who are ready to abandon their property, as men who would even live without a wife if need be" (*Strom.* 3.14.95).

Clement's use of Hebrews in his understanding of faith indicates the importance of this homily for Clement. Both writers undoubtedly share the concerns to place faith within a philosophical context and to portray the faithful as "seeing the invisible." However, Clement demonstrates a far greater range of concerns than one finds in Hebrews. Despite his copious quotations from Hebrews, he discusses a wide range of issues that are not found in Hebrews.

---

35. Eisele, *Ein unerschütterliches Reich*, 378–80.

Conclusion

Although Clement makes abundant use of Hebrews, his usage does not indicate fully the place of Hebrews in the Alexandrian tradition. Many of the verbal echoes of Hebrews in Clement's work do not reflect the context or the significance of the passages in their original contexts. The place of Hebrews in the Alexandrian tradition is most apparent in the number of themes that Philo, Hebrews, and Clement share. All three authors apparently share in the philosophical discussions of the era and adapt these categories into the biblical faith in their own way. Clement draws heavily from Philo on the subject of the high priest, but he shares with Hebrews the christological and cosmological interpretation of the Levitical cult. Clement appeals to Hebrews on the two levels of education but ultimately subverts the claim in Hebrews that the entire community should aspire to the solid food of advanced teaching. While all three writers share major themes in their understanding of faith, each writer has distinctive elements that reflect the issues and controversies of his own time. Thus the Alexandrian tradition to which Hebrews belongs appears to be an extended conversation where the three writers overlap in numerous ways but maintain their own individual perspectives.

CHAPTER 9

THE EPISTLE TO THE HEBREWS AND THE PAULINE LEGACY

The existence of a school that preserved and transmitted the teaching of Paul has been a working assumption of Pauline scholarship for more than a century. With the common distinction between undisputed and pseudepigraphic letters, this assumption has taken on increased importance in the last generation for explaining the reception-history of Pauline theology.[1] Bultmann suggested that in these writings "essential motifs of the Pauline theology have remained alive."[2] Eduard Lohse suggested that "in the circle of the apostle's students, Paul's letters were constantly read and studied again and again" and that a "Pauline school tradition" developed and produced the letters in the Pauline corpus that are considered pseudepigraphic.[3] The existence of this school may account for the preservation and collection of Pauline letters and the continuing transmission of Paul's thought after his death.[4] Nevertheless, the nature and extent of this school leaves many unresolved questions. Did the authors know Paul personally? Did they only know his letters, or did they also have Pauline oral tradition? Did they adapt and interpret Paul's theology for changing situations? Do they represent a congruent Pauline tradition, or do we have competing forms?[5] What was the outcome of the legacy of Paul in the second and third generations?[6]

---

1. Originally published in *Restoration Quarterly* 47 (2005) 197–206. Gese, *Das Vermächtnis des Apostels*, 15. See also Beker, *Heirs of Paul*.

2. Bultmann, *Theology of the New Testament*.

3. Lohse, *Colossians and Philemon*, 182.

4. Schenke, "Das Weiterwirken des Paulus und die Pflege seines Erbes durch die Paulusschule," 233–47.

5. Gese, *Das Vermächtnis des Apostels*, 8.

6. See the articles in Babcock, ed., *Paul and the Legacies of Paul*.

One unresolved question in contemporary scholarship is the place of the Epistle to the Hebrews in the Pauline legacy. With only rare exceptions, no one posits Pauline authorship for Hebrews.[7] The textual tradition indicates the ancient church's assessment of this relationship. Hebrews stands between Romans and 1 Corinthians in p46. It appears between 2 Corinthians and Galatians in the Sahidic translation, and between Paul's letters to churches and the letters to individuals in the Bohairic translation.[8] Clement, Origen, and other church fathers assumed its Pauline character, although Origen maintained that only the νοήματα, not the style are Pauline.[9] At the same time, other canon lists and church fathers did not include Hebrews among the letters of Paul. The final placement of Hebrews in the canon between the Pauline corpus and the general epistles reflects the ambiguity regarding the relationship of Hebrews to the Pauline tradition.

Does Hebrews reflect an awareness of the letters of Paul or belong to the reception-history of Pauline thought? A. E. Barnett examined numerous phrases and concluded that literary reminiscences of Pauline letters are present in Hebrews.[10] C. Spicq and A. Vanhoye made statistical comparisons between Hebrews and the Pauline corpus;[11] Spicq concluded that Hebrews has a close affinity to the Prison Epistles,[12] and Vanhoye saw a close literary relationship between Hebrews and Ephesians. More recently, Ben Witherington argued that we may detect the influence of Galatians on Hebrews.[13] Martin Hengel and Otfried Hofius argued that the descent-ascent motif in Hebrews 1 and 2 is a development of the Philippian hymn.[14] All of these attempts to find a literary relationship between Hebrews and Paul have been unsuccessful, for all of the verbal contacts can be explained by the use of commonplace expressions in early Christian literature. Erich Grässer's conclusion is appropriate:

7. For a contemporary argument for Pauline authorship, see Voulgaris, "Hebrews: Paul's Fifth Epistle from Prison," 199–206.

8. Witherington, "The Influence of Galatians on Hebrews."

9. Eusebius, *HE* 6.25,11–14.

10. Barnett, *Paul Becomes a Literary Influence*, 69–85.

11. Vanhoye, "Epitre aux ephesiens et l'epitre aux Heb."

12. Spicq, *L'Épître aux Hébreux*, 1.162–64.

13. Witherington, "The Influence of Galatians on Hebrews," 146–52.

14. Hengel, *The Son of God*, 87–88. Hengel concludes: "One might almost regard the whole of Hebrews as a large-scale development of the christological theme which is already present in the Philippians hymn" (ibid., 88). See also Hofius, *Der Christushymnus Philipper 2.6–11*, 16: "The same Christology that shapes the Christ hymn in Philippians, also finds its focus in Hebrews." Hofius argues that both the Philippian hymn and Hebrews not only describe the way of Jesus with the schema of "preexistence–incarnation–death–exaltation, but also agree in the understanding of each step of the path of Christ" (ibid., 75).

"If our author knew Paul's letters, he did not use them as sources, for Hebrews has its own vocabulary and stylistic taste."[15]

Others have argued that, while no literary relationship exists between Paul and Hebrews, we can find evidence that the theology of Hebrews belongs to a Pauline tradition. These points of contact include the following christological and soteriological parallels that K. Backhaus summarizes: The preexistent Son (cf. Heb 1:2, 3, 5//1 Cor 8:6; 2 Cor 4:4; Phil 2:5f; Col 1:15-17; 1 Pet 1:20) humbles himself to become like humankind (Heb 2:14-17//Rom 8:3; Gal 4:4; Phil 2:7) and is thus obedient (Heb 5:8//Rom 5:19; Phil 2:8). He offers himself as a sacrifice (cf. Heb 9:28//1 Cor 5:7; Gal 2:20; Eph 5:2) with the giving of his blood (cf. Heb 9:11f, 14; 10:19, 29; 12:24; 13:12, 20// Rom 3:23; 5:9; 1 Cor 10:16; 11:27; Eph 1:7; 2:13; Col 1:20; 1 Pet 1:2, 19) for the people as ἀπολύτρωσις (Heb 9:15; 8:28; Rom 3:24; 1 Cor 1:30; Eph 1:2, 14; 4:30; Col 1:14), as ἱλαστήριον for sin (cf. Heb 2:17; 9:5//Rom 3:25) in a once-for-all act (Heb 7:27; 9:7, 12, 26; 10:10;//Rom 6:9f; 1 Pet 3:18). Thus he defeats the evil cosmic powers (cf. Heb 2:14//Col 2:15), is exalted above the angelic powers (cf. Heb 1:3-14//Eph 1:20f; Col 2:10; 1 Pet 3:22), inherits a new name (cf. Heb 1:4//Phil 2:9-11), the All is laid at his feet (cf. Heb 2;8//Rom 8:20f; 1 Cor 15:25-28; Phil 3:21), and he stands at the right hand of God interceding for the people (ἐντυγχάνω) (cf. Heb 7:25//Rom 8:34). The atoning death of Jesus is for both Paul and Hebrews a key theme; the cultic interpretation of this atoning death develops — in a distinctive way — an interpretation schema that, outside Hebrews, is to be found primarily in Pauline literature (cf. Rom 3:21-26; 1 Cor 5:7; Eph 5:2) and rarely anywhere else. Anyone who looks for literature that corresponds to the tradition-historical outline of Hebrews may find the closest analogies in Philippians, Ephesians, and 1 Peter; in other words, those writings of Paul or the Pauline school which come from a relatively late stage of development.[16]

In addition to the themes that converge in Hebrews and the letters of Paul, the concluding chapter of Hebrews raises questions about the relationship of this homily to Paul. The paraenetic style of 13:1-6 is analogous to the moral instruction in Paul's letters. The concluding words of 13:18-25 are analogous to the parousia, request for prayer, final greetings, and prayer that one finds at the end of Pauline letters. The reference to Timothy's release (from prison?) adds an additional Pauline flavor to the close of the homily. This apparent relationship to the Pauline letters is evidence to many scholars that Hebrews belongs to a Pauline school, while others conclude that the

---

15. Grässer, "Der Hebräerbrief 1938-1963," 157.
16. Backhaus, "Der Hebraerbrief und die Paulus Schule," 187.

closing words are the work of a redactor who added the ending in order to bring Hebrews into the circle of Pauline correspondence.

While many of the parallels can be explained as nothing more than the common tradition of the early church, other points of contact call for explanation. I now turn to the most compelling parallels. These include: a) the Christology of Hebrews in chapters 1–2; b) the atoning work of Christ in chapters 5–10; c) the response of faith in 10:36—12:12; and d) the concluding chapter.

The Christology of Chapters 1–2

The first two chapters, with the celebration of the preexistence, descent, and exaltation of Christ above the angels resonates with the Christology of the Pauline tradition. The use of Ps 110:1 to declare the exaltation of Christ above all intermediary powers appears in Rom 8:34, where the one at God's right hand is the assurance that "neither angels nor principalities nor things to come nor powers" can threaten the believer (8:37). Moreover, the exegetical tradition that binds together the reference to the one who has everything "under this feet" (Ps 8:6) with the claim that the enemies are "a footstool for your feet" (Ps 110:1) in the first two chapters of Hebrews is also present in 1 Cor 15:25–27, according to which Christ now reigns until he has conquered death, the last enemy. These two psalms are also present in Eph 1:20–22 in the declaration that the exalted Christ is supreme over the cosmic powers.

The acknowledgment in Hebrews that "we do not yet see everything in subjection to him" (2:8) has no parallel with the cosmic Christology of Colossians and Ephesians but echoes Paul's claim in 1 Corinthians 15 that Christ has will put all things under his feet only at the end (15:23–28). For both Paul and Hebrews, the coming of Christ anticipates the final victory. According to Hebrews, through death Christ destroyed "the one who has the power of death, that is, the devil" (2:14), while for Paul death is the last enemy (1 Cor 15:26) and will be defeated at the end (1 Cor 15:55).

These points of contact are insufficient to establish either literary dependence of Hebrews on Paul or the trajectory of Pauline thought within a school. The descent-ascent theme belongs not only to Paul but to early Christian tradition. The likelihood that Paul adapted the Philippian hymn from early Christian tradition suggests that the descent-ascent theme was present near the beginning of early Christian reflection. Moreover, the link between Ps 8 and Ps 110 most likely occurred prior to both Paul and Hebrews in early Christian reflection. We may also note the creativity in the themes of the first two chapters of Hebrews that have no parallel in Paul. The motif of Christ as the ἀρχηγός leading his people (2:10) to glory through his own suffering and of the one who is a merciful and faithful high priest are is a distinctive contribution of Hebrews.

The Atoning Work of Christ and the Place of the Torah

In his treatment of the saving significance of the death of Christ in 4:14—10:18, the author does not employ Paul's juridical language of δικαιοσύνη. Indeed, Erich Grässer has analyzed the use δικαιοσύνη in Hebrews, noting that, while Hebrews shares this terminology, it is never used in a Pauline sense.[17] Nevertheless, we may observe a convergence of atonement theology in Paul and Hebrews. Like Paul, the author denies the efficacy of all human deeds and affirms that salvation is sola gratia (cf. Heb 4:16).[18] For both Paul and Hebrews the Christ event is the change of aeons and a once-for-all event (ἐφάπαξ, Rom 6:11; ἅπαξ, Heb 9:26) that takes away sin. Even the cultic interpretation of the work of Christ, which appears to be the unique contribution of Hebrews, has antecedents in Pauline tradition. Paul's claim in Rom 8:34 that the one who is at the right hand of God now intercedes for us (ἐντυγχάνει) anticipates the author's claim that the exalted high priest intercedes for his people (Heb 7:25). This cultic understanding is also present in the interpretation of the death of Christ as a προσφορά and θυσία in Eph 5:2.

This claim necessitates for both Paul and the author of Hebrews an assessment of Israel's traditional means of atonement. If the atoning sacrifice of Christ is the only means of atonement, both writers must explain the place of the first covenant in the divine economy. Both writers insist that the Christ event is the inauguration of the new covenant (cf. 1 Cor 11:25; 2 Cor 3:3-6) of Jeremiah. Although Jeremiah never associates the new covenant with sacrificial blood, both Paul and Hebrews connect Jeremiah's new covenant with the "blood of the covenant" of Exod 24:8. Paul's rendering of the eucharistic words, "the new covenant in my blood" (1 Cor 11:25) implicitly associates the new covenant of Jeremiah with a blood sacrifice, and the author of Hebrews insists that the new covenant was inaugurated with blood (9:18-20). In dependence on Jeremiah, both writers speak of a changed inner disposition of the heart (2 Cor 3.3; 4:6; 5:12; Heb 10:22; 13:9).[19]

While Paul's new covenant theology has a cultic significance only in the Lord's Supper tradition that he inherited, the author of Hebrews

---

17. Grässer, "Rechtfertigung im Hebräerbrief," 80-86.
18. Grässer, "Rechtfertigung im Hebräerbrief," 87.
19. Lehne, *The New Covenant in Hebrews*, 75.

interprets Jeremiah's prophecy exclusively in terms of the cult. Nevertheless, the two writers hold much in common. The inauguration of a new covenant involves the replacement of the old covenant, which both writers associate with the law and the old aeon. Both Paul and the author indicate that the νόμος was weak and associated with the flesh (Heb 7:28; cf. 7:19; Rom 8:3). For Hebrews, the law was "weak and useless" (7:19), and it appointed priests who beset with weakness (7:28). This covenant was not blameless (8:7), for its regulations were only δικαιώματα σαρκός (9:10) that could never take away sins (10:4). The mortality of the priests and the annual repetition of the sacrifices attested to the imperfection of the Levitical system established by the law. Consequently, it failed to perfect (cf. 7:11) or cleanse the conscience of the worshiper (9:9), insofar as it was only a "shadow of the coming good things" (10:1). Because of its imperfection a "change in the law" (νόμου μετάθεσις, 7:12) and priesthood are necessary.

Although the focus of the author of Hebrews is on the sacrificial cultus while Paul's focus is on the rules for admission of gentiles, the two writers offer analogous critiques of the law. When Paul is faced with the imposition of ritual requirements of the law, he insists that the law belongs to the old aeon, and that those who wish to return to its regulations will be under a curse (cf. Gal 3:10). Just as Hebrews insists that "the blood of bulls and goats cannot take away sins" (10:4), Paul insists that the law cannot make one righteous (Rom 3:20; Gal 2:21). Thus both writers have in common a central point derived from the OT by which they make a revolutionary move, challenging the validity of the law. For Paul, it is the promise to Abraham (Gal 3:16ff; Rom 4), while for Hebrews it is the figure of Melchizedek and the oath of God associated with him (Ps 110:4) that calls the law into question.[20]

Nevertheless, despite these points of contact between Paul and Hebrews, the two writers have significant differences in their treatment of the law. Hebrews has no analogy to Paul's insistence that the commandment is "holy and good" (Rom 7:12). The author of Hebrews goes considerably beyond Paul when he insists, not only that the law has been superseded but that it was ineffective from the beginning (9:9–10). For the author of Hebrews, the law belongs not only to the old aeon but also to the earthly sphere within his spatial dualism.[21] The effectiveness of the work of Christ rests on the fact that it takes place within the heavenly world. Consequently, the sacrifice in the heavens is superior to the sacrifice on earth, resulting in the cleansing of the conscience rather than the cleansing of the flesh (cf. 9:11–14).

20. Feld, "Der Hebräerbrief."
21. Grässer, "Rechtfertigung im Hebräerbrief," 88.

These differences between Paul and Hebrews indicate that the author neither reflects the direct influence of any of the Pauline letters nor serves as the slavish imitator of Paul. Nevertheless, we see parallel movements of thought that leave open the possibility that Hebrews has developed motifs of Pauline thought in a creative way. The combination of similarities and differences with the Pauline corpus suggests that the author, who now writes long after the issues of the admission of gentiles has been settled, is taking Pauline theology in a new direction.

The Response of Faith

For the author of Hebrews, as for Paul, πίστις is the appropriate response to God's grace. He challenges his listeners not to follow the example of Israel's ἀπιστία (3:12, 19; cf. 4:2) but to imitate those who through πίστις and μακροθυμία inherited the promises. Indeed, he cites Hab 2:4, a text that Paul cites both in Romans (1:17) and Galatians (3:13). The reference to Hab 2:4 again suggests the possibility that the author of Hebrews belongs to a Pauline school tradition. However, one must note that Heb 10:37 is a mixed citation in which the first line is taken from Isa 26:20.[22] In Heb 10:38, LXX citation is ὁ δὲ δίκαός μου ἐκ πίστεως ζήσεται), in contrast to both citations of Hab 2:4 in Paul, which omit μου.[23] In contrast to the interpretation of Hab 2:4 in the Dead Sea Scrolls, where it refers to those who keep the law,[24] Hebrews and Paul agree that the passage refers to the πίστις of members of the community. However, the author's comments indicate that πίστις in Hebrews is the equivalent of patient endurance (cf. 10:36; cf. 12:1-3). The author contrasts those who have πίστις with those who "shrink back" (10:39). Whereas Paul understands πίστις as the acceptance of the saving events in Jesus Christ, the author of Hebrews understands it as the certainty of the unseen world that becomes the basis for patient endurance.[25] In Hebrews, πίστις never has a christological referent.

For both Paul and Hebrews, Abraham is the primary example of πίστις, and believers are heirs of the promise with him (Rom 4:16; Gal 3:13; Heb 2:16; 6:11-12; 9:15). According to Paul, Abraham trusted God's power to give him an heir even when he considered his body "as good as dead" (Rom 4:19, νενεκρωμένον) and the "deadness" (νεκρώσις) of Sarah's womb. According to Hebrews, Abraham demonstrated faith when both he and Sarah

---

22. Lindemann, *Paulus im ältesten Christentum*, 236.
23. Lindemann, *Paulus im ältesten Christentum*, 236.
24. See Witherington, *Influence of Galatians on Hebrews*, 149.
25. Grässer, *Der Glaube im Hebräerbrief*, 65.

were "as good as dead" (νενεκρωμένου). However, Paul's primary focus in Romans and Galatians is the principle of justification by faith, which he derives from his reading of Gen 15:6 (cf. Rom 4:3; Gal 3:6), while for Hebrews Abraham exemplifies the author's understanding of πίστις. Abraham exemplified this quality through his patient endurance (μακροθυμία, 6:12) when he believed God's oath (6:13–18). When he gave tithes to Melchizedek, he indicated the superiority of the latter (Heb 7:7). By departing his homeland (12:8), living in tents as an alien (11:9), and by looking for the transcendent city and country (11:10, 14–16), he exemplified the author's definition of faith as the "evidence of things not seen" (11:1).

Although Paul and the author of Hebrews call for faith as the appropriate response to God and point to Abraham as the exemplar of this response, the treatment of these themes is remarkably different. The verbal links with Paul's letters are insufficient to establish a relationship between Hebrews and the Pauline letters, and the treatment of both πίστις and the narrative of Abraham depart so much from Paul that they are scarcely evidence that the author belongs to a Pauline school.

The Epistolary Ending and the Letters of Paul

The final chapter of Hebrews has been especially important for a comparison with the letters of the Pauline tradition, for here the homily takes on an epistolary character. The loosely connected ethical instructions in 13:1–6 resemble the paraenetic sections of the letters. Exhortations to practice brotherly love (φιλαδελφία, 13:1), hospitality (φιλοξενία, 13:2), and marital chastity (13:4) and to avoid the love of money (13:5–6) all have parallels in the Pauline tradition.[26] Similarly, the final words in 13:18–25 have numerous parallels to the Pauline tradition. The imperatives of 13:1–17 provide the transition to the imperative "pray for us" (13:18; cf. 1 Thess 5:25; cf. Rom 15:30). The epistolary ending offers an authorial voice for the first time in Hebrews, as the author moves from the "ecclesiological we"[27] that includes author and listeners to the authorial voice of the author, moving from the first person plural to the first person singular with the twofold παρακαλῶ (13:19, 22). The author's prayer (15:20–21; cf. 1 Thess 5:23), the future travel plans of the author and Timothy (13:23; cf. Phil 2:19–30), the final greetings (13:24), the reference to the writing of the book (13:22; cf. Rom 16:22; Gal

---

26. On φιλαδελφία, see Rom 12:10; 1 Thess 4:9; on φιλοξενία, see Rom 12:13; 1 Tim 3:2; Titus 1:8; on chastity, see 1 Thess 4:3–8; on the love of money, see 1 Tim 3:3; 2 Tim 3:2. See also Thuren, *Das Lopopfer der Hebräer*, 57–70.

27. Weiss, *Der Brief an die Hebräer*, 746.

6:10), and the benediction (13:25) resemble the conclusion of a Pauline letter. For some scholars, these similarities are evidence that the author belongs to a Pauline school. For others, the difference in style between chapter 13 and the first twelve chapters is evidence that the final chapter was added by a later hand.[28] Others argue that only 13:22-25 belong to a later hand in an attempt to bring Hebrews under the Pauline umbrella.[29]

Despite the similarities of the ethical instructions in 13:1-6 to Pauline paraenesis, this unit has significant differences as well. In the first place, after the first imperative (13:1), each of the following instructions has a common form that is not found in the letters of the Pauline tradition. Each imperative is followed by a subordinate clause stating the reason for the desired conduct of community members (γάρ, v. 2; ὡς, v. 3; γάρ, v. 4; γάρ, v. 5, ὥστε, v. 6). Inasmuch as the instructions of 13:1-6 are commonplace in early Christian ethical instruction, they are not exclusively Pauline. Furthermore, although the style changes in 13:1-6, numerous points of contact connect the ethical instructions to earlier parts of the book. Hence they do not provide evidence that Hebrews belongs to a Pauline school.

The epistolary closing in 13:18-25 has several elements of the conclusion of a Pauline letter, as I have indicated above. The authorial voice that begins in 13:18 with the request for prayer and the assurance of the writer's good conscience is the first indication in Hebrews of the author's acquaintance with the listeners. The expressed hope that he will be restored to them soon (13:19) indicates the intimacy of his relationship to them. The doxology in 13:20-21 is reminiscent, not only of Pauline doxologies but also of 1 Pet 5:10. Because the language of the doxology probably reflects the church's liturgy, it does not correspond in detail with the vocabulary of Paul or the author of Hebrews. However, the reference to the "blood of the eternal covenant" (13:20) rings with the vocabulary of Hebrews. The epistolary closing indicates only that the author is well acquainted with his audience, and that he leads them in a familiar doxology.

In the postscript in 13:22-25, the author's request that the community bear with his word of exhortation is a reference to the entire homily. The comment about the brevity of the letter, a commonplace in antiquity, appears elsewhere only in 1 Peter (5:12). The final greetings are so common in ancient letters that they cannot be understood as indications of a relationship to the

---

28. See the discussion in Wedderburn, "The 'Letter' to the Hebrews and Its Thirteenth Chapter." Wedderburn argues that the differences in language and style between the first twelve chapters and chapter 13, combined with the references in chapter 13 to the first twelve chapters, suggest that a different author wrote the final chapter to a new situation, but with the knowledge of the content of chapters 1-12.

29. See Grässer, *An die Hebräer*, 1.17-18.

Pauline letters. Only the reference to Timothy's impending visit (v. 23) suggests the author's relationship to a Pauline school. If we assume that Timothy is Paul's companion by that name, the reference indicates only that the author and Timothy share an acquaintance with this community.

If the epistolary ending is insufficiently Pauline to suggest the homily's place within a Pauline school, one must also conclude that it is not the work of a scribe attempting to give it a Pauline flavor. The author of this unit claims neither Pauline authorship nor apostolic authority. If 13:22–25 were the work of a scribe attempting to make this work more Pauline, one must ask why the redactor did not place the Pauline stamp on this unit more clearly.[30] Thus the conclusion to Hebrews is most likely the author's own reflection, not that of a Paulinist, and its content contains both elements that provide a fitting conclusion to the author's message and belong to the liturgical and letter-writing traditions of the church.

Conclusion

A study of these points of convergence between Paul and the author of Hebrews indicates that we have no compelling reason to consider the author of Hebrews a student of Paul or to place the homily within the reception of Pauline theology. The author's creativity and originality precludes a diachronic relationship to Paul.[31] Nevertheless, the cumulative effect of the topics shared by the two authors suggests that a synchronous relationship may exist between parallel theological movements that existed in proximity to each other.[32] Since Hebrews was probably written after the Pauline letters, it is probable that the author was aware of Pauline reflection. While the reference to Timothy in Heb 13:23 is not compelling evidence that the author belonged to the Pauline school with Timothy, it indicates that the author and Timothy knew the same community. If, as the expression ἀπὸ τῆς Ἰταλίας (13:24) suggests, the author is writing to Rome, the recipients are probably members of the Roman community who are acquainted with Paul's coworker.[33] Thus the relationship between Hebrews and the Pauline tradition is minimal.

---

30. Weiss, *Hebräer*, 38.
31. Feld, „Hebraerbrief," 3561.
32. Backhaus, "Paulus-Schule," 192.
33. Backhaus, "Paulus-Schule," 197.

CHAPTER 10

INSIDER ETHICS FOR OUTSIDERS

ETHICS FOR ALIENS IN HEBREWS

Although the author of Hebrews describes his work as a "word of exhortation" (13:22), he offers remarkably few specific guidelines for the behavior of his readers. Until chapter 13, the author's primary hortatory focus is that the readers "hold on" (κατέχειν, 3:6, 14; 10:23; κρατεῖν, 4:14; 6:18) and "draw near" (προσέρχεσθαι, 4:16; 7:25; 10:1, 22; 12:18, 22) rather than fall away (2:3; 3:12; 6:4–6; cf. 10:26–31). Consequently, as interpreters have recognized, the imperatival form and the content of the instructions in Heb 13:1–6 stand apart from the exhortations in the first twelve chapters. The most extended argument of the NT ends with only five specific injunctions. As Knut Backhaus has suggested, "The theological mountain was in labor and gave birth to a moral mouse."[1] Because of this anomaly, the relationship of Heb 13 to the rest of the homily has been a continuing question.

The instructions in Heb 13:1–6 comprise a rhythmic and coherent unity.[2] After the appeal for brotherly love (φιλαδελφία), which is the heading for specific instructions, the author gives four admonitions, adding a reason for each. Brotherly love (φιλαδελφία), hospitality (φιλοξενία), an honorable marriage (τίμιος ὁ γάμος), and a life that is free from the love of money (ἀφιλαργυρία) in Heb 13:1–6 belongs to the common storehouse of early Christian moral instruction and Greco-Roman virtues.[3] Φιλαδελφία,

---

1. Originally published in *Restoration Quarterly* 56 (2014) 137–46. Backhaus, "Auf Ehre und Gewissen!" 215.
2. Thuren, *Das Lobopfer der Hebräer*, 208.
3. See φιλαδελφία in Rom 12:10; ; 1 Thess 4:9; φιλάδελφος in 1 Pet 3:3; φιλόξενος in 1 Tim 3:2; Titus 1:8; 1 Pet 4:9. In Rom 12:10; 1 Pet 4:9, as in Heb 13:2, φιλοξεν- appears under the heading of love within the community. Πορνεία is the most common vice listed in early Christian ethical lists. In 1 Tim 3:2–3, ἀφιλαργυρία appears alongside φιλόξενος. Cf. φιλαργ- in 1 Tim 6:10; 2 Tim 3:2. Cf. also the warnings against the synonymous term πλεονεξία/πλεονέξειν in the undisputed Pauline letters (Rom 1:29;

φιλοξενία, and ἀφιλαργυρία are well-known Hellenistic virtues. Φιλαδελφία appears in the LXX only in 4 Maccabees; φιλοξενία and ἀφιλαργυρία do not appear in the LXX. Only the avoidance of πορνεία is commonplace in the LXX. The care of prisoners (13:3) has no parallel in the moral instruction of the NT, Jewish, or Greek traditions of moral instruction. The ethic of Heb 13:1–6, like the paraenesis of Paul, is an insider ethic that addresses the needs of the community rather than the larger issues of society.[4]

The sudden appearance of these imperatives and the new vocabulary for ethical instruction raises questions that remain unresolved despite the attention that interpreters have given to the topic. What is the relationship between the moral instruction here and the argument of the first twelve chapters? Do the instructions suggest the author's attempt to imitate Pauline paraenesis? Why does the author give only an insider ethic? Why did the author limit the ethical instruction to the five imperatives? Some interpreters conclude that chapter 13 is an addendum to the homily, either by the author or by a later hand.[5] Interpreters who regard chapter 13 as the original conclusion to the homily nevertheless recognize the problem of connecting the ethical instructions in 13:1–6 with the argument of the rest of the homily. In this paper I will argue that the insider ethic presented here is integrally related to the portrayal of the readers as the "wandering people" who are outsiders in their own homeland. It is the expression of the new identity of converts who have lost their old identity. I will also argue that the author follows the pattern already established in Jewish diaspora communities for maintaining cohesion in a hostile climate.

Ethos and Identity in Hebrews

Studies in social identity theory have shown that the identity of a group rests on a shared worldview—"the way things are."[6] A society's worldview ("the assumed structure of reality"), as Clifford Geertz has argued, is inseparable from its ethos ("the approved style of life"). The coercive "ought" grows out

---

1 Cor 5:10; 6:10). See Thuren, *Das Lobopfer der Hebräer*, 57–73.

4. Backhaus, "Auf Ehre und Gewissen," 218–19; cf. Schenck, "Die Paränese Hebr 13,16," 73–106; Horrell, *Solidarity and Difference*, 99–100. "A primary goal of Paul's discourse is to engender communal solidarity, and to attempt to restore and strengthen it in the face of conflict and division" (ibid., 100). See also Wolter, "Identität und Ethos bei Paulus," 168.

5. Cf. Wedderburn, "The 'Letter' to the Hebrews and Its Thirteenth Chapter," 390–405.

6. Horrell, *Solidarity and Difference*, 92.

of a comprehensibly factual "is."[7] The symbolic universe creates cohesion for communities that share in its myths, rituals, and way of life,[8] separating them from others who do not share their symbolic world. Thus those who share in a symbolic world share the moral norms that express their identity. Conversion involves a radical reorientation and resocialization of the convert. If conversion is lasting, it is accompanied by the establishment of a new symbolic world, identity, and ethos.

Hebrews offers abundant evidence of the continuing challenges that confront the readers. Soon after their conversion (φωτισθέντες, 10:32; cf. 6:4), they endured sufferings (παθημάτων). Although the author says little about the persecutors, he places special emphasis on the public humiliation and shame that followed the readers' conversion, as θεατριζόμενοι suggests. They were made a public spectacle, exposed to insults (ὀνειδισμοῖς) and persecutions (θλίψεις). This experience suggests the reasons for the author's consistent focus on suffering, shame, and the outsider status. Conversion had resulted in the loss of the readers' primary relationships and the symbolic world that they had formerly shared with their surroundings, creating a clear boundary between the house church and the world.[9]

The community's suffering is not a thing of the past (12:4-11) but a reality to be endured in the present (10:36; 12:7). Indeed, with the passage of time, the experience of suffering has called the community's alternative symbolic world into question, for they question the claims of the Son's exaltation: "We do not yet see all things in subjection to him" (2:8c). Indeed, the description of them as "refugees" (καταφυγόντες, 6:18) indicates their continuing outsider status. The imagery of a people in the wilderness (3:7—4:11; 12:18-29) that dominates the homily suggests the homelessness of their existence and their outsider status. In challenging his readers to go outside the camp and bear the abuse of Christ (13:13), the author offers no immediate relief from the outsider status but indicates that this existence belongs to the very nature of faith.

The author responds to the community's alienation by presenting the great examples of faith as outsiders in their own time. The world (κόσμος) is an alien place, as Noah demonstrated when he "condemned the world" (11:7) by obeying God's command. Abraham, an alien in his own land (11:9), was among the patriarchs who were "strangers and pilgrims on

---

7. Geertz, *The Interpretation of Cultures*, 126.

8. Berger and Luckmann, *The Social Construction of Reality*, 107.

9. Conversion in antiquity, as in many societies today, resulted in the loss of the primary relationships that had once provided the converts' identity. Numerous examples of conversion to philosophy indicate the disorientation of those who had abandoned their ancestral teaching. See Sandnes, *A New Family*, 21-31.

the earth" (11:13). Like the readers, Moses experienced the ὀνειδισμός of Christ (11:26). Indeed, the author says of all of the patriarchs that the "world was not worthy" of them (11:38). Jesus was the forerunner in enduring suffering (2:9–10) and shame (12:2; 13:13). At the conclusion of the homily, the author invites his readers to follow Jesus "outside the camp, bearing his abuse" (ὀνειδισμός, 13:13).

The marginalization of the community is analogous to the experience of others who lived outside the dominant culture. Jewish communities of the diaspora faced a similar marginalization. Philo speaks of the reduction in status among Alexandrian Jews, whom Flaccus denounced as "foreigners and aliens" (ξένους καὶ ἐπήλυδας, *Flacc.* 54) without basic rights in the city. Like the readers in Hebrews, Jews were robbed of their homes and property and liable to fatal violence (*Flacc.* 53–54). Philo's concern that the violence against Jews would spread to other cities (*Flacc.* 47) suggests the outsider status of Jews elsewhere in the diaspora.

Conversion to Judaism brought severe consequences, transforming insiders into outsiders and causing the painful abandonment by the extended family and abuse directed at the convert. According to Philo, conversion to Judaism meant that the proselytes made a sociological, judicial, and ethnic break with pagan society.[10] This process led to enmity and dangers from their family and neighbors. According to Philo the proselyte experiences severe anguish

> because he has turned his kinsfolk, who in the ordinary course of things would be his sole confederates, into enemies, by coming as a pilgrim to truth and the honouring of One who alone is worthy of honor, and by leaving the mythical fable and multiplicity of sovereigns, so highly honoured by parents and grandparents and ancestors and blood relationships of this immigrant to a better home. (*Spec. Leg.* 4.178 LCL)

Similarly Aseneth, the Egyptian convert and wife of Joseph, cries out, "All people have come to hate me, and on top of these my father and mother, because I too, have come to hate their gods and have destroyed them" (*Jos. Asen.* 11:4–6; cf. 127). Thus converting from one group to another involved cutting ties with family and neighbors, creating the strong need to establish new bonds and a new identity.[11]

Those who were outsiders in their own society had a special interest in recalling biblical narratives of Israelites who lived outside the promised

---

10. Seland, *Strangers in the Light*, 70.
11. Seland, *Strangers in the Light*, 75.

land.[12] Philo describes Abraham, Isaac, and Jacob as sojourners (*Conf. Ling.* 76-82). Abraham asks, "Am I not a wanderer (μετανάστης) from my country, an outcast, an alien from my father's house. Do not all men call me excommunicate, exile, desolate, and disenfranchised" (*Her.* 26). Philo's frequent statements about the estrangement of the wise is occasioned by the estrangement of the Jews in Alexandrian society.[13]

An Insider Identity for Outsiders

The author's challenge in Hebrews is to replace the symbolic world, the identity, and the relationships that the readers have lost. The opening chapter affirms that God has addressed this community of outsiders in a son. As recipients of God's ultimate word, the readers have a status that is qualitatively different from that of the ancestors, who heard God's voice in a partial and piecemeal fashion (1:1-2). The exaltation of the Son above the angels (1:4), as the author will argue, is the occasion for the entrance of the ἀρχηγός (2:10) and πρόδρομος (6:20) into the heavenly sanctuary, the appointment of the Son as heavenly high priest according to the order of Melchizedek (5:5-10; 6:19-20), and the ultimate sacrifice that takes place in heaven (8:1—10:18). Thus the author points disoriented readers to the reality that is "not of this creation" (9:11; cf. 9:1), thus not perceptible to the senses (2:8c; 11:1; 12:18), in an attempt to rebuild their symbolic world. If the readers do not yet see the ultimate victory (2:8c) and currently live as outsiders in this world, they can find assurance in recognizing an alternative reality as their symbolic world.

The author not only insists on the existence of a new reality but provides a new identity for his readers as participants in this alternative reality. The outsiders in this world are the ones who are about to inherit salvation; even angels serve them (1:14). They—not the dominant culture—are "partakers in a heavenly calling" (3:1) who have the opportunity to follow the ἀρχηγός into the heavenly rest (4:3, 9-10). Indeed, the readers may already "draw near" to the heavenly world in worship (προσέρχεσθαι, 4:14; 10:22; 12:18) and "go out" (ἐξέρχεσθαι, 13:13; cf. 11:8-10) from the majority culture.[14] The repeated use of ἔχομεν/ἔχοντες (4:14, 15; 6:19; 8:1; 10:19, 34; 13:14) associated with the heavenly reality indicates that the readers find their identity in belonging to an alternative world. Thus they

---

12. Feldmeier, "The 'Nation' of Strangers," 241.
13. Feldmeier, *Die Christen als Fremdef*, 29.
14. Backhaus, "Auf Ehre und Gewissen," 222.

are like the patriarchs, who are strangers in this world because they are on a journey to another world (cf. 11:13-16).

Those who belong to another world are outsiders who travel together, sharing a common identity as they are homeless in this world. The readers discover their identity not only in belonging to an alternative reality but also in their membership in the family that accompanies them in worship and in the journey to the heavenly κατάπαυσις. They exist in both continuity and discontinuity with Israel. Ancient Israelites are their ancestors (1:1; 3:9; 11:2). Like the Israelites, they are the "seed of Abraham" (2:16), God's house (3:1-6), and the ἅγιοι (3:1; 6:10; 13:24) who have heard the good news (4:2). In their faithfulness they complete the narrative of faithful heroes (11:39-40). However, their participation in the heavenly sacrificial ministry and the ultimate saving event transcends the experience of Israelites, who knew only the provisional and impermanent priestly service (1:1-2; 7:20-28; 9:23—10:4) and the palpable Mount Sinai (12:18-24). The law, the central symbol of Judaism, is a mere shadow of things to come (10:1), and the commandment is "weak and useless" (7:18). The Jewish boundary markers play no role for the community. The only Sabbath of concern to Hebrews is the ultimate place of rest (4:3-11); the earthly cult and the food laws do not benefit the worshiper (9:9-10). Nor does circumcision play any role for the community. Thus the author offers a symbolic world that employs the symbols of Israel but also transcends them.[15]

The family language is pervasive. The listeners are "of one" (2:11)—of the same family—with the ἀρχηγός, who is not ashamed to call them "brothers" (2:11-13). The author says nothing of their ethnic identity; what unites them is the shared confession (3:1; 4:14; 10:23). The one whom they confess is their brother who both shares the suffering of the outsider (cf. 2:17; 4:15) and leads them to the promised land. He is the Son over God's house, and the readers find their identity in being God's house (3:6). The current suffering of the readers may be a sign of their outsider status in this world, but from the alternative perspective it is a sign that they are God's children (12:4-11). The readers have assumed the role of the family, demonstrating love and service to others within the community (6:9-10). The author challenges them to continue the familial roles of offering encouragement to one another (3:12; 10:24-25). Consequently the author addresses the readers as ἀδελφοί (3:1, 12; 10:19; 13:22-23).[16]

---

15. Richard Johnson, *Going outside the Camp*, 129.

16. Some witnesses, including ℵ, have ἀδελφοί in 6:9 rather than ἀγαπητοί. The latter, which appears only here in Hebrews, has the better attestation.

The readers are not only a family united by their confession; they are "holy brothers" (3:1), the community of those who "are being sanctified" (2:11; 10:10, 14) as a result of the ultimate sacrifice of Jesus, who suffered "outside the camp" in order to "sanctify the people" (13:12). Consequently, like ancient Israel, they are "the holy ones" (cf. 6:9) who are set apart from the world and dedicated to God. As a cultic community, they have drawn near to the heavenly Mount Zion rather than the earthly Mount Sinai (12:18-29).[17] They engage in a sacrificial ministry (12:28) but not in the earthly sanctuary (9:1-14). Their participation in the heavenly cultus gives them both an alternative symbolic world and an identity that distinguishes them from the dominant culture.

The images of the family and holy people establish a strong demarcation between insiders and outsiders. The author speaks only obliquely about the insiders in this world, preferring to speak of the community's suffering in the passive voice (cf. 10:33; 13:3) rather than name the offenders. His affirmation "We have an altar, from which those who serve in the tent may not eat" (13:10) demarcates between insiders and outsiders. Thus the insiders in this world become the outsiders, and the outsiders of this world become the insiders in the ultimate reality.

The Insider Ethic of Hebrews

The community's identity as a holy family that is set apart from the majority culture, which the author establishes in 1:1—10:31, becomes the basis for the communal ethos that the author urges his readers to accept in 10:32—13:25. This final section of Hebrews is the *peroratio* that summarizes and states the implications of the argument of 1:1—10:31 for the readers. An *inclusio* shapes the outer frame of the *peroratio*, as the author recalls the communal solidarity of the past when the readers became "partners" (κοινωνοί, 10:33) with those who were mistreated and concludes with the claim that the sacrifice acceptable to God is partnership (κοινωνία, 13:16) among them. The challenge of communal solidarity resonates throughout the *peroratio*. As the *inclusio* marked by ὑπομονή/ὑπομένειν indicates (10:32; 12:7), they have endured suffering in the past (10:32), and they need to continue to do so in the present (10:36-39; 12:4-11), following Jesus, the great model of endurance (12:1-3). The heroes of the past are examples of endurance in the suffering determined by an outsider status (11:13-16, 26-27, 38). Thus, as the *inclusio* indicates, the readers are the outsiders who experience solidarity in both suffering and the sharing of possessions.

17. Gäbel, *Die Kulttheologie des Hebräerbriefes*, 447.

The imperatives in 13:1–6 appear between the reaffirmation that they have come to (12:18, 22, προσεληλύθατε) Mount Zion (12:18–24) and the challenge to "go outside" (ἐξέρχεσθαι) the camp (13:13). They come to the heavenly world and go outside the camp of the majority culture in solidarity with each other. As the author's earlier portrayal of the readers as "refugees" (6:18) and the emphasis on communal suffering indicate, the insider ethic of 13:1–6 is intended for outsiders who belong to an alternative symbolic world and go together "outside the camp." Those who participate in the heavenly cultus adopt a way of life that excludes the material sacrifices. As people who live within Israel's narrative while transcending it, they offer sacrifices that also transcend the earthly cult. The specific norms of 13:1–6 are framed by the cultic language of 12:28—13:16. Using cultic language that implicitly compares their worship to the cultic activity in the earthly sanctuary (cf. λατρεύειν in 8:5; 9:9, 14; 10:2; 13:10), the author challenges the readers to "worship acceptably" (12:28, λατρεύωμεν εὐαρέστως). This encouragement forms an *inclusio* with the statement in 13:16 that doing good (εὐποιΐα) and sharing what one has (κοινωνία) are the sacrifices with which God is pleased (εὐαρεστεῖται θεός). Thus the ethical norms are the expression of the community's identity as joint participants in the heavenly cult.

The specific behavior required of the community of outsiders in 13:1–6 is anticipated in the imperatives that begin in 12:14.[18] The people on the move (12:12–13) share common moral norms, which the author introduces with the injunction "Pursue peace with all, and holiness, without which no one will see the Lord" (12:14). The instructions that follow suggest that "peace with all" refers to the communal solidarity of the listeners. Holiness (ἁγιασμός) suggests their identification with Israel as a holy people (Lev 19:2) and their status as a sanctified people as a result of the work of Christ (cf. 2:11; 9:13; 10:10, 29; 13:12). With the participle ἐπισκοποῦντες followed by three μή τις clauses, the author depicts the nature of communal solidarity of the holy people in the presence of danger.[19] The entire community is responsible for the maintenance of the holy people, as the parallel phrases indicate: that *no one* (μή τις) fail to reach the goal (cf. 4:1), that *not any* (μή τις) root of bitterness spring up, and that *no one* (μή τις) is a fornicator (πόρνος) or indifferent to transcendent matters (βέβηλος).[20] Communal solidarity, therefore, requires both the care for one another and strict boundaries for the sexual behavior of the people.

---

18. See Vanhoye, *Structure and Message of the Epistle to the Hebrews*, 106.

19. See BDAG, 379, on ἐπισκοπεῖν, "to give attention to . . . with implication of hazard awaiting one."

20. On the translation of βέβηλος, see BDAG, 173.

This depiction of communal solidarity anticipates the injunctions in 13:1–6, suggesting the relationship between the five commands. Φιλαδελφία, the heading for the commands, is the expression of the family identity established throughout the homily. Indeed, the readers have already demonstrated their love (ἀγάπη) by serving the saints (6:9), and the author has encouraged them to stir each other up to love and good works (10:24). The readers would express φιλαδελφία by encouraging one another (3:12; 10:24–25) and by ensuring that no one fail to reach the goal (cf. 12:15–16). Unlike Philo, who places high value on φιλανθρωπία, the author encourages the readers to assume the role of the family in caring for one another. The verb μενέτω recalls the readers' past acts of love and connects it with the abiding realities that the author has depicted. Those who have an abiding possession (10:34) and share in the abiding unshakable realities (12:27) "let brotherly love abide."

Although φιλαδελφία was a virtue in the Greco-Roman world,[21] it took on a special significance in early Christianity, where it was employed, not to refer to blood relations, but to those who shared the common confession. The author of Hebrews shares an insider ethic with Paul (cf. Rom 12:10; 1 Thess 4:9) and the authors of 1 and 2 Peter (cf. 1 Pet 4:9; 2 Pet 1:7), and challenges the readers to assume the role of the families from whom they had become alienated.

The value of φιλαδελφία was also expressed by diaspora Jews who, like the readers of Hebrews, lived as minority communities. The seven brothers of 4 Maccabees exemplify φιλαδελφία as they face torture (13:21, 26, 23; 14:1–13, 21; 15:10, 14). In the interpretations of the Torah among diaspora Jews, love for the fellow-Israelite is a major theme. Tobit encourages his son, "Love your kindred" (4:13, ἀγάπα τοὺς ἀδελφούς σου). Similarly, a dominant theme of the Testaments of the Twelve Patriarchs is love for the family of Israelites. The patriarchs frequently instruct their descendants to love their neighbor (T. Iss. 5:2; T. Gad 4:2; 6:1; T. Benj. 3:4), the equivalent of the command to "love one another (T. Sim. 2:4; T. Gad 6:1, 3). Although diaspora writers rarely excluded outsiders from the love command (Lev 19:18), they clearly indicated that love extends to the fellow Israelite and the stranger in their midst.[22]

As in Pauline paraenesis (Rom 12:10–13), the injunction "Do not neglect hospitality" falls under the heading of φιλαδελφία. Φιλοξενία is also a Greek virtue that takes on a new meaning in Christian moral

---

21. See Klauck, "Die Bruderliebe bei Plutarch und im vierten Makkabäerbuch," 94; Söding, *Das Liebesgebot bei Paulus*, 74

22. Söding, *Das Liebesgebot bei Paulus*, 59.

instruction.²³ The term does not appear in the LXX but is common in Jewish instruction. As warrant for hospitality, the author recalls that "some welcomed strangers without knowing it," continuing the association of the readers with Israel's narrative (cf. Gen 18:2-3). Abraham is the example of φιλοξενία in diaspora literature.²⁴ In the Testament of Abraham (recension A), the patriarch is remembered for his φιλοξενία and his ἀγάπη (17.6). The archangel Michael declares that he has seen no one like Abraham: one who is "merciful, hospitable (φιλόξενον), just, true, and reverent, refraining from every kind of evil" (4.25; cf. 1.4, 9). As in Hebrews, his φιλοξενία is an expression of his love.

The placement of φιλοξενία under φιλαδελφία may suggest the author's use of Lev 19, which commands the love of both the neighbor (Lev 19:18) and the stranger (Lev 19:34). The stranger in Hebrews is not an outsider but one who is not immediately recognized as a member of the community.²⁵ The author may include the saints from distant places (cf. 13:24) who come into their midst.

Familial love is also expressed in the care for prisoners, a concern addressed nowhere else in NT paraenesis but a common theme in the second century.²⁶ This injunction reflects the community's situation, for the readers have already shown solidarity to prisoners (10:34). The author has recalled heroes who endured "mocking and flogging, even chains and imprisonment" (11:36). Thus he urges the readers to continue the communal solidarity with prisoners, which they have demonstrated before as an aspect of φιλαδελφία and of the κοινωνία (cf. 10:33; 13:16) of the community of outsiders. They share solidarity not only with each other but with the Israelites, who were also mistreated (cf; 11:37, κακουχούμενοι; 13:3b κακουχουμένων).²⁷ The readers share solidarity, being themselves "in the body."

The transition from expressions of φιλαδελφία to marriage is not a turn from communal to private morality but the expression of the cohesion of the holy community. The relationship between φιλαδελφία and sexual morality is a common theme in early Christian paraenesis (cf. 1 Cor 5:1—11:1; 1 Thess 4:1–12). In Lev 18–19, the life of the holy people is characterized

---

23. Spicq, *Theological Lexicon of the New Testament*, 3.444-45. In the Hellenistic period, φιλοξενία was regarded as an act of φιλανθρωπία (Polybius 4.20; Diodorus Siculus 13.83).

24. Tobit is also an example of one who entertained angels (cf. Tob 12:13).

25. Richard Johnson, *Going outside the Camp*, 82.

26. See Lucian, *Pereg.* 12, "From the very break of day aged widows and orphan children could be seen waiting near the prison, while their officials even slept inside with him after bribing the guards" (trans. Harmon, LCL).

27. Thuren, *Das Lopopfer der Hebräer*, 210.

by the sexual boundaries of the community (Lev 18) and their love of the neighbor (Lev 19:18) and stranger (Lev 19:34). The two most important themes in Jewish paraenesis were the love for one's kindred and the avoidance of sexual immorality.[28] This advice is reminiscent of the instructions in 12:15–16, where care for others within the community is linked with sexual boundaries. The reference to the undefiled bed (ἡ κοίτη ἀμίαντος) employs the language of Scripture, recalling the sin of Reuben, who "went up on his father's bed (κοίτη) and defiled (ἀμίανας) it" (Gen 49:4; cf. 35:22). The language assumes the distinction between ritual purity and impurity. Ἀμίαντος denotes ritual purity in the LXX.[29] Adultery renders one ritually impure.[30] God's judgment on πόρνοι is also reminiscent of the earlier injunction in which Esau, the example of πορνεία, was unable to repent. Thus the instruction on sexual morality calls on the community to live out its identity as a holy people (cf. 12:15), adopting Israel's association of sexual conduct with the love demonstrated by the sanctified people (cf. Lev 18).

The transition from sexual conduct to the life that is free from the love of money (ἀφιλάργυρος ὁ τρόπος) suggests the close connection of these vices in early Christian paraenesis (cf. 1 Cor 5:1—6:11; Eph 5:3-5; Col 3:5). Φιλαργυρία, a classic vice in Greco-Roman discourse,[31] appears elsewhere in the NT only in the Pastoral Epistles (1 Tim 6:10; cf. 1 Tim 3:3; 2 Tim 3:2) and Luke (16:14). Paul prefers the synonymous term πλεονεξία and its cognates (Rom 1:29; 1 Cor 5:10; 6:10; Eph 5:5; Col 3:5). In the paraenesis of diaspora Judaism, sexual immorality and greed regularly appear together in summaries of the law.[32]

Within the context of Hebrews, this injunction corresponds to the community's identity as participants in the heavenly world. The community had accepted the confiscation of property with joy, knowing that they had an "abiding possession" (10:34). Their example is Moses, who counted the sufferings of Christ of greater wealth than the treasures of

---

28. Collins, *Between Athens and Jerusalem*, 137–67.

29. Gäbel, *Die Kulttheologie des Hebräerbriefes*, 401. Cf. Weiss, *Der Brief an die Hebräer*, 703; Grässer, *An die Hebräer*, 3.355.

30. See Wis 3:13, "Blessed is the barren woman who is undefiled, who has not entered into a sinful union." Cf. Niebuhr, *Gesetz und Paränese*, 117. Μιαίνειν is frequently used in the Testaments of the Twelve Patriarchs for sexual offenses (T. Reub. 1:6; T. Lev. 7:3; 9:9; 14:6; 16:1; T. Benj. 8:2–3).

31. Spicq, *Theological Lexicon of the New Testament*, 3.446, cites Plato, *Leg.* 9.870a: "The power that money has to give birth to a thousand and one furies of insatiable, infinite grasping. . . . This love of riches is the first and greatest source of the greatest cases of murder." Luke Johnson, *Hebrews: A Commentary*, 342. See Bion, "The love of money is the mother of all evils" (Diogenes Laertius 6.50).

32. See Reinmuth, *Geist und Gesetz*, 15–47.

Egypt (11:26). As people who, like the heroes of faith, find reality in the unseen (11:1), they are content with what they have. The citations from Scripture in 13:5-6, have special force for a community that lives on the margins of society. God's promise to the people, "I will never fail you or forsake you" (13:5; cf. Deut 31:6, 8; Gen 28:15), is a promise to the outsider community.[33] The citation from Ps 117:6 LXX also has special force for the community of outsiders. Like Moses, the community will not be afraid (13:6; cf. 11:23, 27). Despite the continuing suffering, they ask, "What can man do to me?" Because of this confidence, they can share what they have (13:16), as they have in the past (10:33). Thus ἀφιλαργυρία, a virtue common to antiquity, takes on special significance for the outsider community. Those who go "outside the camp" (13:13) together support one another in a hostile climate as an act of φιλαδελφία.

Moral Instructions within the Context of Diaspora Judaism

These five injunctions depict the life (cf. 12:28; 13:16) that is pleasing to God, summarizing the obligations of a cultic community that has no need of a physical cult. The injunctions provide cohesion for the community and distinguish the ethos of the members from that of the surrounding society. Although the specific injunctions are parallel in many respects to Greco-Roman and early Christian moral instruction, the question remains: Why did the author summarize the obligations with this particular combination of injunctions in 13:1-6? Is the author following existing models for this summary of moral requirements? While earlier Christian tradition, including Paul, offered precedents for the paraenesis of Hebrews, the evidence does not suggest that the author draws directly on any earlier NT document. Indeed, a rich paraenetic tradition developed in Jewish communities of the diaspora, which also faced the challenge of maintaining a common ethos among minority communities.

Jewish teachers in the diaspora summarize the law and contemporize it for their particular situation, including those features that were relevant for their communities. Philo, Josephus, and the unknown author of the Sentences of Pseudo-Phocylides summarize the law's requirements in a remarkably similar fashion,[34] omitting the cultic activities while focusing

---

33. The author's reading is not directly from the LXX, but agrees with Philo's reading (*Conf.* 166).

34. Philo, *Hyp.* 7; Josephus, *C. Ap.* 2; Sentences of Pseudo-Phocylides 48–227; see the synoptic parallels in Niebuhr, *Gesetz*, 45–46.

primarily on sexuality, care for the weak (including animals and birds), and vices that undermine the community. The laws from the holiness code (Lev 17–26) and the Decalogue play an important role in these summaries. Similarly, Tobit summarizes the Torah in the diaspora situation, instructing his son on almsgiving (4:5-11; 4:14-19), warning against fornication (4:12), and encouraging love for kindred (4:13) in the diaspora community, the themes offered in Heb 13:1-6. In his summary of the law, Josephus places the care of strangers among the demands for love (*C. Ap.* 209). Philo maintains that the Decalogue is the summary of the law, indicating that the first tablet describes love for God, while the second tablet is a description of love for humankind (*Spec.* 2.61-63). Thus the prohibitions of adultery and greed fall under the category of love. In The Testaments of the Twelve Patriarchs, the three major vices listed are fornication, hatred of one's brothers, and the love of money. The greatest virtues are chastity and love for one's siblings. Joseph is the model of the great virtues, for he exemplified chastity (T. Reub. 4:8-9), brotherly love, and generosity (T. Reub. 4:6). The Testament of Joseph brings together the themes of chastity and brotherly love. Chapters 3-9 describe the many stratagems used by Potiphar's wife to seduce him. After recalling both the hatred endured from his brothers and the temptations by this woman, Joseph encourages his descendants to "Love one another" (T. Jos. 17:2).

Similarly, πορνεία and φιλαργυρία appear together in the Testaments of the Twelve Patriarchs. In the Testament of Judah the patriarch instructs the children "not to love money or to gaze on the beauty of women" (17:1) and to guard themselves against πορνεία and the love of money (18:2).[35] The same warning against greed and sexual immorality appears in The Testament of Dan (5:5-7). While the vices of adultery and greed are frequently treated separately, they are also treated together as summaries of two commands of the Decalogue.

Cultic requirements recede into the background in the summaries of the law in diaspora Judaism as summaries based on the Decalogue and the holiness code emerge with a special focus on love for others, sexual morality, and the proper care of possessions.[36] Observing these commandments, minority communities cared for one another and maintained community boundaries. They provided a precedent for early Christian communities, which resocialized gentile converts into a new way of life. Although the cultic commandment was "weak and useless" according to the author of

---

35. The two major themes of the Testament of Judah are πορνεία and the love of money (πορνεία in T. Jud. 12:2; 13:3; 14:2-3; 15:1-2); φιλαργυρία in 18:2; 19:1.

36. Niebuhr, *Gesetz und Paränese*, 166.

Hebrews, these summaries of the law provided the basis for the formation of communities who were the holy people of God.

Conclusion: An Ethic for Outsiders

The ethical instructions in Heb 13 cohere with the author's call to "go outside the camp, bearing his shame" (13:13). The task of the readers is to maintain communal solidarity as it experiences abuse from the outside world. Having established the community's identity as family, the author urges them to the familial roles of caring for siblings, ensuring the general welfare of all. In a homily that has demonstrated the inadequacy of worship in an earthly cultus, the author insists that the worship now required of believers is the care for one another. This approach to the moral life had numerous precedents among writers of the Jewish diaspora, who commonly summarized the law without reference to the temple cultus, focusing on the demands for communal cohesion in the midst of a hostile environment.

CHAPTER 11

THE ECCLESIOLOGY OF HEBREWS

Although interpreters have written "in many and various ways" about aspects of the theology of Hebrews, the ecclesiology of this homily has received scarcely any attention. The fact that ἐκκλησία appears only twice in Hebrews—once in a citation from the LXX (2:12) and once for the ἐκκλησία enrolled in heaven (12:23)—has led to the widespread conclusion that ecclesiology is not the author's major concern. The absence of the common Pauline images for the church may also suggest to scholars that the author has no coherent ecclesiology. However, as I shall argue in this article, this "word of exhortation" (13:22) addresses a community gathered for worship, offering a detailed soteriology and Christology as the basis for their communal identity and continuing faithfulness. In the alternation between exposition and exhortation throughout the homily, the author demonstrates the ecclesiological significance of the exposition, moving between third-person exposition and first and second person plural exhortations. In the use of the frequent hortatory subjunctives and the pronouns "we" (or "us") the author offers an ecclesiological vision.[1]

Hebrews, Marginalization, and the Loss of Collective Identity

The author writes to a community that is facing an identity crisis. Conversion has apparently separated this house church from the surrounding society, which has abused them, confiscated their property, and placed some in prison (10:32–34; 13:3). The image of the patriarchs as strangers and pilgrims (11:8–10, 13, 38) suffering marginalization (11:32–40) probably offers models with whom the readers can identify. The growing tendency among

---

1. Originally published in *Restoration Quarterly* 53 (2011) 207–19.
See the first person plural in 1:2; 2:3; 3:6; 4:13; 5:11; 7:26; 10:15, 20, 39; 12:1, 25; 13:15.

the members to abandon the assembly (10:25) indicates the potential threat to the community's cohesion. In earlier days they had shown solidarity with each other when they were partners (κοινωνοί) of those who were mistreated (10:33) and sympathized (συνεπαθήσατε) with prisoners (10:34), but now they need endurance (10:36). The author probably speaks for the community when he says, "But we do not see all things in subjection to him" (2:8).[2] They experience the dissonance between their confession of the exalted and triumphant Son (Heb 1:1–13) and their experience in the house church. The author's challenge is to encourage the community to remain faithful amid the dissonance between their confession and the realities of their lives. Community cohesion is vital for this task.[3]

Rebuilding the Collective Identity

The author opens the homily with a reminder of the community's confession. In the hymnic declaration of 1:1–4 he declares that God has spoken "to us" in a son (1:2), who is both God's ultimate revelation and the one who has become "greater than the angels" (1:4) as the result of the exaltation. The author reaffirms this claim with the catena of Scripture citations in 1:5–13, comparing the exalted Christ to the angels, who have a lower status. This high Christology has ecclesiological implications, for it reaffirms the essential conviction that unites the community. Indeed, references to the community provide the frame for the christological declaration in chapter 1. In the ultimate revelation "to us" (1:2), God has spoken to the believing community, whom the author later describes as "those who are about to inherit salvation" (1:14). The author thus distinguishes between insiders and outsiders—between those who are about to inherit salvation and all others.

Continuity and Discontinuity: Israel and the Church

A People under the Word

The contrast between the word addressed to the ancestors and the word addressed to "us" (1:1–2) indicates the continuity and discontinuity between Israel and the church. The ancestors, several of whom the author mentions in the homily (cf. 3:1–6; 6:12–20; 11:1–40), are "the fathers," with whom the church is connected. Although the author never mentions the ethnicity of his readers, they live in continuity with "the fathers" because they are the

2. Thompson, "Argument and Persuasion in the Epistle to the Hebrews."
3. See DeSilva, "The Epistle to the Hebrews in Social–Scientific Perspective," 10.

descendants in faith. The hearers, like the ancestors, have heard the divine word, but this congregation of hearers has heard the ultimate word (1:1-2). This statement anticipates the later claim that, while Israel received a word delivered by angels, the readers of Hebrews have received a word "spoken by the Lord and confirmed to us by those who heard him" (2:2-3). The good news came to the hearers, just as it had come to the Israelites, but it did not benefit the latter (4:2). The warning, from Ps 95:7 "They shall never enter my rest," spoken in the past to Israel, continues to speak to the church (Heb 4:7). Indeed, God's word is "living and active, sharper than any two-edged sword," as it confronts the readers. In continuity with Abraham, the church has received an irrevocable promise (6:13-20). Like Israel, it now stands before a mountain where it hears the divine voice (12:19-20). However, the assembled church has heard a voice that speaks a better word than that of the blood of Abel (12:24-29), and a voice more powerful than that which caused the Israelites to tremble with fear (12:25-29). With the series of reflections on Israel's Scripture and the comparisons between the two revelations, the author indicates the link between the people of God in the past and present as recipients of God's word.[4] However, as the opening words of the homily indicate, the church has heard a greater word. While the earlier revelation did not benefit their ancestors (4:2), the church stands before a decision about its response to the word (cf. 3:15; 12:25).

Those Who Inherit the Promise

The author describes the community, not with nouns but with participles. The hearers are the people who are about to (μέλλοντας) inherit (κληρονομεῖν) salvation.[5] The identification of the listeners ("us" in 1:2) with "those who are about to inherit salvation" (1:14) introduces a major theme of the book and places the community firmly within Israel's story. The church lives in continuity with Abraham, who went out (13:8) to the place he was about to receive (ἤμελλεν λανβάνειν) as an inheritance (κληρονομίαν) and Moses, who "looked to the reward" (μισθαποδοσία, 11:26). The inheritance is the κατάπαυσις that Israel never entered (3:7-19) and the heavenly πόλις (11:10, 16; 13:14; cf. 12:22) and homeland (πατρίς, 11:14) that the patriarchs never inherited.

---

4. For full treatment of the community under the word, see Wider, *Theozentrik und Bekenntnis*. See also Lewicki, "Weist nicht ab den Sprechenden!"

5. The recipients are "those who are being sanctified" (οἱ ἁγιαζομενοι, 2:11; cf. 10:14), "those who have fled" (καταφυγόντες, 6:18), and those who are called (κεκλημένοι, 9:15). The participial form of μέλλω appears frequently in Hebrews (2:5; 9:11; 10:1; 11:20; 13:14) to describe the future hope. See BDAG, 628.

Unlike the Israelites, who never reached the κατάπαυσις (3:19), and the patriarchs, who never received the promise (11:13, 39), the readers are heirs (κληρονόμοι) of the promise (6:17), provided that they do not forfeit it (2:1–4; 3:6, 12–19; 10:36–39). Those who believe may enter God's κατάπαυσις (4:3–11), where they will participate in God's rest. In the present they are the refugees (καταφυγόντες) who may now grasp the hope (6:18) that enters the heavenly sanctuary through the exaltation of Jesus Christ (6:19–20). Because of the death and exaltation, Jesus is the guarantor (ἔγγυος, 7:22) and mediator (μεσίτης) of the covenant (9:15). As a result, "those who are called may receive the promise of the eternal inheritance" (9:15). Thus they may now receive what the ancestors never received.

The relationship between the church and the inheritance promised to Israel becomes the focal point in the peroration of Hebrews (10:19—13:25), as the author first addresses the church with the three hortatory subjunctive (10:19–23) and the first and second person plural (10:32–39), encouraging the community to draw near (10:19), hold fast to the confession (10:23), stir one another up (10:24), and to continue to participate in the assembly of the community (10:25). He reminds them repeatedly of the promise that the Christ event has guaranteed for them. They have an abiding possession (10:34), and their faith has great reward (μισθαποδοσία, 10:35). If they endure they will receive the promise (10:36). The words once spoken to Israel from Habakkuk now speak to the church, as the author concludes with the distinction between the community and all others: "we are not those who shrink back toward destruction but those of faith for the preservation of life" (10:39).

The connection between the community and the ancestors is evident in the transition from the address to the community (10:39) and the catalogue of heroes of faith in chapter 11, all of whom exhibit the faithful endurance that the author mentions in 10:36–39. The first person plural (10:39; 11:40b) provides the frame for the catalogue of heroes in 11:1–40a as the author recalls the story of the patriarchs in chapter 11 with his own audience in mind. The community that is "about to inherit (κληρονομεῖν) salvation" (1:14) recalls that Noah became an heir (κληρονόμος) of righteousness (11:7). Abraham went out to look for the place he was about to receive as an inheritance (κληρονομία, 11:8), and Isaac and Jacob were coheirs (συγληρονόμοι) of the promise (11:10). Although the heirs looked to the promise and to the reward (11:26), neither the Israelites in the wilderness nor the patriarchs received the promise (3:19; 11:13, 39). This statement recalls earlier comment that Israel did not enter the rest because of unbelief (3:12, 19).

The claim that God has provided "something better" (κρεῖττον τι, 11:40a) develops the earlier comment that God has established a new day (4:7). The better inheritance is undoubtedly the heavenly κατάπαυσις that God has made available (4:1–11), the "better possession and abiding one" (10:34), the "better promises" (8:6), "the better hope" (6:19), and the "greater salvation" (6:9). Consequently, the promise of entering God's rest remains for the community.

According to 11:40b, the link between the ancestors and the community is that "without us they would not be made perfect" (μὴ χωρὶς τελειωθῶσιν), which forms an *inclusio* with the "we" of 10:39. In contrast to the catalogues of heroes in Jewish literature, this list does not conclude with a call to imitate the ancestors in faith.[6] Instead, the author indicates that the church completes Israel's story if it does not repeat its failure. Not only does the author say that the community may now enter God's rest but that the people enter in the company of the patriarchs who neither received the ultimate word (cf. 1:2) nor inherited the promise (11:13, 39). The continuity between Israel and the church suggested in the opening of the homily becomes the central focus. The people of God include believers in the past and present, all of whom have been on the journey to the promise that will be fulfilled only at the end. Jesus has not rejected the old people of God but opens the way for the completion of the journey through the new people of God,[7] which follows Jesus from suffering to glory (12:1–2). The author makes no comment about the Jews of his own day who have not believed in Christ but links his community with the ancestors, who now depend on the church for the completion of their journey. As the author indicates in 1:1–2, the church stands at the end of a sequence of revelations from God, and thus it completes Israel's narrative.

Christ and the Church

As the *inclusio* marked by the first person plural in 1:2 and the reference to "those who are about to inherit salvation" (1:14) indicates, the descent (1:3) and exaltation of Christ above the angels has determined the community's identity. It is thus more than the heir of ancient Israel. The new possibility of inheriting salvation comes only in Christ, as the opening chapter indicates. The church is the recipient of God's ultimate revelation in Christ, whose descent and exaltation (1:1–4) opens the way for believers to inherit salvation (1:14). Because Christ is seated at the right hand of

---

6. Weiß, *Der Brief an die Hebräer*, 625.
7. Backhaus, *Der Hebräerbrief*, 408.

God, the church may enter the heavenly κατάπαυσις (4:3–11). As refugees, they may grasp the hope that has been made available as an anchor of the soul (6:18), the new hope that has been made available by the exaltation. The entrance of Christ into the heavenly sanctuary opens the way for believers to "receive the promise" (9:15) that their ancestors never received. The church is thus a community of hope.

The Son and the Sons

The community's crisis is the occasion for the author to offer further ecclesiological reflections. While the church is on its way to the transcendent inheritance, it still lives on earth, the object of abuse from outsiders and with the temptation to drop out. Thus it has not yet inherited salvation. The triumph described in chapter 1 remains unseen, for the community is only "about to" inherit salvation (1:14) and does not see all things in subjection (2:8). The author responds to the reality of suffering with a response to the community's situation in 2:9–18.

In 2:9, he elaborates on the early confession (1:1–4), indicating that the Son, "because of the suffering of death," is "crowned with glory and honor." The "glory and honor" of the Son is his exaltation to God's right hand (cf. 1:3, 13), his status as a result of being "made perfect through suffering" (2:10). This descent and ascent has significant ecclesiological implications, for Christology here is inseparable from ecclesiology. The author describes God as the one who "leads many sons (υἱοί) to glory" (2:10). The imagery echoes the story of Israel in the wilderness, when God "led" the people toward the promised land under the guidance of Moses.[8] The believing community, like the ancient Israelites, is composed of υἱοί on the way to glory. That God "leads many sons to glory" is consistent with the later description of the community on the way to the heavenly κατάπαυσις (4:1–11).

In a *tour de force* on the ancient concept of "fitting for God,"[9] the author declares that it was "fitting for [God]" that the ἀρχηγός "be made perfect through suffering." Christ was "made perfect" at the exaltation, and the sons follow him to glory. Although it is God who "leads many sons to glory" (2:10), the Son described in 1:1—2:8 plays an important role as ἀρχηγός. Although this title has numerous associations in ancient literature, in Hebrews the word is the equivalent of the forerunner (πρόδρομος)

---

8. Lev 26:13; Deut 8:2, 15; 32:12; Josh 24:8; Ps 78:2; Thompson, *Hebrews*, 73.

9. On the concept of "fitting for God" in Greek philosophy, see Dreyer, *Untersuchungen zum Begrifff des Gottgeziemenden in der Antike*, 152; Thompson, "The Appropriate, the Necessary, and the Impossible," 302–17.

who opens up the way (6:20; cf. 12:2). In this instance, the author focuses on the solidarity of the ἀρχηγός and those who follow. The church is thus the community of sons who follow the Son and pioneer through suffering to ultimate glory (cf. 12:1–2). While ancient Israelites were God's υἱοί, the church lives in solidarity with the υἱός.

The author reinforces this solidarity with a supporting statement (2:11) in the form of a maxim: "The one who sanctifies (ὁ ἁγιάζων) and the ones who are being sanctified (οἱ ἁγιαζόμενοι)" are "of one" (ἐξ ἑνός). Interpreters debate the meaning of ἐξ ἑνός, which can be either masculine or neuter. It could signify the common origin in God, suggesting a cosmic principle of unity derived from Stoicism,[10] or common origin in Adam. In Paul's speech at the Areopagus, he declares that God made "of one" (ἐξ ἑνός) the nations of the earth (Acts 17:26), pointing to a common origin in Adam. Within the context of Hebrews, the phrase describes the common family origin of the Son and the sons—the one who sanctifies (ὁ ἁγιάζων) and those who are being sanctified (οἱ ἁγιαζόμενοι)—who are siblings within the seed of Abraham (cf. 2:16).

The author develops the theme of family solidarity between Jesus and the church, making Christ the speaker in the psalm, "I will announce your name to the brothers" (2:12; cf. Ps 21:23) and ""Behold I and the children (παιδία) God has given me" (2:13; cf. Isa 8:18). The church is thus composed of the siblings of Jesus. According to 2:14–18, the siblings share with Christ the same flesh and blood (2:14). The Son is "like his brothers in every respect" (2:17). Thus the church is not only composed of siblings, but they are also the siblings of Jesus the Son, who is God's agent in leading many sons to glory (2:10). The author's emphasis is twofold: 1) The church follows the destiny of the ἀρχηγός from suffering to glory. The ἀρχηγός led the way, breaching the devil's domain and liberating the siblings from the fear of death (2:15). 2) As the author consistently argues, the Son opened the way into the heavenly world for his siblings to follow (cf. 4:14–16; 6:19–20; 10:19–25). 2) In the present, the Son is able to help those who call on him (2:18). As the author concludes, he is the Son over God's house, and the church is the house (3:1–6).

The imagery of the community as "sons" recalls the consistent designation of the ancestors as the "sons of Israel" under the leadership of Moses.[11] Indeed, the author maintains the family imagery, addressing the church as

10. See Backhaus, *Der Hebräerbrief*, 123.

11. An important theme in the OT is that God leads the people out of Egypt and through the wilderness (Lev 26:13; Deut 8:2, 15; 32:12; Josh 24:8; Ps 78:52). See Thompson, *Hebrews*, 73. On Paul's use of υἱός for the church, see Rom 8:14; 9:26; 2 Cor 6:18; Gal 3:7, 26; 4:6–7.

"holy brothers" (3:1; cf. 10:19; 13:22) and declaring that it is God's house (3:6; cf. 10:21) in which Moses is a servant (3:5) and Jesus is the Son (3:6).[12] The church's suffering is nothing less than the discipline that a father gives to his son (12:5–11; cf. Prov 3:11–12). Just as God once disciplined Israel (cf. Deut 8:5), God now disciplines the people of God. In the reflections on the wilderness journey, he urges the readers to take responsibility for one another, assuming the role of family members,[13] ensuring that "not anyone" (μήποτε . . . ἐν τινι ὑμῶν, 3:12) among them fail to complete the journey, "exhorting one another each day" (3:13). Using the language once spoken to ancient Israel, he encourages them "to see that no one (μή τις) fails to obtain the grace of God" (12;15), that "no root of bitterness (μή τις ῥίζα) spring," and that "no one (μη τις) becomes like the profane Esau." The frequent μή τις indicates the communal responsibility that no members abandon the long journey in the wilderness. This familial relationship is especially evident in the author's encouragement for members to practice brotherly love (13:1), hospitality (13:2), and care for prisoners (13:3).

Holy Ones and Outsiders

The author interprets the readers' alienation from the larger society with the images derived from Israel's Scriptures. While he does not, like Paul, address his readers as "saints" (ἅγιοι), he describes the readers both as "those who are being sanctified" (οἱ ἁγιαζόμενοι, 2:11) and "those who have been sanctified" (ἡγιασμένοι, 10:10). This imagery is drawn from Israel's experience. Just as the Levitical sacrifices "sanctify" (ἁγιάζει) for the purification of the flesh (9:13), the community has been sanctified (ἡγιάσθη, 10:29) by the blood of Christ (13:12). Consequently, just as God instructed Israel to "be holy" (Lev 19:2), the author encourages the listeners to "pursue holiness" (12:14). Like Israel, the church is set apart from its surroundings. Christ has made them holy and instructed them to pursue the path of holiness.

The heritage of Israel suggests that marginalization is not the community's misfortune but its *calling*. The community's pilgrimage toward the heavenly κατάπαυσις is analogous to the patriarch's desire for the heavenly πόλις

---

12. οἶκος is commonly used both for the dwelling and the household. In the LXX, it is used for a the family or race (e.g., Gen 7:1) or the sanctuary (Gen 28:17; 1 Kgs 5:14a; 6:1c). While the family was Paul's most frequent image for the church, he never describes it as an οἶκος. He uses the term for the household (1 Cor 1:16; cf. Heb 3:4). The church is described as an οἶκος in 1 Pet 2:5; 4:17. See Michel, "οἶκος, κτλ."

13. On mutual encouragement as the responsibility of the family in antiquity, see Thompson, *Moral Formation according to Paul*, 57. Thompson, "Paul, Plutarch, and the Ethic of the Family," 223–26.

(11:10, 16) and πατρίς (11:14). Recalling the patriarchs' story with his own readers in mind, the author recalls that Abraham was an ἀλλοτρίος (11:9), and that the patriarchs were ξένοι καὶ παρεπίδημοι (11:13) on the earth. This description, derived from Gen 23:4, recalls the consistent portrayal of the ancestors as people without a homeland (cf. Exod 2:2; Deut 23:7) or strangers in their own land (Pss 39:12; 105:12-13; 119:19). This image becomes especially compelling in the final exhortation of the homily, where the author indicates that the outsider status is the community's calling. "We have an altar" in contrast to "those who serve in the tent" (13:10). While the imagery is a matter of debate, it is evident that the author demarcates the church from others. By recalling that Jesus suffered "outside the gate" (13:12), the author focuses on Jesus as the outsider, who sanctified his people (13:12). The task of the church, therefore, is "to go outside the camp" (13:13), following Jesus. Thus, like the patriarchs, who "went out" (11:8), the community accepts as its calling the alienation from the rest of society.

Worship and the Heavenly Community

While the church lives on earth in the midst of suffering, believers are nevertheless "partakers of the heavenly calling" (3:1), the people whom angels serve (1:14). While believers continue the long pilgrimage, they are now able to "approach the throne of grace" (4:16) where they will find mercy and grace in time of need. Here they follow the path of the one who has "gone through the heavens" (4:14). Indeed, the author's frequent use of προσέρχομαί (cf. 4:16; 7:25; 10:1; 12:18) belongs to the larger context of the claim that the Son and high priest has opened the way into the heavenly world. Whereas the ancient sacrifices were not able to perfect those who drew near (10:1) because the way was not yet open (9:6-8), at the exaltation, Christ became the high priest who opened the way into the sanctuary (10:19). Thus with the hortatory subjunctive προσερχώμεθα (4:16; 10:22), the author invites the church to follow the one who entered the heavenly world and to come into his presence. In corporate worship, the community on earth sees beyond its own marginalization as it approaches the heavenly throne of grace.

The three hortatory subjunctives in 10:19-25 indicate the nature of the community's response to the high priest who opened up the way. These appeals to the readers are not three separate challenges but an insight into the nature of worship and community life. The challenge, "let us draw near" (10:22), "let us hold fast to the confession" (10:23), and "let us stir one another up to love and good works" (10:24) indicate the relationship between worship and service. In worship, the community holds on to the confession and encourages others to love and good works. Thus attendance at the assembly is vital (10:25), for here members encourage one another.

With the frequent use of προσέρχ-, a term used in the OT for the entrance of priests in the sanctuary,[14] the author describes the task of all believers. The author does not, like the author of 1 Peter, describe the community as "a royal priesthood" (1 Pet 2:10). Although Jesus is the high priest, no one in the community is described as priest. The author uses cultic language to describe the whole community, which performs priestly tasks. They "draw near" to the presence of God, and they offer a "sacrifice of praise" (13:15). When they do good works and share with those who are in need, they offer the sacrifices that are pleasing to God (13:16).

In the climactic statement in 12:18-25, the author no longer employs the hortatory subjunctive to invite the community to draw near to God but speaks in the perfect tense, declaring, "You have not come (προσηλύθατε, 12:18) . . . , you have come . . . (προσληλύθατε)" (12:22), comparing the ancient assembly at Sinai with the assembly of believers in the heavenly Mount Zion. Although the inheritance of the heavenly city lies in the future (11:10; 13:14), the community is already the participant in worship that spans heaven and earth. Despite appearances, the community worships with the myriads of angels (12:22), the universal church composed of those whose names are written in heaven (12:23), and the spirits of the just made perfect (12:23), and comes to God the judge (12:23). It hears a voice that is greater than the voice at Sinai and greater than the sound of Abel's cry (12:25). The experience of the "unshakable kingdom" is the basis for the church's priestly task. Unlike priests whose worship (λατρεία) was unable to perfect the conscience (Heb 9:1, 6, 9; 10:2; cf. 8:6), believers may now "worship in reverence and awe" (12:28), knowing that God is a consuming fire.

Worship is the occasion for hearing the word of God. The author assumes that the community will hear this "word of exhortation" (13:22) in the assembly. As the author's frequent invitation to the "hearing" of God's word indicates, the ancient Scriptures continue to speak to the church.

Polity and the Sacraments

While the members of the community all encourage one another (3:12; 10:25) and engage in pastoral activities (12:15-17), the author assumes that the community recognizes specific leaders. Indeed, he mentions ἡγούμενοι

---

14. Lev 9:7-8; 21:17-24; 22:3; cf. Exod 16:9; Lev 9:5; Num 18:4.

three times in the final chapter,[15] first instructing the hearers to "remember [their] leaders who taught them the word of God (13:7) and "consider the outcome of their way of life, and imitate their faith." While the readers remember past leaders, their task is "obey" the current leaders because they "watch over [their] souls" (13:17). At the conclusion he greets the leaders (13:24) along with all of the saints. The task of leaders appears to be threefold: a) they are the community's teachers and examples (13:7); b) they hold authority over the community, which obeys them (13:17);[16] c) they also "watch out over the souls" of the believers. That is, while the whole community has pastoral responsibilities (cf. 12:15–17), some leaders have emerged whose responsibility is acknowledged in the community.

The author does not mention sacerdotal responsibilities of the leaders, referring only to their task of teaching and pastoral care. He speaks obliquely, if at all, about baptism and the Lord's Supper. Despite the argument for the ineffectiveness of washings as "regulations of the flesh" (9:10), he assumes that baptism is the entry into Christian existence, for he recalls the occasion when the hearers were "washed with pure water" (10:22). With its focus on the sacrifice of Christ in the sanctuary, the homily is filled with language that interpreters have described as eucharistic. The description of Christ as the mediator of the new covenant (9:15) echoes the words of institution in the Lord's Supper (cf. Matt 26:28; Mark 14:24; Luke 22-20; 1 Cor 11:25). Interpreters have maintained that the affirmation that "we have an altar from which those who officiate in the tent have no right to eat" (Heb 13:10) refers to the Eucharist.[17] However, the author never speaks unambiguously of the Eucharist. The altar that believers have (13:10) is the death of Jesus in the heavenly sanctuary (cf. 9:1—10:18). While the community probably observes both baptism and the Lord's Supper, the author's focus is not on the sacraments but on the word that the community hears in worship. Indeed, his own "word of exhortation" (13:22) reflects the importance of the spoken word in the assembly of the community.

---

15. On ἡγούμενοι as "leading men" of the community, see Acts 15:22. See also Luke 22:26, ὁ ἡγούμενος ὡς ὁ διάκονος. The term is used for men in any leading position, including those who have military or political positions (BDAG, 434).

16. Πείθεσθε (13:17) is used to mean "to win over as the result of persuasion." BDAG, 792; ὑπείκετε ("to give way" or "yield to someone's authority") is not used elsewhere in the NT. Cf. 4 Macc 6:35, for the argument that reason does not "yield to" the passions.

17. See Swetnam, "Christology and the Eucharist in the Epistle to the Hebrews," 74–75. See the discussion of the Eucharist in Hebrews in Weiß, *Hebräer*, 726-46.

Conclusion: The Wandering People of God

The title of Ernst Käsemann's classic work *The Wandering People of God* is a suitable description of the ecclesiology of Hebrews. The community addressed in Hebrews is the heir of the children of Israel. The narrative of the people of God culminates in this community, composed of the "sons" who live in solidarity with the Son. The Christology and soteriology of this homily are inseparable from the ecclesiology, in which the people of God follow the path of Jesus from earthly alienation to heavenly worship. The author addresses the marginalization of the community, reminding the hearers that, while they are the objects of ridicule in the present, they are "partakers of a heavenly calling." They are united, not only with ancient Israel, but also with the Son as they share both his sufferings and his exaltation in the present, living in hope for the ultimate realization of the promise.

BIBLIOGRAPHY

Adams, Edward. "The Cosmology of Hebrews." In *Reading the Epistle to the Hebrews: A Resource for Students*, edited by Eric F. Mason and Kevin B. McCruden, 53-76. Atlanta: Society of Biblical Literature, 2011.

Alexandre Jr., Manuel. *Rhetorical Argumentation in Philo of Alexandra*. Atlanta: Scholars, 1999.

Almqvist, H. *Plutarch und das Neue Testament: Ein Beitrag zum Corpus Hellenisticum novi Testamenti*. Uppsala: Appelbergs Boktryckeri, 1946.

Amir, Y. *Die hellenistische Gestalt des Judentums bei Philon von Alexandrien*. FJCD 5. Neukirchen-Vluyn: Neukirchener, 1983.

Anderson, R. Dean. *Rhetorical Theory and Paul*. Kampen: Kok Pharos, 1996.

Andresen, Carl. "Antike und Christentum." In *Theologische Realenzyklopädie*. 36 vols, edited by G. Krause and G. Müller, 50-99 in vol. 3. Berlin: de Gruyter, 1978.

———. "Justin und der Mittelplatonismus." *Zeitschrift für die neutestamentliche Wissenschaft und die Kunde der älteren Kirche* 44 (153) 159-95.

Attridge, Harold. *Hebrews*. Hermeneia. Philadelphia: Fortress, 1989.

Aune, David. E., ed. *The Westminster Dictionary of New Testament and Early Christian Literature and Rhetoric*. Louisville: Westminster John Knox, 2003.

Babcock, William S., ed. *Paul and the Legacies of Paul*. Dallas: Southern Methodist University Press, 1990.

Backhaus, Knut. "Auf Ehre und Gewissen! Die Ethik des Hebräerbriefs." In *Der sprechende Gott: Gesammelte Studien zum Hebräerbrief*. Wissenschaftliche Untersuchungen zum Neuen Testament 240, 215-37. Tübingen: Mohr Siebeck, 2009.

———. "Aufbruch ins Evangelium: Unruhe als urchristliches Existential." In *Der sprechenden Gott: Gesammelte Studien zum Hebräerbrief*, 287-99. Wissenschaftliche Untersuchungen zum Neuen Testament 240. Tübingen: Mohr Siebeck, 2009.

———. "Der Hebäerbrief: Potential und Profil, Eine Hinführung." In *Der sprechende Gott: gesammelte Studien zum Hebräerbrief*, 1-19. Wissenschaftliche Untersuchungen zum Neuen Testament 240. Tübingen: Mohr Siebeck, 2009.

———. "Der Hebraerbrief und die Paulus Schule." *Biblische Zeitschrift* 37 (1993) 183-208.

———. *Der Hebräerbrief*. Regensburger Neues Testament. Regensburg: Pustet, 2009.

———. "Das Land der Verheißung: Die Heimat der Glaubenden im Hebräerbrief." *New Testament Studies* 47 (2001) 171-88.

———. *Der neue Bund und das Werden der Kirche: Die Diatheke Deutung des Hebräerbriefs im Rahmen der frühchristlichen Theologiegeschichte*. Neutestamentliche Abhandlungen n.s. 29. Münster: Aschendorff, 1996.

———. "Per Christum in Deum: Zur theozentrischen Funktion der Christologie im Hebräerbrief." In *Der lebendige Gott: Studien zur Theologie des Neuen Testaments; Festschrift für Wilhelm Thüsing zum 75. Geburtstag*, edited by Thomas Söding, 258–84. Münster: Aschendorff, 1996.

Baltes, M. "Middle Platonism." In *Brill's New Pauly, Chronologies of the Ancient World: Names, Dates and Dynasties*, edited by Walter Eder and Johannes Renger, 8.858–63. Translated and edited by Wouter Henkelman. Leiden: Brill, 2007.

Barnett, A. E. *Paul Becomes a Literary Influence*. Chicago: University of Chicago Press, 1941.

Bateman IV, Herbert W. *Early Jewish Hermeneutics and Hebrews 1:5–13. The Impact of Early Jewish Exegesis on a Significant New Testament Passage*. New York: Peter Lang, 1997.

Bauer, J. "Πολλοι Luk 1,1." *Novum Testamentum* 4 (1960) 263–64.

Beker, J. Christiaan. *Heirs of Paul: Paul's Legacy in the New Testament and in the Church Today*. Minneapolis: Fortress, 1991.

Berger, Klaus. *Die Gesetzauslegung Jesu*. Wissenschaftliche Untersuchungen zum Neuen Testament 40. Tübingen: Mohr (Siebeck) 1972.

Berger, Peter, and Thomas Luckmann. *The Social Construction of Reality: A Treatise on the Sociology of Knowledge*. Garden City, NY: Doubleday, 1967.

Bianchi, Ugo. "Plutarch und der Dualismus." In *Aufstieg und Niedergang der römischen Welt*, 36.1. 2; edited by Wolfgang Haase, 350–65. Berlin: de Gruyter, 1987.

Birnbaum, Ellen. *The Place of Judaism in Philo's Thought: Israel, Jews, and Proselytes*. Brown Judaic Studies 290; Studia Philonica Monographs 2. Atlanta: Scholars, 1996.

Bousset, W. *Jüdisch-christlicher Schulbetrieb in Alexandria und Rom*. Reprint, Hildesheim: Georg Olms, 1975.

Brawley, Robert L. "Discoursive Structure and the Unseen in Hebrews 2:8 and 11:1: A Neglected Aspect of the Context." *Catholic Biblical Quarterly* 55 (1993) 81–98.

Brenk, Frederick E. "The Imperial Heritage: The Religious Spirit of Plutarch." In *Aufstieg und Niedergang der römischen Welt*, 36.1. 2; edited by Wolfgang Haase, 1300–1332. Berlin: de Gruyter, 1987.

Brooks, James A. "Clement of Alexandria as a Witness to the Development of the New Testament Canon." *Second Century* 9 (1992) 41–55.

Buell, Denise Kimber. *Making Christians: Clement of Alexandria and the Rhetoric of Legitimacy*. Princeton: Princeton University Press, 1997.

Bultmann, Rudolph. "δηλόω." In *TDNT* 2.61–62.

Bultmann, Rudolf. *Theology of the New Testament*. 2 vols. Translated by Kendrick Grobel. London: SCM, 1952.

Busch, Peter. "Der mitleidende Hohepriester. Zur Rezeption der mittelplatonischen Dämonologie in Hebr 4,14f." In *Religionsgeschichte des Neuen Tesstament. Festschrift für Klaus Berger*, edited by Axel Dobbeler, Kurt Erlemann, and Roman Heiligenthal, 19–30. Tübingen: Francke, 2000.

Casey, Robert Pierce. *The Excerpta ex Theodoto of Clement of Alexandria*. London: Christophers, 1934.

Church, Philip. "Hebrews 1:10-12 and the Renewal of the Cosmos." *Tyndale Bulletin* 67 (2016) 269-86.

Collins, John J. *Between Athens and Jerusalem: Jewish Identity in the Hellenistic Diaspora.* New York: Crossroad, 1986.

Compton, Jared. *Psalm 110 and the Logic of Hebrews.* Library of New Testament Studies 537. London: Bloomsbury T. & T. Clark, 2015.

Conley, Thomas M. "Philo of Alexandria." In *Handbook of Classical Rhetoric in the Greco-Roman Period*, edited by Stanley E. Porter, 695-714. Leiden: Brill, 1997.

Cox, Ronald. *By the Same Word: Creation and Salvation in Hellenistic Judaism and Early Christianity.* Beihefte zur Zeitschrift für neutestamentliche Wissenschaft und die Kunde der älteren Kirche. Berlin: de Gruyter, 2007.

Daley, Brian E. *The Hope of the Early Church.* Peabody, MA: Hendrickson, 2003.

De Silva, David. "The Epistle to the Hebrews in Social-Scientific Perspective." *Restoration Quarterly* 36 (1994) 1-21.

De Vogel, C. J. "Platonism and Christianity: A Mere Antagonism or a Profound Common Ground?" *Vigiliae Christianae* 39 (1985) 1-62.

Decock, Paul D. "Migration as a Basic Image for the Life of Faith: The Letter to the Hebrews, Philo, and Origen." *Neotestamentica* 51 (2017) 129-50.

Dey, Kalyan Kumar. *The Intermediary World and Patterns of Perfection in Philo and Hebrews.* Society of Biblical Literature Dissertation Series 25. Missoula, MT: Scholars, 1975.

Dillon, John. *The Middle Platonists.* London: Duckworth, 1977.

———. "The Nature of God in the 'Quod Deus.'" In *Two Treatises of Philo*, edited by John Dillon and David Winston, 217-27. Brown Judaic Studies 25. Chico, CA: Scholars, 1983.

Docherty, Susan E. *The Use of the Old Testament in Hebrews: A Case Study in Early Jewish Bible Interpretation.* Wissenschaftliche Untersuchungen zum Neuen Testament 2.260. Tübingen: Mohr Siebeck, 2009.

Dörrie, H. "Was ist 'spätantike Platonismus'?" *Theologische Rundschau* 36 (1971) 285-302.

Dreyer, O. *Untersuchungen zum Begrifff des Gottgeziemenden in der Antike*, Spudasmata 24. Hildesheim: Olms, 1970.

Dunnill, John. *Covenant and Sacrifice in the Letter to the Hebrews.* SNTSMS 15. Cambridge: Cambridge University Press, 1992.

Edwards, M. J. "On the Platonic Schooling of Justin Martyr." *Journal of Theological Studies* 42 (1991) 17-34.

Eggs, E. "Argumentation." In *Historisches Wörterbuch der Rhetorik*, edited by Gert Ueding, 914-19. Darmstadt: Wissenschaftliche Buchgesellschaft, 1992.

Eisele, Wilfried. *Ein unerschütterliches Reich: Die mittelplatonische Umformung des Parusiegedankens im Hebräerbrief.* BZNW 116. Berlin: de Gruyter, 2003.

Eisenbaum, Pamela Michelle. *The Jewish Heroes of Christian History: Hebrews 11 in Its Literary Context.* Society of Biblical Literature Dissertation Series 156. Atlanta: Scholars, 1997.

Erbse, Hartmut. "Die Bedeutung der Synkrisis in den Parallelbiographen Plutarchs." *Hermes* 84 (1956) 398-424.

Eusebius. *Preparation for the Gospel.* Translated by Edwin H. Gifford. Reprint, Grand Rapids: Eerdmans, 1981.

Fascher, E. "Theologische Beobachtungen zu δεῖ." In *Neutestamentliche Studien für Rudolf Bultmann*, edited by W. Elstester, 228–54. BZNW 21. Berlin: Töpelmann, 1957.

Feld, Helmut. "Der Hebräerbrief: Literarische Form, religionsgeschichtliche Hintergrund, theologische Fragen." In *Aufstieg und Niedergang der römischen Welt*, II.25.4, edited by Wolfgang Haase, 3522–3601. Berlin: de Gruyter, 1987.

Feldmeier, Reinhard. *Die Christen als Fremde: Die Metapher der Fremde in der antiken Welt, im Urchristentum und im 1. Petrusbrief*. Wissenschaftliche Untersuchungen zum Neuen Testament 2.212. Tübingen: Mohr Siebeck, 1992.

———. "The 'Nation' of Strangers: Social Contempt and Its Theological Interpretation in Ancient Judaism and Early Christianity." In *Ethnicity and the Bible*, edited by Mark G. Brett, 241–70. Biblical Interpretation Series 19. Leiden: Brill, 1996.

Ferguson, Everett. "Spiritual Sacrifice in Early Christianity and Its Environment." In *Aufstieg und Niedergang der römischen Welt*, Part 2, edited by H. Temporini and W. Hasse, 2.23.2, 1151–89. Berlin: De Gruyter, 1972–.

Ferrari, Franco. "Der Gott Plutarchs und der Gott Platons." In *Gott und die Götter bei Plutarch: Götterbilder-Gottesbilder-Weltbilder*, edited by Rainer Hirsch-Luipold, 13–26. Berlin: de Gruyter, 2005.

Focke, F. "Synkrisis." *Hermes* 51(1923) 326–68.

Frevel, Christian. "σήμερον—Understanding Psalm 95 within, and without, Hebrews." In *Psalms and Hebrews: Studies in Reception*, edited by Dirk J. Human and Gert J. Steyn, 165–93. London: Bloomsbury T. & T. Clark, 2012.

Gäbel, Georg. *Die Kulttheologie des Hebräerbriefes: Eine exegetisch-religionsgeschichtliche Studie*. Wissenschaftliche Untersuchungen zum Neuen Testament 2.212. Tübingen: Mohr Siebeck, 2006.

Geertz, Clifford. *The Interpretation of Cultures*. New York: Basic Books, 1973.

Gese, Michael. *Das Vermächtnis des Apostels*. Wissenschaftliche Untersuchungen zum Neuen Testament 2.99. Tübingen: Mohr Siebeck, 1997.

Goppelt, L. *Typos*. Grand Rapids: Eerdmans, 1982.

Gorman, Heather M. "The Power of Pathos: Emotional Appeal in Hebrews." M.A. thesis, Abilene Christian University, 2009.

Grässer, Erich. *Der Glaube im Hebräerbrief*. Marburg: Elwert, 1965.

———. *An die Hebräer*. Evangelisch-katholischer Kommenhtr zum Neuen Testament. 3 vols. Zurich: Benziger; Neukirchen-Vluyn: Neukirchener, 1993.

———."Der Hebräerbrief 1938–1963." *Theologische Rundschau* n.s. 30 (1964) 138–236.

———. "Hebräer 1:1–4: Ein exegetischer Versuch." In *Text und Situation: Gesammelte Aufsätze zum Neuen Testament*, 183–230. Gütersloh: Gerd Mohn, 973.

———. "Rechtfertigung im Hebräerbrief." In *Rechtfertigung: Festschrift für Ernst Käsemann zum 70. Geburtstag*, edited by Johannes Friedrich, Wolfgang Pöhlmann and Peter Stuhlmacher, 79–93. Tübingen: Mohr (Siebeck), 1976.

Greer, Rowan. *The Captain of Our Salvation: A Study of the Patristic Exegesis of Hebrews*. Beiträge zur Geschichte der biblischen Exegese 15. Tubingen: Mohr, 1973.

Griffiths, J. Gwyn. *Plutarch's De Iside et Osiride*. Cardiff: University of Wales Press, 1970.

Groningen, E. A. van. *In the Grip of the Past: Essay on an Aspect of Greek Thought*. Philosophia antiqua 6. Leiden: Brill, 1953.

Guthrie, George. *The Structure of Hebrews: A Text-Linguistic Analysis*. NovTSupp 73. Leiden: Brill, 1994.

Harding, Fletcher. "Christ as Greater than Moses in Clement of Alexndria's *Stromateis* I–II." *Studia Patristica* 31 (1997) 397–400.
Harnack, Adolf. *History of Dogma*. Reprint, New York: Dover, 1961.
Hauck, Friedrich. "Παραβολή." *TDNT* 5.745–46.
Hellholm, David. "Amplificatio in the Macro-Structure of Rom." In *Rhetoric in the New Testament*, 23–51. JSNTS 90. Sheffield, UK: JSOT, 1993.
Hengel, Martin. *The Son of God: The Origin of Christology and the History of Jewish-Hellenistic Religion*. Philadelphia: Fortress, 1976.
Hofius, Otfried. *Der Christushymnus Philipper 2.6–11: Untersuchungen zu Gestalt u. Aussage e. urchristl. Psalms*.Tübingen: Mohr Siebeck, 1976.
———. *Katapausis: Die Vorstellung von endzeitlichen Ruheort im Hebräerbrief*. Wissenschaftliche Untersuchungen zum Neuen Testament 2. Tübingen: Mohr, 1970.
Holtz, Gudrun. "Besser und doch gleich—zur doppelten Hermeneutik des Hebraerbriefes." *Kerygma und Dogma* 58 (2012) 159–77.
Hopfner, Theodor. *Plutarch über Isis und Osiris*. 1940–41. Reprint, Hildesheim: Georg Olms, 1991.
Horrell, David G. *Solidarity and Difference: A Contemporary Reading of Paul's Ethics*. London: T. & T. Clark, 2005.
Horsley, Richard A. "The Law of Nature in Philo and Cicero." *Harvard Theological Review* 71 (1978) 35–59.
Hübner, Hans. *Hebräerbrief, Evangelien und Offenbarung; Epilegomena*. Vol. 3 of *Biblische Theologie des Neuen Testaments*. Göttingen: Vandenheock & Ruprecht, 1995.
Hughes, Graham. *Hebrews and Hermeneutics*. Society for New Testament Studies Monograph Series 36. Cambridge: Cambridge University Press, 1979.
Hurst, Lincoln D. *The Epistle to the Hebrews: Its Background of Thought*. Society for New Testament Studies Monograph Series 65. Cambridge: Cambridge University Press, 1990.
Jaeger, W. *The Theology of the Early Greek Philosophers*. Oxford: Clarendon, 1947.
Johnson, Luke Timothy. *Hebrews: A Commentary*. New Testament Library. Louisville: Westminster John Knox, 2006.
Johnson, Richard W. *Going outside the Camp: The Sociological Function of the Levitical Critique in the Epistle to the Hebrews*. Journal for the Study of the New Testament. Supplement Series 209. Sheffield, UK: Sheffield Academic Press, 2001.
Karrer, Martin. "Die Schriften Israels im Hebräerbriefs." *Theologische Literaturzeitung* 138 (2013) 1181–96.
———. "Der Weltkreis und Christus, der Hohepriester: Blicke auf die Schriftrezeption des Heb." In *Frühjudentum und Neues Testament im Horizont Biblischer Theologie*, edited by Wolfgang Kraus, Karl-Wilhelm Niebuhr, and Lutz Doering, 151–79. Tübingen: Mohr Siebeck, 2003.
Käsemann, Ernst. *The Wandering People of God: An Investigation of the Letter to the Hebrews*. Translated by R. A. Harrisville and I. L. Sandberg. Minneapolis: Augsburg, 1984.
———. *Das wandernde Gottesvolk: Eine Untersuchung zum Hebräerbrief*. FRLANT 37. Göttingen: Vandenhoeck & Ruprecht, 1938.
Kennedy, George A. *A History of Classical Rhetoric*. Princeton: Princeton University Press, 1994.

———, trans. and ed. *Progymnasmata: Greek Textbooks of Prose Composition and Rhetoric*. Atlanta: Society of Biblical Literature, 2003.

Kistemaker, S. *The Psalm Citations in Hebrews*. Amsterdam: Wed. G. van Soest, 1961.

Klauck, Hans-Josef. *Alte Welt und neuer Glaube, Beiträge zur Religionsgeschichte, Forschungsgeschichte und Theologie des Neuen Testaments*. Göttingen: Vandenhoeck & Ruprecht, 1994.

———. "Die Bruderliebe bei Plutarch und im vierten Makkabäerbuch." In *Alte Welt und neuer Glaube: Beiträge zur Religionsgeschichte, Forschungsgeschichte und Theologie des Neuen Testaments*, 83–98. Novum Testamentum et Orbis Antiquus 29. Göttingen: Vandenhoeck & Ruprecht, 1994.

Kneepkens, C. H. "Comparatio." In *Historisches Wörterbuch der Rhetorik*, vol. 2, edited by Gert Ueding, 293–99. Tübingen: Niemeyer, 1994.

Koester, Craig. *Hebrews*. Anchor Bible 36. New York: Doubleday, 2001.

Kurianal, James. *Jesus Our High Priest: Ps 110,4 as the Substructure of Heb 5,1–7,28*. Frankfurt am Main: Lang, 1999.

Lamberton, Robert. *Homer the Theologian: Neoplatonist Allegorical Reading and the Growth of the Epic Tradition*. Berkeley: University of California Press, 1989.

Lanziger, Daniel. "'A Sabbath Rest for the People of God' (Heb 4:9): Hebrews and Philo on the Seventh Day of Creation." *New Testament Studies* 64 (2018) 94–107.

Larmour, David H. J. "Making Parallels: Synkrisis and Plutarch's 'Themistocles and Camillus.'" In *Aufstieg und Niedergang der römischen Welt* 33.6. Part 2, *Principat*, 33.6, edited by H. Temporini and W. Haase, 4143–4200. Berlin: de Gruyter, 1992.

Lausberg, Heinrich. *Handbook of Literary Rhetoric: A Foundation for Literary Study*. Leiden: Brill, 1998.

Lehne, Susanne. *The New Covenant in Hebrews*. Journal for the Study of the New Testament Supplement Series 44. Sheffield, UK: JSOT, 1990.

Lewicki, Tomasz. *"Weist nicht ab den Sprechenden!": Wort Gottes und Paraklese im Hebräerbrief*. Paderborner theologische Studien 41. Paderborn: Schöningh, 2004.

Lindemann, Andreas. *Paulus im ältesten Christentum*. Beiträge zur historischen Theologie. Tübingen: Mohr Siebeck, 1979.

Löhr, Hermut. "Reflections on Rhetorical Terminology in Hebrews." In *Hebrews: Contemporary Methods, New Insight*, edited by Gabriella Gelardini, 199–210. Biblical Interpretation Series 75. Leiden: Brill, 2005.

Lohse, Eduard. *Colossians and Philemon*. Hermeneia. Philadelphia: Fortress, 1971.

Maas, Wilhelm. *Unveränderlichkeit Gottes: zum Verhältnis von griechisch-philosophischer und christlicher Gotteslehre*. Paderborner theologische Studien 1. Munich: Schöningh, 1974.

Mackie, Scott D. *Eschatology and Exhortation in the Epistle to the Hebrews*. Wissenschaftliche Untersuchungen zum Neuen Testament. Tübingen: Mohr Siebeck, 2007.

Martin, Josef. *Antike Rhetorik: Technik und Methode*. Munich: Beck, 1974.

Martin, Hubert. "Plutarch." In *Handbook of Classical Rhetoric in the Greco-Roman Period*, edited by Stanley E. Porter, 724–25. Leiden: Brill, 1997.

Martin, Michael W. "Philo's Use of Syncrisis: An Examination of Philonic Composition in the Light of the Progymnasmata." *Perspectives in Religious Studies* 30 (2003) 271–97.

Martin, Michael W., and Jason A. Whitlark. "The Encomiastic Topics of Synkrisis as the Key to the Structure and Argument of Hebrews." *New Testament Studies* 57 (2011) 415–39.

———. *Inventing Hebrews: Design and Purpose in Ancient Rhetoric.* Society for New Testament Studies Monograph Series 171. New York: Cambridge University Press, 2018.

März, Claus-Peter ". . . Nur für kurze Zeit under die Engel gestellt (Hebr 2,7): Anthropologie und Christologie in Hebr 2,5–9." In *Von Gott Reden in säkularer Gesellschaft: Festschrift für Konrad Feiereis zum 65. Geburtstag*, edited by Emerech Coreth, Wilhelm Ernst, and Eberhard Tiefensee, 29–42. Erfurter theologische Studien 71. Leipzig: Benno, 1996.

Mees, M. *Die Zitate aus dem Neuen Testament bei Clemens von Alexandrien.* Quaderni di "Vetera Christianorum" 2. Rome: Typis Pontificiae Universitatis Gregorianae, 1972.

Meier, John. "Structure and Theology in Heb 1:1–14." *Biblica* 66 (1985) 168–89.

Meijering, E. P. "Wie Platonisierten Christen? Zur Grenzziehung zwischen Platonismus, kirchlichem Credo und patristischer Theologie." *Vigiliae Christianae* 28 (1974) 15–28.

Michel, Otto. *Der Brief an die Hebräer.* Kritisch-Exegetischer Kommentar über das Neue Testament. Göttingen: Vandenhoeck & Ruprecht, 1966.

Mitchell, Alan C. "The Use of Πρέπειν and Rhetorical Propriety in Hebrews 2:10." *Catholic Biblical Quarterly* 54 (1992) 681–701.

Moffatt, James. *A Critical and Exegetical Commentary on the Epistle to the Hebrews.* International Critical Commentary. Edinburgh: T. & T. Clark, 1924.

Moore, Nicholas J. *Repetition in Hebrews: Plurality and Singularity in the Letter to the Hebrews, Its Ancient Context, and the Early Church.* Wissenschaftliche Untersuchungen zum Neuen Testament. Tübingen: Mohr-Siebeck, 2015.

Nauck, Wilhelm. "Zum Aufbau des Hebräerbriefes." In *Judentum, Urchristentum, Kirche: Festschrift für Joachim Jeremias*, edited by Walther Eltester, 199–206. Berlin: Töpelmann, 1960.

Neyrey, J. H. "'Without Beginning of Days or End of Life,' (Heb 7:3): Topos for a True Deity." *Catholic Biblical Quarterly* 53 (1991) 439–55.

Niebuhr, Karl-Wilhelm. *Gesetz und Paränese: Katechismusartige Weisungsreihen in der frühjüdischen Literatur.* Wissenschaftliche Untersuchungen zum Neuen Testament 2.228. Tübingen: Mohr (Siebeck), 1987.

Nikiprowetzky, Valentin. *Le commentaire de l'Écriture chez Philon d'Alexandrie; son caractère et sa portée; observations philologiques.* Arbeiten zur Literatur und Geschichte des hellenistischen Judentums 11. Leiden: Brill, 1977.

Nongbri, Brent. "A Touch of Condemnation in a Word of Exhortation: Apocalyptic Language and Graeco-Roman Rhetoric in Hebrews 6:4–12." *Novum Testamentum* 45 (2003) 265–79.

Norden, Eduard. *Die antike Kunstprosa vom vi. Jahrhundert v. Chr. bis in die Zeit der Renaissance.* Reprint, Darmstadt: Wissenschaftiche Buchgesellschaft, 1958.

Olbricht, Thomas H. "Anticipating and Presenting the Case for Christ as High Priest in Hebrews." In *Rhetorical Argumentation in Biblical Texts: Essays from the Lund 2000 Conference*, edited by Anders Eriksson, Thomas H. Olbricht, and Walter Walter Übelacker, 355–72. Emory Studies in Early Christianity. Harrisburg, PA: Trinity, 2002.

———. "Hebrews as Amplification." In *Rhetoric and the New Testament*, edited by Stanley E. Porter and Thomas H. Olbricht, 375–87. Journal for the Study of the New Testament Supplement Series 90. Sheffield, UK: Journal for the Study of the Old Testament, 1993.

Osborn, Eric. "Arguments for Faith in Clement of Alexandria." *Vigiliae Christianae* 48 (1994) 1–24.

———. *The Philosophy of Clement of Alexandria*. Cambridge: Cambridge University Press, 1981.

Otto Michel. "οἶκος, κτλ." In *Theological Dictionary of the New Testament*, 5.119–25. 10 vols. Grand Rapids: Eerdmans, 1967.

Oulton, J. E. L., and Henry Chadwick. *Alexandrian Christianity*. London: SCM, 1954.

Overbeck, Franz. *Zur Geschichte des Kanons*. Chemnitz, Germany: Schmeitzner, 1870.

Perelman, Ch., and L. Olbrechts-Tyteca. *The New Rhetoric*. Notre Dame, IN: University of Notre Dame Press, 1969.

Pilhofer, Peter. *Presbyterion Kreitton: Der Altersbeweis tier judischen und christlichen Apologeten und seine Vorgeschichte*, Wissenschaftliche Untersuchungen zum Neuen Testament 2.39. Tubingen: Mohr (Siebeck), 1990.

Pohlenz, M. "τὸ Πρέπον. Ein Beitrag zur Geschichte des griechischen Geistes." In *Kleine Schriften*, edited by H. Dörrie, 1.100–115. Hildesheim: Olms, 1965.

Ramsaran, Rollin A. *Liberating Words: Rhetorical Maxims in 1 Corinthians 1–10*. Harrisburg, PA: Trinity, 1996.

———. "Living and Dying, Living is Dying (Phil. 1:21)." In *Rhetorical Argumentation of Biblical Texts*, edited by Anders Eriksson, Thomas H. Olbricht, and Walter Übelacker, 325–38. Emory Studies in Early Christianity. Harrisburg, PA: Trinity, 2002.

Rascher, Angela. *Schriftauslegung und Christologie im Hebräerbrief*. Beihefte Zeitschrift für die neutestamentliche Wissenschaft und die Kunde der älteren Kirche 153. Berlin: de Gruyter, 2007.

Reinmuth, Eckart. *Geist und Gesetz: Studien zu Voraussetzungen und Inhalt der paulinischen Paränese*. Theologische Arbeiten 44. Berlin: Evangelische Verlagsanstalt, 1985.

Rissi, Matthias. *Die Theologie des Hebräerbriefes*. Wissenschaftliche Untersuchungen zum Neuen Testament 41. Tübingen: Mohr (Siebeck), 1987.

Rose, Christian. "Verheißung und Erfüllung: Zum Verständnis der ἐπαγγελία im Hebräerbrief." *Biblische Zeitschrift* 33 (1989) 60–80, 178–91.

———. *Die Wolke der Zeugen: eine exegetisch-traditionsgeschichtliche Untersuchung zu Hebräer 10,32–12,3*. Wissenschaftliche Untersuchungen zum Neuen Testament 60. Tübingen: Mohr (Siebeck), 1993.

Runia, David T. "Philo and Middle Platonism Revisited." *Studia Philonica* 5 (1993) 112–40.

———. *Philo in Early Christian Literature*. CRINT 3.3. Minneapolis: Fortress, 1993

———. *Philo of Alexandria, On the Creation of the Cosmos according to Moses*. Leiden: Brill, 2001.

———. "The Theme of Flight and Exile in the Allegorical Thought-World of Philo of Alexandria." *Studia Philonica Annual* 21 (2009) 1–24.

Russell, D. A. *Plutarch*. London: Duckworth, 1973.

Salevao, Iutiosone. *Legitimation in the Letter to the Hebrews: The Construction and Maintenance of a Symbolic Universe*. Journal for the Study of the New Testament Supplements. London: Sheffield Academic Press, 2002.

Sand, A. "ἐπαγγελία." In *Exegetical Dictionary of the New Testament*. Grand Rapids: Eerdmans, 1991.

Sandnes, Karl. *A New Family: Conversion and Ecclesiology in the Early Church with Cross-Cultural Comparisons*. New York: Lang, 1993.

Schenck, Kenneth L. *Cosmology and Eschatology in Hebrews: The Settings of the Sacrifice.* Society for the Study of the New Testament Monograph Series 143. Cambridge: University Press, 2010.

Schenck, W. "Die Paränese Hebr 13,16 im Kontext des Hebräerbriefes—Einer Fallstudie semiotisch-orientierter Textinterpretation und Sachkritik." *Studia Theologica* 39 (1985) 73–106.

Schenk, Kenneth. *Understanding the Book of Hebrews.* Louisville: Westminster John Knox, 2003.

Schenke, H-M. "Das Weiterwirken des Paulus und die Pflege seines Erbes durch die Paulusschule." In *Einleitung in die Schriften des Neuen Testaments,* edited by H. M. Schenke and K. M. Fischer, 233–47. Gütersloh: Mohn, 1978.

Schierse, F. J. *Verheißung und Heilsvollendung: Zur theologischen Grundfrage des Hebräerbriefes.* Münchener theologische Studien. Munich: Karl Zink, 1955.

Schniewind, J., and G. Friedrich. "ἐπαγγελία." In *Theological Dictionary of the New Testament,* vol. 2, edited by Gerhard Kittel, 576–86. Grand Rapids: Eerdmans, 1964.

Schröger, F. *Der Verfasser des Hebräerbriefs als Schriftausleger.* Regensburg: Pustet, 1968.

Seland, Torrey. *Strangers in the Light: Philonic Perspectives on Christian Identity in 1 Peter.* Biblical Interpretation Series 76. Leiden: Brill, 2005.

Smillie, Gene R. "Contrast or Continuity in Hebrews 1.1–2." *New Testament Studies* 51 (2005) 543–60.

Soden, H. von. *Hebräerbrief, Briefe des Petrus, Jakobus, Judas. Hand-Commentar zum Neuen Testament,* vol. 3.2, edited by H. J. Holtzmann, R. A. Lipsius, P. W. Schmiedel, H. von Soden. 3rd ed. Freiburg: Mohr, 1899.

Söding, Thomas. *Das Liebesgebot bei Paulus: Die Mahnung zur Agape im Rahmen der paulinischen Ethik.* Neutestamentliche Abhandlungen 26. Münster: Aschendorff, 1995.

Son, Kiwoon. *Zion Symbolism in Hebrews: Hebrews 12:18–24 as a Hermeneutical Key to the Epistle.* Paternoster Biblical Monographs. Milton Keynes, UK: Paternoster, 2005.

Spicq, Ceslas. *L'Epitre aux Hébreux.* Paris: Lecoffre, 1952.

———. *Theological Lexicon of the New Testament.* 3 vols. Peabody, MA: Hendrickson, 1994.

Sterling, Gregory. "Ontology vs. Eschatology: Tensions between Author and Community in Hebrews." *Studia Philonica Annual* 13 (2001) 190–211."

Strack, H. L. *Introduction to the Talmud and Midrash.* New York: Athenaeum, 1969.

Strack, H. L., and Paul Billerbeck. *Kommentar zum Neuen Testament aus Talmud und Midrasch.* Munich: Beck, 1926.

Svensen, S. N. *Allegory Transformed: The Appropriation of Philonic.* Hermeneutics in the Letter to the Hebrews. Tübingen: Mohr Siebeck, 2009.

Swetnam, James. "Christology and the Eucharist in the Epistle to the Hebrews." *Biblica* 70 (1989) 74–95.

———. "Ἐξ ἑνός in Hebrews 2,11." *Biblica* 88 (2007) 521–22.

Theobald, Michael. "Vom Text zum 'lebendigen Wort' (Hebr 4,12). Beobachtungen zur Schrifthermeneutik des Hebräerbriefs." In *Jesus Christus als die Mitte der Schrift: Studien zur Hermeneutik des Evangeliums,* edited by Christof Landmesser, Hans-Joachim Eckstein, and Hermann Lichtenberger, 751–90. Beihefte zur Zeitschrift für die neutestamentliche Wissenschaft und die Kunde der älteren Kirche 86. Berlin: de Gruyter, 1997.

Thompson, James W. "The Appropriate, the Necessary, and the Impossible: Faith and Reason in Hebrews." In *The Early Church in Its Context: Essays in Honor of Everett Ferguson*, edited by Abraham J. Malherbe, Frederick W. Norris, and James W. Thompson, 302–17. Supplements to Novum Testamentum 90. Leiden: Brill, 1998.

———. "Argument and Persuasion in the Epistle to the Hebrews." *Perspectives in Religious Studies* 39 (2012) 361–77.

———. *The Beginnings of Christian Philosophy*. Catholic Biblical Quarterly Monograph Series 13. Washington, DC: Catholic Biblical Association, 1982.

———. "*Ephapax*: The One and the Many in Hebrews." *New Testament Studies* 53 (2007) 566–81.

———. "The Epistle to the Hebrews in the Works of Clement of Alexandria." In *Transmission and Reception: New Testament Text-Critical and Exegetical Studies*, edited by J. W. Childers and D. C. Parker, 239–54. Piscataway, NJ: Gorgias, 2006.

———. *Hebrews*. Paideia. Grand Rapids: Baker Academic, 2008.

———. *Moral Formation according to Paul: The Context and Coherence of Paul's Ethics*. Grand Rapids: Baker Academic, 2011.

———. "Paul, Plutarch, and the Ethic of the Family." *Restoration Quarterly* 52 (2010) 223–26.

———. "Strangers on the Earth: Philosophical Perspective on the Promise in Hebrews." *Restoration Quarterly* 57 (2015) 193–212.

———. "What Does Hebrews Have to Do with Middle Platonism?" In *Reading the Epistle to the Hebrews: A Resource for Students*, edited by Eric F. Mason and Kevin B. McCruden, 31–52. Atlanta: Society of Biblical Literature, 2011.

Thuren, J. *Das Lopofer der Hebräer: Studien zum Aufbau und Anliegen von Hebräerbrief* 13. Abo, Finland: Abo Akademi, 1973.

Thuren, Lauri. *Argument and Theology in 1 Peter: The Origins of Christian Paraenesis*. JSNTS 114. Sheffield, UK: Sheffield Academic Press, 1995.

———. "Is There Biblical Argumentation?" In *Rhetorical Argumentation in Biblical Texts*, edited by Anders Eriksson, Thomas H. Olbricht, and Walter Übelacker, 77–92. Emory Studies in Early Christianity. Harrisburg, PA: Trinity, 2002.

———. "On Studying Ethical Argumentation and Persuasion in the New Testament." In *Rhetoric and the New Testament*, edited by Stanley E. Porter and Thomas H. Olbricht, 464–78. Journal for the Study of the New Testament Supplement Series 90. Sheffield, UK: JSOT, 1993.

Toulmin, Stephen. *The Uses of Argument*. Cambridge: Cambridge University Press, 2005.

Übelacker, Walter. *Der Hebräerbrief als Appell: Untersuchungen zu Exordium, Narratio, und Postscriptum (Heb 1–2 and 13:22–25)*. Stockholm: Almqvist and Wiksell, 1989.

———. "Hebrews and the Implied Author's Rhetorical Ethos." In *Rhetoric, Ethic, and Moral Persuasion in Biblical Discourse: Essays from the 2002 Heidelberg Conference*, edited by Thomas H. Olbricht and Anders Erikson, 316–34. Emory Studies in Early Christianity. London: T. & T. Clark, 2005.

Van den Hoek, Annewies. *Clement of Alexandria and His Use of Philo in the Stromateis*. Supplements to Vigiliae Christianae 3. Leiden: Brill, 1988.

Van Groningen, E. A. *In the Grip of the Past: Essay on an Aspect of Greek Thought*. Philosophia Antiqua 6. Leiden: Brill, 1953.

Vandergrif, Kenneth A. "ΔΙΑΘΗΚΗ ΚΑΙΝΗ: New Covenant and Jewish Apocalypticism in Heb 8." *Catholic Biblical Quarterly* 79 (2017) 97–110.
Vanhoye, Albert. "Épître aux Ephésiens et l'epître aux Heb." *Biblica* 59 (1978) 198–230.
———. *La structure littéraire de l'Epître aux Hébreux*. StudNeot 1. Paris: Desclée de Brouwer, 1976.
———. *Structure and Message of the Epistle to the Hebrews*. Subsidia Biblica 12. Rome: Pontificio Istituto Biblico, 1965.
Veit, W. F. "Argumentatio." In *Historisches Wörterbuch der Rhetorik*, edited by Gert Ueding, 904–14. Darmstadt: Wissenschaftliche Buchgesellschaft, 1992.
Vos, J. S. "Die hermeneutische Antinomie be Paulus (Galater 3.11–12; Römer 10.5–10)." *New Testament Studies* 38 (1992) 254–70.
———. *Die Kunst der Argumentation bei Paulus*. Wissenschaftliche Untersuchungen zum Neuen Testament 149. Tübingen: Mohr Siebeck, 2002.
Voulgaris, Christos Sp. "Hebrews: Paul's Fifth Epistle from Prison." *Greek Orthodox Theological Review* 44 (1999) 199–206.
Walter, N. "'Hellenistische Eschatologie' im Frühjudentum—ein Beitrag zur 'biblischen Theologie'?" *Theologische Literaturzeitung* 110 (1985) 331–47.
Wedderburn, A. J. M. "The 'Letter' to the Hebrews and Its Thirteenth Chapter." *New Testament Studies* 50 (2004) 395–99.
Weiss, Hans-Friedrich. *Der Brief an die Hebräer*, Kritisch-Exegetischer Kommentar über das Neue Testament. Göttingen: Vandenhoeck & Ruprecht. Göttingen: Vandenhoeck & Ruprecht, 1991.
Westfall, Cynthia. *A Discourse Analysis of the Letter to the Hebrews: The Relationship between Form and Meaning*. SNTSMS 75. Cambridge: Cambridge University Press, 1992.
Whittaker, John. "Plutarch, Platonism, and Christianity." In *Neoplatonism and Early Christian Thought*, essays in honour of A. H. Armstrong, edited by H. J. Blumenthal and R. A. Markus, 50–63. London: Variorum, 1981.
Wider, David. *Theozentrik und Bekenntnis: untersuchungen zur Theologie des Redens Gottes im Hebräerbrief*. Zeitschrift für die neutestamentliche Wissenschaft und die Kunde der älteren Kirche 87. Berlin: de Gruyter, 1997.
Williamson, Ronald. *Philo and the Epistle to the Hebrews*. Arbeiten zur Literatur und Geschichte des hellenistischen Judentums 4. Leiden: Brill, 1970.
Windisch, Hans. *Der Hebräerbrief*. Handbuch zum Neuen Testament 14. Tübingen: Mohr, 1931.
Witherington, Ben. "The Influence of Galatians on Hebrews." *New Testament Studies* 37 (1991) 146–52.
Wolfson, Harry A. "Albinus and Plotinus on Divine Attributes." *Harvard Theological Review* 45 (1952) 115–30.
Wolter, M. "Identität und Ethos bei Paulus." In *Theologie und Ethos im frühen Christentum: Studien zu Jesus, Paulus und Lukas*, edited by M. Wolter, 121–69. Wissenschaftliche Untersuchungen zum Neuen Testament 236. Tübingen: Mohr Siebeck, 2009.
Wrede, William. *Das literarische Rätsel des Hebräerbriefs*. Göttingen: Vandenhoeck & Ruprecht, 1906.
Wyller, Egil A. "Plato/Platonismus II." In *Theologische Realenzyklopädie*, vol. 26, edited by G. Krause and G. Müller, 677–702. 36 vols. Berlin: de Gruyter, 1976–2004.